The Lost Mother

이 윤호 장로님과 사모님께!

길 군자 드림

2008년 Xmas에

The Lost Mother

By Iltang (Kim Tae Shin)

Translated from the Korean by
Joon Ja Kim
and
Dona M. Dietz

iUniverse, Inc.
New York Lincoln Shanghai

The Lost Mother

iUniverse books may be ordered through booksellers or by contacting:

iUniverse
2021 Pine Lake Road, Suite 100
Lincoln, NE 68512
www.iuniverse.com
1-800-Authors (1-800-288-4677)

ISBN: 978-0-595-44194-5 (pbk)
ISBN: 978-0-595-69724-3 (cloth)
ISBN: 978-0-595-88525-1 (ebk)

Printed in the United States of America

Contents

Translators' introduction for English-speaking readers of *The Lost Mother*

The Lost Mother is the memoir of Iltang (Kim Tae Shin), a man of mixed Korean and Japanese descent, who grew up in an era of conflict and chaos, and developed into a noted artist and cultural figure. His mother was a well-known feminist poet in Korea, who turned her back on the fame of her accomplishments to become a Buddhist monk. Her spiritual journey required her to renounce the world and its emotional ties for a life of contemplation. Her decision caused much pain for Iltang over the years, and his own path was largely determined by his need to come to peace with his feelings of abandonment. The continual conflict marking the history of the two nations of his heritage was the second factor which both limited and ultimately enriched his life.

The history of the Korean Peninsula is not very familiar to Americans, although it became a part of our own history during World War II and the Korean War. Korea has the historical misfortune of being located between two powerful and periodically expansionist neighbors, China and Japan. At the time of World War II, Korea had been occupied by Japan for more than thirty years. An active independence movement existed in Korea during this time which was strongly suppressed by the occupiers, and which plays a part in Iltang's memoir. In connection with its efforts to expand further onto the continent of Asia beginning in 1937, Japan severely exploited Korean resources, both human and material.

During WWII, Korea was recognized by the Allies as an independent nation, and was promised its independence at the end of the war, but ideological and political issues resulted in its partition at the 38th Parallel, and it was occupied south of that line by United States forces, and north of it by those of communist Russia, tragically frustrating Korean hopes for autonomy. On June 24, 1950, South Korea was invaded without warning by troops from the North, thus initiating that most bitter of all conflicts, a civil war. North Korean forces, armed by Russia, took Seoul within three days, and overran almost all of the rest of the country within a month. Korea appealed to the United Nations, and U.N. troops were dispatched to reinforce the Korean army, gradually managing to push the communist forces back to the 38th Parallel. In October of that year, China intervened with such large numbers of fighters that the defenders of South Korea were once more obliged to retreat, and Seoul again fell into communist hands on January 4, 1951, and remained under occupation until being retaken in March of that year.

Kim Tae Shin, who later took the name Iltang for professional purposes, was born in 1922, and was a young man at the start of World War II. His life-story is representative of a generation of Koreans whose lives were warped by war and by resentment against the Japan of their harsh occupation. His life was doubly affected because his heritage was a mixed one, Japanese and Korean.

In the beginning of his story, Iltang imagines the romance between his Japanese father, and his poet-mother, who was a strong advocate of Korean independence from Japanese domination. A marriage between these people would have been unheard of in that place and time, and was made completely impossible by Ilyeop's decision to leave the family after Iltang's birth to pursue the path of spiritual enlightenment as a Buddhist monk.

This decision of his mother's was the pivotal event in Iltang's life. He was reared in a series of loving foster families, friends of his father's, and only found out that he had a "real mother" when he was fourteen years old. He longed for a relationship with her, which, according to her tenets, she could not permit. He was ultimately able to sublimate his longing for mother-love into his development as an artist.

When as a child, Iltang's artistic talents were recognized, he was sent to a Korean foster father, the master-artist Idang, Kim Eunho, who taught and mentored him, and he later studied with Ito Shinsui, one of Japan's most prominent portraitists. He obtained his higher education in Japan, and was graduated from the National College of Art just in time to be drafted into the army of Japan, for whom the war had begun to go badly.

After Japan's surrender, Iltang, with much difficulty, returned to Korea, but was soon caught up in the chaos of ideological conflict. He attempted to enter North Korea in order to bring the members of one of his foster families to the South, but was apprehended and imprisoned. His artistic abilities were discovered by his captors, and he was required to join a Russian artist in making propaganda portraits of Stalin and Kim Ilseong, the Korean communist leader. This duty required traveling from place to place in North Korea, and after patiently biding his time to gain the trust of his Russian colleague, he managed to take advantage of this requirement to escape into South Korea once again.

He later traveled to Japan in search of art supplies which he had not been able to procure in Korea, but the civil war intervened, and he found himself unable to get back. Forced to make a life in Japan, he taught school to support himself, and gradually became known for his abilities as an artist, eventually becoming able to make a living from his art.

In a psychological sense, his dual national identity was always very significant in Iltang's life. As his own reputation grew, he was able to establish cultural exchanges which he hoped would begin to heal the resentments which continued to boil between the Japanese and the Koreans. Most psychologically significant in his life, however, was his inability to overcome his feeling of having been deserted by his mother. He turned, as an elderly man, to his own search for spiritual enlightenment, and became a monk, following in her footsteps. Critical appraisals of his work have frequently commented on his ability to represent in art the emotions aroused by the beauty of nature, which was for him symbolic of "Mother."

Although he married and had a family, the rigors of his artistic development and his later quest for spiritual growth seem to have been more significant in his life, and it is these areas which he chooses to emphasize in his memoir, with little mention of his wife and sons.

Iltang has ample reason to be proud of his accomplishments in the world of art. His work as a stone-color artist is widely known and respected in Japan and elsewhere, and he has at least in some measure, been able to fulfill his ambition of increasing the appreciation of Korean artistic techniques and accomplishments in his second nation. He has received numerous national and international honors for his professional attainments. His has not been an easy life, but it has been a rich and eventful one.

His memoir affords insight into the effects of history on the lives of the peoples of his two nations, as well as a window into the private lives of interesting individuals who were important in the cultural life of his time and place.

For this translation, the conversion of Korean into English by the translators was done in accordance with the Revised Romanization of Korean which were provided for us by the Korean Cultural Center of Los Angeles; we thank them. Any inconsistencies which may have slipped in are wholly our responsibility.

We also wish to thank the following for the help and advice they have afforded: Dr. Chong Hae Chung, Professor of Japanese Language and Literature; Yongjin Choi, Senior Director of the Korea Society; Dr. Hyangsoon Yi, Professor of Literature; Dr. Linda Carr, USC Writing Program; Carol Willner, School Principal and Administrator; Mrs. Grace Kim, Retired Teacher; Dr. Kwangja Park. OC International; William Kil, Board of Directors of the Korean-America Education Foundation; Jamoon Koo, President of Korean Education Center in Los Angeles; Charles J Kim, National President of Korean American Coalition.

Attached are endorsements of the book from Dr. Carr and Ms. Willner.

Joon Ja Kim, M.S.
Dona M. Dietz, Ph.D.
Seal Beach, California, October 19, 2007

*Letter dated October 11, 2007, from Linda P. Carr, Ph.D.

In his inspiring memoir, The Lost Mother, Iltang has given us a compelling portrait of the development of an artist who remains true to his core identity in spite of loss and change. His mother's tragic decision to sacrifice her personal happiness in the face of cultural animosity sets him on a lifelong quest for the connections that he alone can create. As an orphan, even his name changes each time he must adapt to changing circumstances. Now he is known as Iltang—an internationally known artist—and writes with the artist's eye for detail, painting for us the unique world he inhabits between Korean values and Japanese education.

With vivid brush strokes, the writer and painter Iltang enables the reader to step inside the Buddhist monastery, the homes of Japanese artists, and the artist's studio. He makes his boyhood journey to see his mother so real that the reader, too, is breathless from the climb up the mountain in the mist. From the reflective vantage of a mature artist, Iltang shows the triumph of the human spirit.

The Lost Mother is more that the poignant tale of a boy who travels the long road to achievement; the book is larger than the sensitive and stirring relationships between the strong characters. This is a story of our millennium, when individual struggle with the conflict between guarding national pride and becoming a citizen of the world.

Bravo! This book will appeal to both young people and those old enough to reflect of the complexity of their lives. I think of J.D. Salinger's scene in his American classic Catcher in the Rye when young Holden Caulfield finished reading Far From the Madding Crowd and he wanted to call up the heroine to talk to her. And as I finished The Lost Mother, I had come to know such closeness with the characters that I felt like Holden Caulfield—I wished that I could call up Iltang and talk to him. Such are the connections that a beautiful book can create!

*Comments from Carol Eckert Willner, teacher and school administrator:

Secondary school administrators have extreme difficulty finding appropriate literature that illuminates distant lives, experiences and cultures. The Lost

Mother is such a book. This autobiography of Korean/Japanese artist Iltang tells a universal story of longing while also describing a world completely unknown to most of us in the West. With vivid imagery and heartfelt emotion, Iltang describes his valiant quest to find his mother, and after locating her, his painful attempts to gain acceptance and affection from her.

A very human drama unfolds, with challenges modern youth can identify with: prejudice, poverty, marginalization, feelings of not truly belonging anywhere. Yet there also is maturation, striving, the dawning of acceptance, determination, and the joy of discovering and developing a powerful means of expression.

Through Iltang's life story, the reader learns about Japanese and Korean geography, history, art, poetry, religions, philosophy, and political struggle. Many issues and concepts that would otherwise be difficult to understand become clearer when embedded within the context of the life described by the author.

Skilled teachers (and parents) can use this book to guide high school-age students' understanding ad appreciation of the world as it was in Japan and Korea in the 1940's.

VOLUME 1

1

Rahula: Problem Child of an Impossible Love

Encounter

Oda Seizo, a law student at Kyushu National University, was a splendid youth despite being somewhat short. In reality, his short stature could be a symbol of pride, since it was emblematic of his pure Japanese heritage. He was both intellectual and passionate. His house was in Yamaguchi-ken, Honshu. That house was as big as the Imperial Palace, dignified and luxurious. His father, Oda Hosaku, was a bank president. He was a direct descendant of Oda Token, Edo era Master, and had inherited huge wealth. Oda Token, along with Tokugawa Ieyasu, united Japan into one nation. The Oda clan was well-known all over Japan. In the middle of January 1921, Oda Seizo, then a sophomore in law school, was given ample money by his father for a winter vacation tour to Tokyo. He took a first-class train from the Kyushu station to Tokyo, and he was relaxed and was enjoying his trip.

When the train stopped at the Shimonoseki station, a woman appeared in the aisle with a huge trunk. As soon as she boarded the train, everything became brighter. Oda Seizo could not take his eyes off of her. She was looking at each seat number, and stopped beside him. At that moment he felt a pain in his chest.

"May I help you?" But even as he said it, he was already on his feet, lifting her trunk onto the shelf.

"Thank you."

She smiled, and sat down next to the window. He sat down beside her.

"Pardon me. May I ask where you are going?"

"Oh, to Tokyo."

"Is that so? I am going to Tokyo, too."

She didn't answer, and he wondered whether she had heard his delight in the fact that they were going to the same place. She just continued to look out of the window. Oda Seizo stole a glance at her profile. She appeared to be less than twenty-five years old. She had straight eyebrows and even features. He thought she looked beautiful and intelligent. She carried herself with nobility and grace. He felt lucky to have met such a woman at the beginning of his trip.

"I'm Oda Seizo. If I'm not being too forward, may I ask your name?" The woman did not answer right away, but she slowly turned toward him, and gazed at him.

"Kim Ilyeop."

He knew that "Kim" was a Korean name. One of his acquaintances was of that name, and was studying with him in the Kyushu Middle School.

"Are you a Korean student studying in Tokyo?" he asked in a tense voice. He was praying she would say no, but she gave a little nod, and he felt a sudden chill. He had never contemplated dating a Korean woman; he had the sense of pride from being the descendant of Oda Token. He pretended nothing had happened, but did not pursue his conversation with her, and opened his book. He told himself that it would be wiser to not even consider the possibility of what he had wished for a few minutes earlier. He looked down at his book, but since he could think of nothing but her, he did not know what he was reading. He was conscious of trembling and breathing very fast. Realizing that trying to read was useless, he closed the book and cleared his throat to get her attention.

"Umm ... what do Korean women think of Japanese men? Even though they are of different nationalities, would they consider dating one?"

Hearing the abrupt question, she looked at him, and clearly knew what was on his mind. He felt his face get hot, but waited patiently for her answer. Finally, she spoke.

"It is not an easy thing to do."

"Why would that be so?"

"Don't you think that relationships are possible only when there is understanding and trust? How could a Korean woman understand and trust a man who is one of the colonizers of her country?"

Her voice sounded cold. He considered abandoning his expectation, but could not help feeling disappointed.

"Do you hate all Japanese?"

"Then, do you think I could respect them?"

Her cold smile did not reach her clear eyes, and again he felt a pain in his chest. When he spoke, his voice sounded high and edgy to his ears.

"All Japanese do not agree with the plundering of Korea. Anyway, that has nothing to do with me—I'm only a student."

"A college student now will soon join the generation in power. The historical crimes committed by Japan will relate to you in any case. If you are a student, I hope you will become a man who understands the pain of the oppressed Koreans." She was clearly demonstrating her rejection of him. Even so, he was not angry, and actually felt closer to her than ever.

"If ... I become like what you said, could I become your friend?"

"I don't know ... maybe ..."

She did not promise, but neither did she refuse.

They conversed about many things until the train arrived at Tokyo. Kim Ilyeop spoke polished Japanese, and was knowledgeable about many things, and had her own ideas about them. When the moment arrived to separate, he felt desperate.

"Miss Ilyeop, could you let me know how to contact you? I will write you a letter."

".... If we have Karma, we will meet again. Goodbye, and have a wonderful trip."

She did not share her address with him before she disappeared into the crowd. That was a refusal without words. That was their first encounter, and they parted with no promises about the future.

Prisoner of Love

On the day before he was to return to his home town, Oda Seizo had lunch with Shindo Araki, a hometown friend and schoolmate. The restaurant was next to Hibiya Park.

After lunch, Oda Seizo and Shindo Araki said their goodbyes.

"Have a safe trip back."

"Take care, and we'll get together again next time."

Shindo Araki went back to work, but Oda Seizo had no wish to return to his hotel. The winter sky was so clear and bright that he felt an intimation of springtime, and walked to the park, without true intention to go there. Many people were in the park enjoying the fine weather. He roamed without direction or purpose.

The sun was bright and the breeze was warm.

Oda Seizo stopped to watch pigeons being fed. Then, his eyes turned toward the fountain. In front of the fountain, two women were sitting on a bench. His heart started pounding. One of the women was drawing and the other was reading a book. The breeze was blowing her hair, and she smoothed it back, and turned the page of her book.

It was surely Kim Ilyeop, the girl from the train! When they had parted at the train without making plans to meet again, he had vowed to abandon thoughts of her; but now, he felt that God, who controls all of life, had willed that he should meet her again.

"How are you?" At his sudden greeting, she lifted her head, clearly surprised.

"Where … how …?"

"By accident, I happened to walk in the park. It must be our Karma to meet again."

Kim Ilyeop had a perplexed expression, but said nothing.

The lady who was drawing was interested.

"Who is he?" she asked.

"Oh, well, um … Just someone I know…." Kim Ilyeop's words trailed off.

"Oh, how do you do? I am Oda Seizo."

"How are you? I am Na Hyeseok. I am a friend of Ilyeop's."

She began gathering up her drawing materials. Oda Seizo said, "I hope I'm not interrupting you."

"No, no. We were about to leave. Let's go get a cup of tea."

Na Hyeseok's suggestion delighted Oda Seizo, since it was his very wish. The three went into the tearoom in the park. While they drank their fragrant tea, they talked about literature and world affairs. Oda Seizo talked passionately, addressing Kim Ilyeop, but whenever he looked at her, she quickly looked away.

The more she avoided his gaze the more intensely he tried to get her attention. He thought that by tomorrow they would be separated again. Finally he got up the courage to speak:

"Tomorrow I am leaving to go back to Kyushu."

"Yes…." Her response was not very encouraging.

"This is not enough. I wish we had more time. If we separate now, we don't know when we will ever see each other again. I want to share thoughts in letters, so, this time, you will give me your address, right?"

"If you, Mr. Oda, will give me your address, I will write to you."

He was upset that she did not give him her address, but there was nothing he could do. Still, the rejection was not so complete that he had no hope. He wrote down his address and gave it to her.

"Please write to me. I'll be waiting for your letter."

There was nothing left to do but just to turn around and leave.

Back in Kyushu, he awaited Kim Ilyeop's letter nervously. A week passed, fifteen days, one month, but still the letter did not come. The experience began to feel hazy to him, like he may have met her in a dream.

"I can only think that I must have been of no consequence to her," he thought.

Oda's self-respect had been crushed. He had previously had little experience with the opposite sex. His first attempt at making a date had resulted in a severe wound. His hurt pride changed to a continual yearning to see her that only became stronger as time went by. He could not rationalize this ache away. The fact that he had no way to contact her made him feel helpless.

"Anyway," he told himself, "she is a Korean woman and not someone I could marry."

He admonished himself in that way, but his thirst still grew. He couldn't sleep, his delicious food was tasteless to him. When he tried to read a book it was meaningless to him, and everything in his life was like that.

"I can't live like this. I have to find her."

Finally, one spring day in his junior year Oda Seizo took the express train to Tokyo. He prayed that fate would lead him to another meeting with her. When the train arrived at Shimonoseki station he wished to meet her accidentally, like last time, but that was just a dream. His dream led him to Hibiya Park. There the cherry blossoms were everywhere, dazzling, covering the trees and scattered over the ground. Under the shadow of the blossoms, women were strolling in their fresh spring colors. On the bench where he had seen Kim Ilyeop and Na Hyeseok were sitting a pair of unknown lovers. For three days, he roamed aimlessly around the park and nearby tearooms. He began to look like a defeated soldier back from the wars. He had become a prisoner of love. He could not prepare for his law examinations. There was not a moment of the day that Kim Ilyeop's face did not disturb him.

He had almost given up in despair when one day he had a glimmer of hope.

"Maybe I might be able to find her. If Kim Ilyeop, a woman, was able to go abroad to study, she must come from a prominent family."

Immediately, he wrote a letter to Song Gisu, a close friend, who had returned to his home in Sincheon, Hwanghae-do, after finishing Kyushu high school. They had remained in contact.

"I want to find out about a woman, Kim Ilyeop. I want to know details. Can you find out for me?" That was the main point of the letter. After fifteen days an answer came back from Song Gisu:

> "Kim Ilyeop's hometown is Dukdong-ri, Sanwhe myeon, Yongang-gun, Pyongannam-do. Her real name is Kim Wonju; Ilyeop is her pen name. She is

a famous poet who is known to the literary and intellectual worlds as a modern woman. Her activities and her family relationships are well known.

"Kim Ilyeop is the first born daughter of a Christian minister named Kim Yonggyeon and his wife, Lee Madae. She had four younger siblings who all died at an early age. Her parents, too, have passed away, so she is all alone in the world.

"She wrote a poem about the loss of her brothers and sisters when she was still in grade school, which became emblematic of the new Korean literature. Probably, since she was born into a Christian family, she might have had a good education, even though she is a woman. After that she went to Ehwa Hakdang, and then to Younghwa University in Tokyo. After she came back, she taught in elementary school, and published *New Woman*, the first Korean women's magazine. She also participated in publishing the famous *Pyeheo.* She and her colleagues hoped to renew the culture after the destruction of war in Korea.

"A while back, she published "Sin Jung Jo Ron" and surprised everyone. Here is a part of it for you to read: '… There is no problem with having love shared between a man and a woman. If a woman can completely erase the man from her mind, she can return to the status of a virgin. The man who can accept that kind of woman can create a new life. That kind of woman is who I am….'

"She is emphasizing the mental purity of woman as a part of her position as a feminist, but in my opinion it also reflects her own experience. I understand that she was married and divorced from her husband. Rumor has it that her husband was handicapped by having an artificial leg, which she didn't know until after they had married. In Korea, couples don't meet, except in the case of a romantic as opposed to an arranged marriage. In general, the matchmaker deals with both sets of parents, who may or may not know each other, and sometimes the parents don't even meet each other. The clans may know of each other, and the parents have wisdom and experience, so usually the children just go along with their decision. Usually the marriage works out all right. The problem is that the matchmaker sometimes hides things, and Ilyeop is an example of someone who suffered at the hands of an unscrupulous matchmaker. Once married, wives must be submissive—that is an accepted concept. Women cannot even think about requesting a divorce. If the husband divorces her, she is looked down upon and despised. In view of that, you can imagine how much hurt Ilyeop must have gone through. She had a wounded heart, and, I believe, because of experiencing all that rejection, she wrote 'Sin Jung Jo Ron.'

"At present, Kim Ilyeop has stopped publishing her women's magazine, and I heard that she was going to continue her education at Younghwa University.

"Dear Oda!

"I don't know what your interest is in Kim Ilyeop, but, if you should happen to be in love with her, to give her up would be a wise decision. There are more than a few reasons for this.

"First, she failed in her marriage. You are a respectable bachelor, and it would not be common sense to marry a divorced woman.

"Second, and most important, she would never marry a Japanese man. It would be unheard of for a Korean girl to marry a foreigner, much less a Japanese! She is a famous poet, with a long history of nationalism, who supports the independence of Korea from Japan. In the 1919 Kimi Independence Movement, she made a Korean flag, and distributed printed matter which strongly advocated the ideal of independence. Would that kind of woman consent to marry a Japanese?

"There are other reasons, but those are the most important. Please accept my advice, block out distractions, and concentrate on your studies. That is my sincere wish for you."

After Oda Seizo read Song Gisu's letter, he was overwhelmed with complex feelings. He was glad to have the information about Kim Ilyeop, but he agreed with Song Gisu that there were many obstacles to be overcome. He was astounded to hear that she was a woman poet. He had thought that she was a smart lady, but had not imagined her to be a famous poet at such a young age. When he remembered her shining eyes, his heart ached. Then that ache changed to impatience that twisted inside him. She was a Korean woman with a history of divorce—he knew all that, but still longed for her. But, as a descendant of Oda Token, that was an incredibly foolish idea. Song Gisu's advice was right. The problem was that his feelings did not obey his reasoning. He kept telling himself to forget her, but her features floated before his eyes. A face of both nobility and beauty, and eyes that could be either cold or warm; he shook his head, but her image refused to be erased.

"A different nationality, a failed marriage—that kind of woman. And you are still yearning for her?...."

Oda Seizo's mind became more and more confused. He tried to understand about her feminist article "Sin Jung Jo Ron." Clearly, she had been oppressed by the social structure and long established customs. He could understand her emphasis on this subject, and felt sympathetic toward her point of view. When he went to bed, his eyes refused to close throughout the night. It was no longer simply a matter of dating; he was now seriously thinking about marriage to Kim Ilyeop. Even though he could understand and accept her, he knew his obstinate parents would never do so. When his thinking had reached that point, a flame of rebelliousness was kindled in him. "Right. To overcome all of those obstacles and succeed: that is real love." After that determination, he wrote a letter to Kim Ilyeop at the Younghwa University. Whatever happened, he wanted to let her know that he was sincerely in love with her. He edited his writing to make clearer his sincerity about his love. He had believed her promise to write to him, and indicated his disappointment at not hearing from her. He wanted her to know that he was one Japanese man who could love and understand Korea. He wanted to be seen not as a temporary lover only, but as one who hoped that they could love one another sincerely. His heart was filled with passionate and genuine feelings. In spite of Seizo's impassioned writing, Kim Ilyeop did not respond. Maybe she didn't get the letter. But, no—the letter hadn't come back. She must have received it. Not receiving an answer made Seizo even more impatient. He wrote twice, three times, five times—still the same result.

"That is too much," he said to himself. Sometimes he felt resentful and angry, but then his thoughts turned to the feelings he could not deny or give up, and his determination became even stronger. He could not step back. In all his more than twenty years, he had never been so fascinated by a woman. She would be the only love in his life.

"If she won't answer my letter, I will have to go to meet her." He gathered all his zeal and enthusiasm, and wrote with a flourish even more fervently and honestly than he ever had before: "I'll go to Tokyo right away. I wish for us to meet at the bench in Hibiya Park where we ran into each other before. I know you are thinking that you will not go there. But, if you won't come, I will go to visit the school. I know this is not a satisfactory way to meet, but I must see you. Please understand." He included the meeting date and hour. It was a somewhat threatening letter, but he felt he had no choice, since otherwise she would not meet him.

Loneliness and Fate

After she read Oda Seizo's latest letter, Ilyeop frowned. She had received all of the letters and had read every one. Of course, she understood his passion, but she wanted to concentrate on her studies. Moreover, she had never considered falling in love with a Japanese man.

"What shall I do? …" Kim Ilyeop realized that this was not a simple matter. The volley of letters he had sent had burdened her, like a baptism. She had thought that unrequited love would soon run its course, but that did not appear to be happening. Instead of fading away, he appeared to be becoming increasingly determined. Since he was threatening to come to the school, she would have to meet him at the time and place he had specified.

She thought that Seizo was one or two years younger than herself, so, perhaps she could convince him, like an elder sister, of what would be the best course of action. She put his letters between the pages of various books, and noted on the calendar the date on which he was planning to arrive.

"If I tell him in the right way, it will be OK."

Kim Ilyeop arrived at the park thirty minutes later than Seizo had specified. It had taken longer to get there from her rooming house than she had expected. Inside of the park the air was crisp and refreshing as it touched her face. She walked toward the bench where they had met before. He had arrived earlier, and she could see him sitting there. He was flushed and breathing deeply as he repeatedly consulted his watch. As she approached, he leapt to his feet.

"Ah, you came!" he shouted. Kim Ilyeop's heart sank as she saw his misery turn into joy in that instant. Maybe it was not going to be as easy as she had thought to solve this problem. She had planned how she was going to persuade him, but when the time came, she could not open her mouth.

His face had changed a lot. Though he was not tall, he had appeared commanding and healthy. Now his eyes were hollow, his shoulders slumped and he seemed thin and ill, and she knew immediately that it was because of her. She dropped her head, and when she did so she saw that his feet were surrounded by a smattering of cigarette butts; he had tried to appease his impatience with tobacco, and these were the remains. She sat down on the bench without speaking, and Seizo seated himself close to her. For a while they sat in silence. He had come from far away to see her, but now he felt powerless to affect her. For her, too, the powers of persuasion she had thought she had, had deserted her. The early-summer sunlight was flooding the park, and the pigeons were peacefully pecking at their crumbs, as they had been that other time. In the sky cumulous clouds floated gently, and around them roses were dazzlingly red. Finally, Oda Seizo spoke first.

"I'm sure you got my letters. I have been waiting for your answer."

"What could I say to you?"

"Do you mean that you could not accept my sincere feelings?"

Kim Ilyeop took a deep breath. Finally she had to tell him that she could not, under any circumstances, accept his confession.

"Mr. Seizo, I don't want to discount your feelings of love. I am not the kind of person who could do that. But, we are not suitable for each other. I do not think that we can love each other."

"Why, what is the reason?" His throat was dry. He had been expecting her to feel this way, but when he actually heard her statement, his whole body became tense. She said slowly and clearly:

"First of all, we have different nationalities. This means different life styles and different values. We should not expect to be able to reconcile these differences or get along well together."

"Do you have any other reasons?" he asked, trying to control his trembling. She was silent.

"There could possibly be problems, as you are pointing out," he said. "But, isn't overcoming problems what real love is all about?"

"I think that love should look for a future of guaranteed happiness."

"Do you think we would become unhappy?"

Now he had control of himself, and his trembling had stopped, but still passion had him in its grip.

"Now, Mr. Seizo, even if you don't change your mind, things change, and you would be surrounded by opposition."

"I'm ready for any opposition."

She also had expected his determination. She sighed.

"As a matter of fact, there are more important reasons than those."

Oda Seizo knew what she was going to say.

"Is it because you have been married before and therefore could not accept me? Is that the story?"

"Ah … how did you know?" Her eyes were wide.

"Did you think I would come here to meet you without some knowledge?"

"Then, after you know everything, are you still trying to court me?"

Seizo nodded his head. When Ilyeop heard what he had to say, her heart grew heavy. She was almost convinced that his feelings were not merely temporary, and he had begun to work his way into her heart. She was not a heartless woman who could turn her back on his sincerity, but neither was she one to act impulsively. She tightened her control over her emotions.

"I believe what you are saying, Mr. Seizo, but I am not ready, even so, to accept your reasoning."

"If so, if you understand me now, that is enough."

After saying this, his eyes blazed, and Ilyeop felt penetrated by that flame.

They left the park, and walked around without a destination. They ate dinner together.

He followed Ilyeop to her rooming house, under the pretense of escorting her there.

"OK, that's enough. Are you going to stay at your hotel tonight?" Ilyeop asked, looking into his deep eyes.

"No. I have a hometown friend, Shindo Araki. I am going to sleep at his house."

"Oh, good. You should get back there before it gets too late." But Seizo did not move from his position. Instead, he addressed her in a very low and strong voice.

"Promise to meet me again tomorrow. I came here only to see you. I cannot go back after seeing you only once." His will overcame her resistance, and she nodded her head.

After they had decided the place and time, Seizo came close to her, and she reflexively took a step backward, retreating step by step until her back was against the wall. He continued to move toward her, and she pushed him away, but for a moment he embraced her, and she could not prevent it. He was trembling. Ilyeop felt dizzy. His hug was awkward, but she could feel his warmth and sincerity; she remained immobile, and the stars were shining in the sky.

When she went inside, her friend Na Hyeseok was waiting for her.

"Where did you go? Why are you so late? I've been waiting for a long time." As Ilyeop regarded the cheerful face of her friend, her own feelings became more complicated. Nothing had been resolved: he had not given up, and she, against her better judgment, had finally agreed to meet him again.

"Hyeseok, will you listen to me for a while?" She told her everything about the relationship between her and Oda Seizo. Hyeseok's eyes widened.

"Wow! Kim Ilyeop the proud and stubborn one conquered by a Japanese man! I can't believe it." Hyeseok was a good enough friend to be able to such things.

"I'm not so arrogant that I could condemn someone's sincerity," Ilyeop said.

Na Hyeseok saw how serious she was. She sat up straight and asked, "Then are you thinking about marrying him?"

"No."

"If you are not going to marry him, are you just going to play with fire?"

"I couldn't do that." Ilyeop sighed deeply. "I tried to persuade him to separate without hurting him too much."

Na Hyeseok eyed her with concern.

"But if you can't get out of it, what are you going to do?"

"That's absolutely not going to happen." She emphasized these words like she was trying to convince herself. That night she had not been able to say cold-hearted words to Seizo. She had been so driven by his passion that she had not been able to push him away, but she had not expected things to lead to thoughts of marriage with him.

As promised, the next day these two people met again, and Oda Seizo's face reflected his happiness. Like any other lovers, they strolled through the Ueno Art Gallery, and went to a movie theater. While they roamed around the streets, they talked and shared many stories. Mostly Seizo talked and Ilyeop listened.

"I'm the oldest of three sons in the Oda family, so my parents expect a lot out of me." A dark shadow passed over his face, a fact that did not go unnoticed by Ilyeop; an unmistakable expression of just one of the challenges they faced. She thought that there would be no way that he could go against his family and would never want to be the cause of something like that.

The day that Seizo went back to Yamaguchi, Ilyeop saw him off at the station.

"Then, from now on, if I send a letter, will you answer it?" Seizo asked before they parted.

"Yes." Kim Ilyeop had not changed her mind about him, but there was no way that she could tell him that.

From the beginning, she had no intention of accepting Seizo's declaration of love. A distinguished and well-known Japanese family would never accept her as a daughter-in-law, and she could never dream of becoming the wife of a Japanese man. If things became too serious between them, Seizo would be the one that would suffer more. If the relationship was broken off now, it could be kept as a beautiful memory. She was thinking of putting all these things in a letter, then telling him good-bye.

The End of the Relationship

Before she could write the letter, she received one from him:

"I knew I loved you, but until I saw you again, I didn't know how much.

Now, I can see clearly how much I love. I want to marry you. This is my pledge toward you.

"Dear Ilyeop! I'm determined to marry you. Since I know only my own feelings, I am not sure it could really happen. First of all, you might not agree with me, my father might prevent it, or the gods of fate might be against us. Even so, if I cannot marry you, I would rather be alone in my life—that is my vow to myself. You might laugh at that kind of promise, but if I didn't have this strong determination, I might lose my love.

"As you said, we are of different nationalities. Moreover, my nation has trampled over your country. That happened—it has nothing to do with us, but it may be an obstacle to our getting together. But we can overcome all of those things; it could be a beautiful victory of love.

"Ilyeop, you are one year and five months older than I. This age difference doesn't matter to us. If I can marry you, I will be a faithful husband, and be a good provider.

"I know your first marriage failed, but I have no concern about that. I have no wish or expectation for you to become different than you are. Please marry me—that is all I want …"

Ilyeop gripped the letter and stared into one corner of her room. She felt that the cool rationality of her mind was threatened. His letter was utterly sincere. She thought that his vows and promises to her were completely honest. He hadn't even condemned her past marriage, and her eyes filled with tears as she felt the scope of his love. Typically a Korean man might have considered her as a second wife or lover, but not in terms of someone with whom he could make a family or home. Women agreed with the viewpoint of her magazine "Sin Jung Jo Ron," but no man did.

"Even though my earlier marriage failed, if I could have a real marriage now, could I still come to a foreign country to study?" she asked herself. She was not confident she could answer that question.

"Probably, I would try to have a family before I got too old. I would have a child from the man I love, and would try to make a happy home." Even though she had tried to portray herself as a cold person, she was a woman who wanted love. Ilyeop caught herself and shook her head. "What am I thinking? This makes no sense."

There was no way in which she could be married to Oda Seizo. It could not be done. There were so many patriotic people who had given their lives in the struggle for independence. How could a feminist poet marry the enemy and live only for herself? She could not accept such a thing. His honest love made her feel like crying, but she could not accept it. She pulled her chair up to the desk and sat there. She carefully lined up a sheet of white paper, and took hold of her pen. She tried to write what she had in her mind, but somehow could not do so.

"How can I put this so he won't be hurt?" She hesitated for a while, then began writing, word by word, with careful concentration. She was concerned about his feelings, but she was not qualified to accept his huge and noble love. She tried her best to express her sincerity. As she expected, he answered back that whatever she said, his love was not going to change.

She received one other similar letter, then came summer vacation, and Seizo showed up again in Tokyo. She couldn't refuse his suggestion to meet; not only was he burning with love, but also he had come all the way from Yamaguchi to Tokyo to see her.

In 1921 Ilyeop did not go home to Korea over summer vacation. Even if she had, there would be no parents there to greet her. She was alone in the world, and indeed had a pen name meaning "one leaf." The name had been given to her by the famous Korean author, Chun Won, whose real name was Lee Gwang Soo. There had been a poem:

> One fragile leaf
> Dropped into a water fall
> And was dashed to bits;
> The spirit of that leaf reached the ocean.
> Ilyeop: One Leaf

Ilyeop was a strong person who hid her loneliness, but still she was a woman. All of her friends had gone to their respective home towns, leaving her in an empty school, and, at times, she felt her isolation keenly. Her heart would ache, and she would hug herself and weep silently.

"If only Seizo and I could love each other…." When that thought entered her mind, she would shake her head.

"That is futile thinking!" She could reason clearly, but her heart, not listening to reason, wanted only to be joined with Seizo's, ending her loneliness.

One day Oda Seizo came to Tokyo to see her again. Ever since love had opened his eyes he seemed more alert and manly. Maybe this change was reflecting his determination and readiness to choose and secure that love.

They finished a simple lunch and strolled around the park, conversing about this and that. Suddenly he stopped, and looking directly at her, began speaking in a formal way:

"I'm staying at the house of my friend, Shindo Araki. He works in a bank, and was recently married. I told them about Ilyeop, and they invited us to visit Saturday afternoon. Please do not refuse." She was a little bit flustered and uneasy.

"Invitation…." She had not ended her relationship with him, but neither did she wish it to proceed further. "That would be a real burden for me."

"My father, who is a bank president, used his influence to help Shindo Araki get his job. He is my best friend—you don't have to feel reluctant." Seizo had misunderstood her to mean that she had a problem with his friend, when actually she was trying to protect herself from being further attracted to Seizo. She was afraid that she would be inextricably tied to him, but still her loneliness drove her toward his passion. Finally she nodded.

"I'll go; I knew I would end up going."

Shindo Araki's house was neat and cozy, permeated by the charming atmosphere of a new marriage. The bride's cooking skills were very good. For Ilyeop, being surrounded by this sweet environment, eating such delicious food, felt strange. For her, the idea of such a home life was a distant dream. It was a little painful and sad, and she felt herself isolated in the happy world of others. She glanced at Seizo, who was talking with his friend in a relaxed and comfortable manner. Looking at his strong profile, she sighed without meaning to.

They left after the tea service. It was already getting late, and outside it was very dark.

"It is too late, we must get going." She looked up at the sky, but could see only darkness, where clouds were hiding the stars.

"It looks like we are going to get some rain soon. Let's hurry up." As soon as he had spoken, a strong wind blew. It was not just an ordinary wind, but brought with it lightning that slashed through the darkness, and crashing thunder that shook the earth. They hurried, but before they had taken more than a few steps, the rain started, so hard that they could scarcely walk into it. This happened in the blink of an eye.

"We've got to get out of this rain—come in here!"

He pulled her under the corner of the eaves, and they hugged the wall to avoid getting wet. Her thin summer dress was soon drenched and clinging to her body, and Ilyeop crossed her arms over her chest, in an unconscious effort to conceal herself. It didn't look like the rain was likely to stop soon, and there were no rickshawws in sight. When the rain slowed down a bit, they started walking, but immediately it started to pour again. They were at a loss, and could do nothing but watch the pounding rain.

"I'm very sorry to put you through this...."

"Oh, no. It's not your fault; the sky is doing it. What can we do?"

In reality, she looked perplexed as she stared at the weather. If this storm had begun before they had left Shindo's house, perhaps they would not feel so bewildered. There was not likely to be a rickshaww to be found in such a strong rain, and it was too far to go to Ilyeop's boarding house.

"There is no choice—we can't get home tonight. What do you think about staying in a hotel?" Seizo asked this of Ilyeop with a very careful face. She could not answer easily, but neither could she keep standing in the rain. Seizo understood her feelings, and looked at her face without saying anything.

"It doesn't look like the rain is going to stop any time soon...." Ilyeop bit her lip, and they stood in silence for a while, in the rain. Ilyeop was shivering, and Seizo could not let her go on that way.

"We can't keep this up. You will catch cold. Let's go in somewhere until the rain stops, and get dry." Seizo took hold of her arm and Ilyeop let herself be pulled into a hotel.

"Two rooms, please."

"There is only one room remaining...." The clerk looked sorry.

"Oh, dear, what shall we do?" Seizo looked at Ilyeop again, and she looked into his face. Maybe this was the kind of situation that could be described as an impossible choice. She did not disapprove of an unmarried man and woman spending the night in a hotel room, but this was Oda Seizo, and that was different. What was fate doing to her? She was trying hard to get away from him and they kept being bound up together. She was exhausted from the struggle going on in her brain. In fact, it was fortunate to have even one room so late at night and in such bad weather. In this rain, how could one find a hotel with two rooms? Ilyeop's thinking was so conflicted that she put her hand on her brow. Seizo saw how tired she was becoming and took her arm.

"Ilyeop, you are not feeling well. Let's go into the room."

"No, no—I'm OK."

"Do not make this too complicated. You don't want to catch a cold. Think how bad I would feel if you were ill—do it for me." Seizo saw how perplexed she was, and spoke sweetly to her. Seizo urged the hotel clerk to guide them. Ilyeop went to the room with Seizo supporting her. In the room were two beds made up side by side on the floor. Ilyeop sat down quietly in one corner. Their clothes were so wet that they began steaming in the indoor heat.

"If you stay like that you will catch a cold. Change into this." Seizo handed her a robe. Then he took off his own wet clothes, but Ilyeop could not bring herself to disrobe. Up to now, Seizo had been a perfect gentleman, but seeing her in this closed room with only the two of them, he was filled with heat. She looked so pretty, her wet hair dripping on her forehead, her milky white earlobes, her round wet shoulders clearly showing through her transparent attire. He had always thought her very pretty, but now her form enraptured him.

"She didn't refuse me, but she didn't accept me either. If it's not tonight, I might lose her forever," he thought. There might never be another such God-given opportunity. Perhaps now Ilyeop would accept him. There might never be another chance. He stopped in the midst of putting on his robe, and grabbed her in an embrace. When he felt her breathing against his chest, he felt faint, unable to think clearly.

Ilyeop was trembling like a wild bird and his passion consumed him. He embraced her like she was a fragile, dear and precious object. But suddenly his embrace became as strong as a tidal wave, and he could no longer control himself. The solitary leaf could not prevail against such an all-encompassing wave. She could not even breathe, and, thinking of fate, love, loneliness, she became helpless. She threw her body into that hot and passionate ocean.

Like a lone leaf in the sea, Ilyeop was engulfed by the flood.

Foreseeing Disaster

When Oda Seizo told his father Oda Hosaku about his plan to marry Kim Ilyeop, it was shortly after he had found out that she was pregnant. The reaction was to be expected.

"You, the descendant of Oda Token, you didn't study *and* you made a Korean woman pregnant?"

"I love the woman." Seizo's gaze did not retreat an inch; he was like his father in this respect; stubbornness was a character trait handed down through the generations.

"What did you say? How could you talk so heedlessly in front of your father about such a worthless love!" Seizo was silent.

"No marriage!" Hosaku did not back down.

"Why is it not possible?"

"Are you telling me you don't know?"

"Please give us your consent."

"Do not forget that you are from such a distinguished family that you could marry into Japanese royalty. Maybe you don't care, but the daughter-in-law of Oda Hosaku cannot be just anybody. Even a Japanese woman would have to come from appropriate stock, but a Korean? This cannot even be considered. Absolutely not! Never bring it up again!"

Hosaku's voice was filled, not just with anger, but with rage. Seizo's heart shattered. Maybe this was the end. He again appealed ardently to his father.

"In her belly, the blood of the Oda family is growing."

"Termination, then, is the only course of action."

"It is already too late for that. Even if it wasn't, it could not be done."

While the verbal battle was going on between father and son, Seizo's mother watched his face with a worried expression. Poor Mother. Seizo hoped that his mother at least would understand him. Hosaku's tirade continued.

"You will marry the woman I designate, and leave the matter of this other person to me."

"That cannot happen."

"That means you will sever the ties between father and son." Seizo thought about the consequences, but spoke calmly and serenely, recalling his freely given promise of love.

"If we cannot find a point of compromise, there is no way this problem can be resolved."

"What? You good-for-nothing! I have patiently explained it so you could understand how immense your disobedience in this matter would be! Now get out of here at once!"

When his mother heard Seizo's father threaten to expel him from the family, she tried to intervene with tears streaming down her cheeks, but neither could she change his father's will, nor was Seizo's determination to be shaken.

"Please forgive my disobedience. If you cannot accept her, Father, I must bid you farewell."

"Didn't I already tell you to get out of here?" The negotiation was broken off at this point and Seizo departed.

"Seizo! Seizo! Does it have to be this way? It is not too late—please apologize to your father, and ask his forgiveness," his mother pleaded with her tears. Seizo's heart ached, but he could not do what she asked. He looked at her tears, and said lovingly,

"This might be the last time I see you. I am sorry to pain you so, Mother. Please take good care of yourself.... Good-bye."

"Seizo!"

He could hear her entreaties, but he did not look back. Once he had made a promise, the promise must be kept, and this was indeed the last time he saw his parents. He never attempted to see them, nor they, him.

Oda Seizo was not a person to change his mind, and resolved to go ahead with the marriage despite the wishes of his family. He left the Kyushu National University without finishing his degree, and went to Tokyo to be with Ilyeop. Ilyeop saw things differently. Even though she was pregnant, she felt that this marriage should not take place; rather, she believed that she should not marry him at all. When she found out about the pregnancy, she almost fainted. Who would have imagined that one unexpected night could end up like this? However, in a corner of her mind, she could hear the whisper of temptation:

"Why are you hesitating?" she asked herself. "Have the baby, marry, have a good life; everything will turn out well. Seizo is trustworthy and will be a good husband."

"No, let's not dwell on useless expectations. To do that, I would have to pay too heavy a price. He and I have different ways, and for a brief moment, our paths simply crossed." She knew that the temptation was coming from her own weakness. She was especially unhappy that Seizo had broken off with his parents because of her, and she could not picture herself living comfortably in a marriage to a Japanese man.

"You must go back home," she told Seizo. "That is the right thing for you to do." Seizo strongly rejected her persuasion. She sighed silently, wondering how she could change his mind.

"Well, there is no choice. If he won't leave me, I have to leave him." She was already determined.

In September 1922, Ilyeop gave birth to a boy in the home of Seizo's friend, Shindo Araki. Seizo's happiness was extreme. He named his son Oda Masao. When she had recovered her strength, she could no longer postpone that which she had been thinking about for a long time. She wrote a long letter to Seizo:

"Dear Seizo, I am so sorry.

"To marry me you have given up your relationship with your parents. But there is no way that I can accept that love. I would be comfortable with you, but it would always bother me to have acted against my country.

"Dear Seizo, I know how much you love me; that is why I am leaving. Your love is too big, and I must not let myself be absorbed by it.

"I am sorry, and am heartsick to leave Masao, but I think this will be best for you both. Please raise him well, poor Masao, and I hope you will reconcile with your parents. For you to sever the most basic and natural relationship, both of the past and the future; all because of me, should not happen. Please seek forgiveness from your parents; marry a nice woman, and live a happy life. I am sure you can start a happy home again…."

She held her baby son, wrapped up like a bundle, and cried without a sound. Maybe Seizo and Masao would have offered her a last chance for a happy family life, despite her previous failure at marriage. The child, Masao, could be the symbol of a new life; but her own happiness could not be her ultimate goal. To sit down in a comfortable life would be a betrayal of her dreams.

"I'm sorry, Masao." Without delay, she took a train toward her home country. Oda Seizo was in despair when he found out Ilyeop had left. He realized for the first time the depth of the differences between them. He had given up everything to be with her, but she had left him anyway.

When he had begun to think clearly again after his bitter disappointment, he did not return to his family, although it had been Ilyeop's dearest wish that he do so. First, he asked Shindo Araki and his wife to raise Masao; fortunately, they had no children of their own as yet. Since he had made the decision not to go back home, he had to discover a way to make a living, for Masao as well as for himself. Even though Ilyeop was not at his side, Masao was not only a part of him, but also a part of her, whom he loved.

He entered the Nakano School, which did not require tuition, and which trained officers for the intelligence service. After finishing school, he got a job working in Korea for the viceroy as a reporter. He brought Masao to Korea with him. He began to see in young Masao an increasing resemblance to Ilyeop, and Seizo became more nostalgic for her as time went on.

"Kim Ilyeop … how was she getting along?" He wondered. "Has she met a Korean man, and is she living happily with him? If not, perhaps she would accept me by now."

He brought Masao to Song Gisu, who now lived in Sincheon, Hwanghae-do.

"I hate to ask, but would you look after this child for a while? It is not easy to raise a child alone."

"Is that the one? What can you do?—It happened. Don't worry."

Song Gisu took the child in without hesitation. From then on, Seizo looked for Kim Ilyeop, but then he received an unexpected blow: Kim Ilyeop had renounced the world and become a Buddhist monk.

Oda Seizo despaired when he realized that Ilyeop had cut her hair and had withdrawn from the world. The dream of finding her and making a happy home—he could hear it shattering into bits, and no other dream was possible for him. Why, why had she done that? Maybe she felt guilty about abandoning her newborn, and that led her Buddhism. He murmured to himself his determination: "I cannot embrace you forever, but I have promised you eternal love, so in all my life there will be no possibility of holding another woman. Don't worry about Masao. I will bring him up to be honorable and respectable."

As he had promised Ilyeop, he never married, and lived as a single man all of his life.

2

In the Garden of Youth

My Story

This is the story of the love between my mother Ilyeop, and my father Oda Seizo, as I heard it. It seems like fiction, but it is true; my mother and father lived lives that were more complex and dramatic than any novel that could be written. Whenever I think about those two people and their unfulfilled love, I recognize that the fruit of that love is me. Both of them were very proud and strong willed. Once their decisions were made they never wavered, and their pride and determination went to the grave with them. Because of that, I was abandoned; I grew up an orphan, hungry for love, even though I was not really an orphan.

When I was young, I had no way of knowing about these things; I could not even have guessed. I learned about them when I was quite a bit older, and having sifted through the memories of my eighty years, I am finally able to present the full picture of my life.

Leader of the Street Kids

I have a clear memory of being the second son of a family with a rice-polishing business in Sincheon, Hwanghae-do, Korea. I remember my address still: Mujeong-ri, Sincheon-eup, Sincheon-gun. At that time my name was Song Yeongeop. My father was Song Gisu; some people called him Songjaesu. That is clear; but I am frustrated that I can't remember the names of my mother, my sister and my younger and older brothers. Father owned a large rice polishing factory and an orchard. He was in the trading business, as well, exporting rice to Japan. He was a big-business man. I went to grade school in Sincheon, where other students envied me.

I was an average student. However, I remember having a leading part in a play, and representing my school in a swim competition. Like everyone else, I was excited to participate in sports or the school picnics in the spring and fall. My parents worried about my poor grades, but they never forced me to study. They wished for me to grow up healthy, with good food and clothing, and they figured that when I grew older I would have the sense to study.

The family had two houses, one in the orchard, as well as a big, tile-roofed house near the factory. These houses were not far apart, and I played between them. In the orchard, when the peach and apple trees were in bloom, their fragrance and the sunlight through the trees made it peaceful and beautiful. In the fall, the rich beauty of this spot was like a watercolor painting.

When I was young, I had another name: Chief of the Bad Boys. It was during the Japanese occupation, but that dark time had nothing to do with a child of the age of Song Yeongeop. In those days we fished in the creek for crawfish. We played at war, riding horseback on each other's backs. That was one game. Another was flipping cards by hitting them; another was playing shuttlecock using our feet. We spent that time in play, not knowing how fast it would go by. I hated to lose to anyone. Never once did I surrender to my friends. Even those bigger and stronger than I, I knocked down and made my subordinates. Even so, I would never fight without a good reason. If the other boy made a mistake but would not acknowledge it, I would flourish my fist in his face. Especially, I would never let it pass if a Japanese boy hurt a Korean boy. Even as a youngster, I had a clear concept of justice. I was the leader of the neighborhood kids, and, when I look back, I remember that as the happiest time of my life.

Unexpected Guest

Even now, my speech has the ghost of a Hwanghae-do accent; what we learn well in childhood we never lose. But, if I compare life as a youngster with painting, it is like the viewing the basic outlines, with the details impossible to perceive: in my eighties, it is impossible to recall all the details of my youth.

It is frustrating not to be able to remember details, but there are some things etched sharply in my memory, which I can reproduce over and over, like a woodblock print. One of those memories is of New Years Day of my fourth year in grade school. We all got new clothes and special food for the New Year, and counted on our fingers in anticipation of its arrival. That year, we were given new clothes as a gift. But, I remember clearly that I noticed my older brother's things were new and even included a vest, whereas mine were very clean, starched and neatly ironed to look new, but they clearly were not. I was such an envious person that I could not let that go by. I started complaining and asking why I should be slighted. I cried and shouted, and demanded new clothes. My older brother responded to my anger by saying that I should be grateful for what I had. All of my anger toward my parents was then directed at my brother. I followed him outside, and threw mud on his new vest.

"You brat!" My brother kicked my leg, and I fought back. As we wrestled, we both fell down. My brother, who had a gentle character, had always let me win, and our parents always took my side. Maybe that was the reason that at that moment my brother exploded in anger, and could not stop kicking me. Even as he kicked, I fought back, and he was finally provoked into yelling:

"You're not really a part of this family—you are just a stray we picked up under the bridge! Why should you be so angry with me?!"

"NO!"

"You are, you are! We rescued you…." At that moment, Father came out to stop the fight, and began shouting at Brother.

"You, Boy! Who told you you could say that? Shut your mouth!" My brother was shocked. He stopped what he was doing and backed up. Mother, who had followed Father out, was also frowning at him. If my parents had just let it go, I might have regarded what he said as just angry words, but their strong reaction gave me an unexpected frightened feeling. It flashed upon my mind that maybe I was indeed a picked-up child. I was uneasy, and asked,

"Mother, is it true? Am I really just a picked-up child?" Mother brushed me off, and gave me a warm hug. She said with a smile,

"Your brother was just trying to make you angry. I love you so much; how could you be a picked-up child?" Father had not stopped shouting, and whipped Brother's legs with a stick. So New Year turned into chaos. Even though I was young, I sensed that my parents were hiding something. I sank into anxiety for a while, but it did not last long. I was not of an age to think deeply, and my parents' love was the same as ever. I soon became the same innocent and naughty boy as before.

My second clear memory is of the fall when I was in fifth grade. At that time, there was a grade school art competition. The preliminary selection was done in Gun, and the final competition, for drawings from nature, took place in Hwanghae-do. I was not a particularly good student, but I had always loved to draw. The contest was quite democratic. Our art teacher collected the art works of all the students and displayed them on the board, where the students could view them, and pick out what they thought the best. The teacher also made her selection, and asked the opinion of the students. If they agreed with her, that work was submitted to Gun; if they made another choice, both works were submitted.

The students picked mine, but I realized that two works had been sent, so I supposed the teacher had chosen the work of another student. In Gun, the judges picked mine. I was very proud, and, in the further Hwanghae-do competition, I won the top prize. This was the discovery of my talent, which I had not appreciated myself up to then. I was surprised, and the teacher and my parents were equally surprised. After that occasion, without my planning it, my education became aimed at my becoming an artist. I didn't realize that fact until much later. I had received a big award, but I did not have any intention of becoming a painter; maybe I was too young to develop that kind of determination. In spite of myself, I was led by my elders to become a painter. Even though I was not the one to choose this path in life, I have never for a moment regretted being an artist. If I had made the choice of an occupation after I had grown up, perhaps I still would have turned out to be an artist.

I met the person most responsible for my studying art during the winter of the year in which I won the award in the Hwanghae-do competition. That is my third most clearly recalled memory. One short winter day, I had played so hard that I fell asleep early. Mother woke me abruptly.

"Yeongeop, wake up! You need to go to the sarang-bang." That was the room where guests were greeted. I asked, "Why, Mom?"

"Go there, eat your naengmyeon noodles, then go back to bed." I had never before eaten cold noodles in the sarang-bang. Always before, Mother had brought my food to me in my room. I complained, "Bring the naengmyeon here.…" But she had a serious expression.

"There is a guest in the sarang-bang with Father. Greet him politely, and eat naengmyeon with them." Mother spoke so strongly that I could not argue with her. I went to the sarang-bang where I found Father, and a Japanese man of Father's age dressed in a western style suit. They were sitting together. I greeted him politely. Father and the guest conversed in Japanese.

"This is Yeongeop. He won the first prize in the whole Hwanghae-do art competition." The guest was nodding his head and studying me. He appeared to be satisfied with me, and asked Father, "So—he has artistic talent?"

"In the future he might be a famous master. Who knows?"

"Painter … artist.…" He kept repeating that, even forgetting to eat his noodles. I had been called in from a deep sleep, so I ate my naengmyeon quickly, and went back to bed. The next day, when I woke up, the guest was already gone, and I soon forgot his face.

Near the time of grade school graduation, I found that I never should have forgotten that face.

Sad Separation

It was the night before graduation, and Father, Mother and I were sitting in the sarang-bang. Father was looking at me with misty eyes and deep emotion. Finally, he called my name in a low voice.

"Yeongeop."

"Yes?"

"Now, listen well to what I have to tell you." I was tense because his expression was so unusual. Mother was sitting with lowered head.

"Yeongeop, you were born in Tokyo, Japan."

"Wha-....?" Father told a completely unexpected story.

"You came here when you were three years old. Until then, Shindo Araki, a Japanese man, raised you. You are my adopted son, coming into my family when you were three years old." I was deeply shocked, and felt like I had been hit with a iron bar. I could hardly breathe, and my insides were roiling. My face became very hot. My mouth was so dry I could barely lick my lips. I asked Father, "Then, are you saying that Shindo Araki is my real father?"

"No. He is not your real father. I was in the Kyushu High School with your real father. Shindo Araki was also, like me, the friend of your real father. When you were born, your father was a student and could not support you. Please understand that point. When you were born, you were left with Shindo Araki, and, when you were three, you came to Korea to live with me."

If a person is shocked they are often at a loss for words, and I couldn't say anything.

"Maybe you find it hard to believe, but it is all true." There was no reason for Father to lie to me. Elder Brother had teased me about being a picked-up child; now I knew that was not a lie. Mother was wiping away her tears with a handkerchief. Tears were running down my cheeks as well. I was choked up, but I managed to ask:

"Then, who are my real parents?" Father thought for a while, and the silence was heavy. I asked again, "Who are the real parents I was born to?"

"You might remember—a year or so or ago, you were called to this room and ate naengmyeon. Do you remember that?"

"Yes. I do recall that."

"The guest that night was your father."

I remembered that night when I greeted a guest and ate naengmyeon, but I could not remember the guest's face. Later, I recalled that the guest was a Japanese man. Then, I was the son of a Japanese man? In school, I was known as the tough Korean boy who could beat up the Japanese kids; instead of being a Korean child who got beaten up, I was the one who could vent all of the anger. Because of that, I was often called to the principal's office, and was often the target of condemnation by Japanese parents. Could I really be a Japanese? That was a terrible trick of fate! Father continued.

"Yeongeop, your father still lives alone, so he cannot take you home yet." If my father was not married, then who is my mother, and where is she?

"So, the mother who gave birth to me has passed away?"

".... Not exactly."

"Then, why did Father and Mother not marry?"

"Your mother is Korean. She is a daughter of a good family, and worked in the Independence Movement. Your father and mother loved each other, but because of being of different nationalities, they could not marry."

"Then, where is she now?"

"She relinquished the family."

At my young age, I did not understand the concept of renouncing the world to become a monk, so when my father said that, I thought he meant that she had married another man. That made another wound in my heart. There was no need for me to try to find a mother who was married to another man. I believed it to be so, and I felt so mortified and so victimized that I could not control my tears. Mother embraced me and we sobbed together. Then she wiped away my tears with her warm hand. Father cleared his throat, and continued.

"Yeongeop, I raised you as my real son, but the reason I am telling you this story is that we have to separate now. If that were not the case, I might not ever have told you. From now on, you will be living in Seoul."

"What? I have to go to Seoul?"

"Yes. Tomorrow, right after the graduation ceremony, there will be someone who will take you there. You will have to leave right away."

"My real father called for me?"

"No. You will go to Master Idang in Seoul. He is a famous artist. Your father decided to send you there to make the most of your talent. Go, study hard and become a famous artist."

I had hardly ever seen my father, he had left me to someone else to raise, and now he decides that I must leave this place ... I couldn't accept it.

"No. I don't want to be an artist. I just want to live here. I prefer not to be an artist." Then Mother, who to that point had said nothing, opened her mouth.

"Yeongeop, Mother doesn't want this separation either. You know how dearly we have loved you...."

"So—please let me live here."

"But, Yeongeop, you can become somebody. Here in this countryside, you would never have this opportunity."

Father's voice was even softer.

"Your mother is right. For you to study in Seoul is your father's wish, but it is our wish, too. Nothing will be changed; you are still my son, and you will have to come home on vacations"

"Yes. Please do not forget me and your father, and your sister and brothers. You can come home any time when you want to see us, or if you are having problems."

I couldn't sleep at all that night. That these people who raised me were not my real parents had shocked and saddened me. My heart was broken and the pain cut into my bones. I was wracked with disappointment and the feeling that I was all alone.

The sadness of separation was the same for my parents as for me. The next morning, Mother's eyes were red and bloodshot. She was trying to make me eat a good meal, but I couldn't swallow a bite. I felt like a bone was stuck in my throat. Mother kept repeating that I should come back after I became an important person. There were tears in the eyes of my sister and brothers. I went to school, but my feet were dragging, and I kept turning around to look back at the house.

Waryong-dong Father

All during the graduation ceremony I was very depressed, not because I was graduating, but because my circumstances were so pathetic. After the ceremony, my classmates were surrounded by flowers and laughing with their parents and their brothers and sisters. But I was taken by the hand by my father and was pulled reluctantly to the playground. There, a monk in a Buddhist robe was waiting for us. In Sincheon-eup, there was a Japanese temple called Nishihongan. This monk's name was Kanegio, and he was the head monk of that temple. Father introduced me to him, and asked him to take good care of me.

"Yeongeop, go well!" Those were the last words that Father said to me. He turned away then, with misty eyes.

"Father, take care of yourself. I will be back to see you."

"Of course. I'll be waiting for you." Father had turned his back so that I would not see his tears. This was my separation from Father.

I had been in the Nishihongan temple for a few days when Master Park Seungmu, whose name as an artist was Simhyang, visited us. He was an old friend of the head monk, Kanegio, and he was staying at the hot springs in Sincheon to treat an ailment he had. Master Simhyang was happy to hear from Kanegio that I had a talent for art.

"Hah, you cannot fool blood." When I heard this, my ears perked up. Because I heard it, I was able, in later days, to find my birth mother. For Master Simhyang to come there at that time was no accident, but rather was fated to happen.

I graduated from elementary school in Sincheon in 1936, Showa, the eleventh era of the Japanese calendar. The spring day I left Sincheon with the Monk Kanegio was cold and blustery. As we went into the Sincheon train station, I kept looking back at the sky over Mujeong-ri, where was located the house of my parents.

My first impression of Seoul was that it was a flourishing city. It was twilight, but the sidewalks were crowded, and buildings were big and beautiful. We took a streetcar, and got out at Third street in Jong-ro. We walked past the Danseongsa theater, and a little further on we came to Waryong-dong street and the house gate of Master Idang, Kim Eunho.

His servant led us past three doors, then into the main quarters. There one man was seated on the floor looking at us. He was Master Idang.

"You look very smart. Did you have a hard trip?" Master Idang was so pleased to meet me that he patted me on the head.

"From today, this is your house. It might seem strange at first, but you will get used to it. Next year, you will go to Tokyo to enter middle school there. Now, study what you learned in sixth grade, and concentrate on your art-studies."

At that time, Master Idang lived with his old mother, his wife, and his two daughters. The women lived in separate quarters. Master Idang took me in to meet his family. Master Idang did not have a son, and I had been sent to him as an adopted one. He asked me to call him Father, and his wife Mother. Grandmother treated me like I was her own grandson. I started my second life in Father Idang's house.

Idang gave me a new name, Seolcheon. I was no longer Song Yeongeop; I had now become Kim Seolcheon.

First, Father Idang taught me how to make ink from an ink stick, and how to hold the brush. To have power in the brush stroke, he said, you must practice drawing orchids, one of the four gracious plants, and he demonstrated that for me.

Master Haegang and Master Cheongjeon

The fragrance of ink permeated that house, one that was often was visited by other great Korean artists. Among them were Master Haegang, Kim Kyujin, and Master Cheongjeon, Lee Sangbeom, who treated me especially well. One day, Master Haegang was watching me draw an orchid. He took my brush and wrote a poem in one flourish, then asked me the meaning of it.

"The apricot blooms in the cold, its blossoms fresh, clean and regal. In the orchid, silence becomes a flower, subtle and profound."

"Right! Great!"

Then he told me that one must appreciate the character of the four gracious plants before one could create freely. He explained to me in detail how to draw an orchid, and explained that the beauty of the orchid flower depends on elegance.

"What is 'elegance'?"

"It is the configuration of the orchid's leaf and petal that makes it elegant."

He explained that it would take an exquisite and original skill to portray that, and emphasized the importance of keeping in mind the meaning of calligraphy. The technique of calligraphy must be light and airy, and must reach the state of absolute ease. As a child, I could not fully understand Master Haegang's teaching, but it remains in my memory. Master Cheongjeon also taught me well. He taught me the special technique of landscape painting. I learned to draw mountains and water by wetting the brush. That is a technique that I use even now.

They often made samples that I could look at while I drew. Naughty boy that I was, because of their mystic powers, I could concentrate on the four gracious plants. That ability to concentrate I used to treat the loneliness and estrangement I had felt since discovering the secret of my birth. All of those sample drawings the masters made for me disappeared during the Korean War, which I felt very sad about.

"When you draw a stem of apricot flowers, try to convey the mood of a woman."

"The brush stroke must be as sharp as the slash of a dagger."

"The bamboo leaf is like the Chinese character for bamboo."

"The segments of the bamboo can be expressed as the Chinese character for the heart on one."

"Draw completely. If you cannot sketch well, it would be silly to expect to be an artist."

Even now, if I close my eyes I can hear the masters' voices in my ear. The two masters asked my Idang father to let me become their disciple, but he refused.

The Name That I Call Silently

My Idang father looked at my talent as something very valuable that should not be wasted. Of all the family, I alone had the honor of dining with him at his table. That meant that I was not merely a student, but that he accepted me as a son. Occasionally if I tried to help around the house, he would scold me, saying,

"I told you that your job is to study." Idang Father was an elder in the church, so every Sunday I had to go to church, too. Looking back on that from my life now, as a Buddhist monk, it seems a very special time for me. I was just following the family tradition, but I know now that experiencing the beliefs of Christianity added to the depth of my spirituality.

Often in the early morning my Idang father would take me to the public bathhouse where we would wash each other's back. In the evening, the three of us, Father, Mother and I, would often go out. Walking with them, holding their hands, I felt love from both parents. Everyone treated me well, but still, in my heart, was an empty, windy, space. In the wide back yard garden, I watched the flowers bloom and fade, and the bees and butterflies flying busily about, and I felt a deep loneliness. Sometimes I would throw myself passionately into my drawing and painting, but sometimes I would fall suddenly, and for no reason, into a swamp of lassitude, and become helpless and unable to do anything.

Without my birth parents I could not exist. I felt isolated, aimless, and helpless, constantly obsessing about my birth parents. Father was still single and Mother had left the home. That was all I knew about my parents. I believed that Mother had married another man, so I resented her, but still I missed her, and that made me resent her all the more.

I thought that Father was still single because of being shocked by Mother marrying another man. I didn't like it that Father was Japanese, but the fact that he had remained faithful, and had never married made me feel sorry for him. In this way, many months passed.

One day in late spring, Master Simhyang, whom I had met in Sincheon, visited us. He told us that he had regained his health, so he had returned to Seoul. He was pleased to see me, and told me that my family in Sincheon were all well, as was the monk, Kanegio.

Clearly, this person knew the secret of my birth. I was sure that Simhyang knew my birth parents because it was he who had remarked that blood would tell. I followed him when he left the house because I didn't want to miss the opportunity. I caught up with him as he reached the Secret Garden.

"Master!"

"Did you follow me because you had something to tell me?" He opened his eyes widely.

"Master, you know who my birth parents are, right?" I asked him without hesitation.

"Why did you think that?"

"Everybody knows, but no one will tell me. But, I trust that you will grant my wish, so I was waiting for you." Simhyang started to walk on.

"I do not know."

"Then why did you say that blood will tell? I'm sure that you know about my heritage. Is it true that my mother left the home?" Master Simhyang looked at me and nodded without saying anything. I noticed how blue the sky was, but his words had only added to my sadness. He took out a cigarette, lit it, and looked at me sideways.

"You knew that already? Well, your mother is a very famous person, a poet. Do you know her name?"

"No, I don't."

"Well, you'll find out eventually.... Your mother's name is Kim Ilyeop."

"..."

"I do not know whether that is a pen name or her Buddhist name. Her real name is Kim Wonju. I have met her—she is a wonderful person."

"What is a 'pen name,' or a 'Buddhist name?'"

"Boy, oh, boy.... A pen name is what is used by writers. Didn't I tell you that your mother is a poet? A Buddhist name is taken when someone becomes a monk." When I heard that I was shocked.

"Monk? Then my mother became a monk?"

"Well, you already knew that she had left home. Why do you keep asking about it?"

"I thought that leaving home meant that she had married someone."

"Oh, is that so? It might mean that, but another meaning might be that someone chose to shave her head and become a Buddhist monk."

Finally, I had discovered that Mother had become a monk. I was ashamed that I had misunderstood the meaning of those words, but I was so glad that she had not married another man that I blushed with joy. I tried to control my breathing, and hurriedly asked him, "Then, which temple is the one where my mother stays?"

"I heard that she is in Sudeok-sa."

I silently called my mother's name, Kim Ilyeop, and when I did so, all of my pent up longing burst out like a tidal wave, and hot tears rolled down my cheeks.

3

One Fallen Leaf

Looking for Mother

Sometimes I was positive that I had arrived at the certain truth, but then my certainty would fade away, and I couldn't recapture the meaning of it. At those times, I would recite to myself the following poem:

> Under a pine tree, when asked, a young man answered:
> "My master has gone to find an herb.
> I know he is on this mountain,
> But, because of the clouds, I am not sure where."

This poem symbolized my distress, knowing that my birth parents existed, yet having no way to reach them. They were surrounded by clouds, and I did not know where they were or what they looked like, and I agonized about it.

Now I knew that my mother's name was Kim Ilyeop, and that she was in Sudeok-sa, but she and that place were obscured by deep clouds and mountain peaks. There were a few who knew about my birth, but it seemed that they must have promised to keep the secrets. That much I had figured out. Now I knew where my mother was, but next I needed to find out where Sudeok-sa was located. I was stymied, because at that time it was difficult to get ahold of a map, and there was no public transportation available. Finally, I thought one way to find out would be to ask Master Simhyang. I waited until he came again, and then, when no one else was around, I brought up the subject.

"Master! Where is the Sudeok-sa temple?"

"Why? Are you going to look for your mother?"

"Not exactly. But I do want to know where my mother is. You are the only one who can tell me." Master's face showed his discomfort, but he was compassionate, and spoke:

"Sudeok-sa is a very famous temple in Chung Nam province. You take a train from the Seoul station and get out at Sapgyo station. From there you have to walk. If you ask someone in Sapgyo, they will tell you the way." Master was silent for a while, then said, "I think it would be better not to go right away. Later, when you are an adult, then go. Do not forget that your mother is a monk, who has committed herself to ascetic religious practices."

That is what Master Simhyang told me, but my mind was too impatient. I thought of my mother every moment of the day. I couldn't quiet my mind to draw an orchid. I saw my mother in dreams, even though I had never seen her face. In my dream, she was always so kind, warm, and comforting that I hated to wake up. I tried to keep thinking that she was a heartless mother who had abandoned me, and I tried to hate her, but the yearning for Mother was not disappearing; the more time that passed, the more intense it became. I lost my appetite, and my mouth was dry. If I could not slake my thirst, I would probably just burn up.

At last, I got my chance. Idang Father was to be gone on a sketching trip for ten days, and, the morning after he left home; so did I. I could easily get the train ticket from the Seoul station to Sapgyo. I had quite a bit of money at that time, because my Sincheon father had given me some before I left, and the monk, Kanegio, had also given me some pocket money.

The problem was getting from the Sapgyo station to Sudeok-sa. I found out that the distance was about seven and one half miles, and the only way to get there was to walk. I hesitated for a while, but, had it been seventy-five miles, I still would have had to make the walk.

"If you don't hurry, you won't make it before dark."

"Thank you." As soon as I had said my thanks, I began running down the gravel road. When I got out of breath, I would walk for a while, then resume running. As I came closer to the place where my mother was, I became more and more eager and anxious, and I tried hard to calm myself. It was a day in late spring, and I could hear the cuckoo crying in the distance, and smell the smoke from village chimneys, already bearing the scent of dinners cooking. I began to fear that I could not get there before dark. My legs became heavier and heavier, but the urgency in my mind drove me on. When I got to the area of the Sudeok-sa with my tired body, the sun was already gone, and it was dark. I could hear a bell ringing, breaking the dark silence. I ran to the bell pavilion. A monk, who had finished ringing the bell, came down from the pavilion.

"Seu-nim, is this the place where Seu-nim Kim Ilyeop stays?"

"Seu-nim Ilyeop is in Gyeonseong-am...."

"You said 'Gyeonseong-am'....?"

It was not usual for a boy to be looking for a Seu-nim at such a late hour. The bell-ringing Seu-nim was studying me carefully.

"You have to climb more than a mile from here.... By the way, why are you looking for Seu-nim Ilyeop?"

"I came here with an urgent message." At that moment, I made a lie. The Seu-nim did not address me as a child, but rather spoke to me with respect, and kindly showed me the road.

"If you follow that path, you will see a separate cottage where lives Seu-nim Mangong. A little further, there is Cheonghye-sa, and, going past that temple, and up to the top of the mountain, you will find Gyeonseong-am."

Gyeonseong-am was located at the top of Deokseung-san Mountain. I followed the narrow trail to the top. The trail was so steep and rough, and the forest so thick that I thought a tiger might come out at any minute. When I looked up at the night sky, the stars were clear and bright. I took a deep breath, and ran up the path. The cottage of Seu-nim Mangong looked like a magpie house. I followed the stone fence of Cheonghye-sa, and at the top was Gyeonseong-am. When I saw it, my heart was pounding. Finally, I had arrived at the place where my mother was.

Mother

I took a deep breath, and went into the yard of Gyeonseong-am, which was completely dark and silent. Even though I had arrived there, I didn't know what to do next. I wanted to yell, "Mother!" but I couldn't do it, and I just roamed around the yard. In a while, a woman emerged from the one room in which there was a lantern. She looked at me suspiciously, and asked me what I was doing there.

"I came here to meet Seu-nim Kim Ilyeop with an urgent message."

She told me to wait a while, and she disappeared. After while, a female Buddhist monk came out of the wooden-floored prayer room. I couldn't even breathe, and I did not know what to say, and the Seu-nim spoke first.

"I am Kim Ilyeop. What brought you here?"

Tears were pouring down, and without willing it, I went up to where she was standing.

"Mother!" My voice trembled.

My mother stepped back and looked around. It was clear that she was astonished.

When she saw that no one was near, she asked me in a low voice, "Then, are you Yeongeop?"

"Yes. But now I'm known as Seolcheon."

"You came from Master Idang in Seoul?"

Mother was living in the remote mountains, but she seemed to know what was going on with me. That meant that someone was keeping her informed. She thought for a minute, and said quietly, "Follow me."

I went into the room where Mother stayed. She sat down, and I honored her with a deep bow; I looked at her silently. Under the light her shaved head had a bluish tinge, and she looked like any other monk. But in her eyes was a warm that only a mother could show.

"Come closer."

When I came close to her, she took my hand, and lightly caressed my cheek and shoulder. Mother's hand was warm, and her eyes were wet and sad.

"You have grown up enough that you could come looking for me by yourself."

She seemed to be proud of me.

After a while, it suddenly burst upon me how much I had missed her, and I threw myself into her lap and sobbed.

> All life is transient:
>
> Someone we love dies, and we mourn.
>
> But should we ourselves abandon what we love—
>
> Ah, then the tears can never stop.
>
> *The Love I Left*, by Ilyeop

I discovered this poem much later.

Mother wiped her tears with her monk's robe, and said in a stern voice, "Stop crying! This is a mountain temple. There is a saying that when in Rome we must do as the Romans do. When you are in a temple, you must abide by the temple's customs and etiquette. First, you must not say 'Mother' to me. Do you understand?"

I was shocked, and asked her, "Do not call you 'Mother' when you are my mother?"

"You have to call me 'Seu-nim'"

Mother's voice was firm. Her attitude was the complete opposite of what it had been a few moments before. My heart grew chilled. In a while, in a softer voice, Mother asked, "Did you eat dinner?"

"…" Dinner? I hadn't even had lunch.

"This place is for female monks only. You are a boy, and so, even though you are young, you cannot sleep here. Let's go to the cottage of the head monk.

There, you can have dinner and sleep."

I followed Mother, but things were hazy in front of my eyes. I had met the mother of my dream, but I had never thought that I could not sleep in her arms.

New grief and sadness engulfed me. Not only could I not sleep with her, I had to hear her say that I could not even call her 'mother'. Even now, that memory makes me sad.

The Sadness of Rahula

While we were walking down to the monk's quarters, Mother did not speak, and that silence made me uncomfortable. When we got to the cottage, she said toward a room that was lighted, "Seu-nim, this is Ilyeop."

I heard the answer from inside, "Come on in."

In the room were two monks. Mother bowed three times before the older of them, and he asked, "Who is this child?"

"Seu-nim.... I'm sorry to say that...."

Mother stopped speaking for a moment, then forced herself to continue.

"This child is my flesh and blood; he was born before I left the secular world to become a Buddhist."

I could read the surprise on the faces of the two monks.

"Aha, Ilyeop has an offspring...."

The monk examined me carefully, then closed his eyes murmuring,

"Karma...."

Mother instructed me to bow to Great Seu-nim Mangong and Seu-nim Byeokcho.

Then she asked Seu-nim Byeokcho for food for me. When he left to get the meal, the Great Seu-nim Mangong asked Mother, "The child's father....?"

"A Japanese man, Oda Seizo. During my studies in a foreign country, I got this child. At that time, his father gave him the name Masao."

Mother explained in detail to the Great Seu-nim about my growing up, telling him that I was at present staying with Master Idang to study drawing. "I kept track of what was happening through letters, but I have not seen him since he was a newborn baby."

That was the first time that I found out that my father's name was Oda Seizo, and that I, myself, had had another name, Masao.

When I finished eating, Great Seu-nim Mangong said, "It's better not to let either the Buddhist or the secular world know that Ilyeop has a son. Don't tell anyone. Keep in mind that he is a Rahula."

Seu-nim Byeokcho promised that he would keep that in mind.

I had no idea what a Rahula was, but I realized that it must be kept secret that Mother had a child. Only a few people knew about it for many years, through World War II, the regaining of Korean independence from Japan, and the Korean War.

Mother called me by my real name. "Masao!

I have to go to my quarters, but you stay here and sleep."

This was the first name my mother had called me, but it did not sound strange to me, probably because I was hearing it from my own mother. From then on, Mother, Mangong, and Seu-nim Byeokcho all called me 'Masao'.

It did not happen that I could sleep in Mother's arms. My love and thirst for her went still unsatisfied. But, my body, tired from my long trip, dropped me into a deep and dreamless sleep.

"Great Seu-nim, what is Rahula?" I asked Mangong after breakfast, since I was still curious from the night before.

"The Buddha, before he became a holy man, was a prince of India. Of course, he married, and had a son. The name of the son Buddha had in the secular world was 'Rahula'."

"...."

"Buddha was frustrated because of Rahula, because, even though he was doing penance, he wanted to return to the world. The love of flesh and blood makes it very difficult to cut off relationships."

"...."

"To be spiritually awakened one must sever the relationship even between father and son. Your mother is a devout Seu-nim in Buddha. Because of that, personal love should not draw her back into the secular world."

My heart burned in my chest. "To my mother, I'm the Rahula who is disturbing her penance?"

"You must try hard not to disturb your mother."

I could not readily understand what the Great Seu-nim was saying. I wanted to say that I was surely not the cause of her worries. I was confident that I would never reflect badly on my mother's name, and that, if I could live with her, I could make her comfortable and devout. I wanted to deliver all my sincerity and truth to my mother.

In the morning Byeokcho took me to Sudeok-sa. When I saw the temple in the light of day, it seemed huge and majestic. Later, when I was a student at the art university, I visited Horyu-ji temple at Asuka, in the Nara region. It is famous for the Kumdang wall paintings which depict four Buddhas serenely seated, done by Damjing, who is a famous Buddhist monk painter, from Goguryeo, who worked sometimes in Baekje. I was surprised when I saw them that they were so similar to those in the temple at Sudeok-sa. Maybe Damjing went to Japan after doing the murals at Sudeok-sa, then painted the ones at Horyu-ji. If so, Sudeok-sa was constructed by Abiji, who built Hwangryong-sa temple's nine-story tower, which is one of the three treasures of Silla. The wooden construction of Sudeok-sa is similar in many ways to the art work in Baekje, so I must conclude that they were created by the same hand. Of course, in those days, I knew nothing of any of this, and just gazed around everywhere Byeokcho took me.

"You go now to the men's quarters; I have something I must attend to here."

After leaving Byeokcho, I followed the path to the Chodang, but I couldn't stand not seeing my mother. Seeing her the night before seemed like a dream. I thirsted for her, so I passed by the men's quarters, and went up to the Gyeonseong-am

But our meeting was only my daydream. I was eager to be embraced by her, but her expression was like ice.

"Follow me this way," she said.

Mother took me to the back of the house where no one was.

"Didn't I tell you that this is the quarters of the women Seu-nims? That means that you may not come in and out. Never come to see me in the Gyeonseong-am."

"...."

"I will visit you in the Chodang after dinner."

"...."

"Did you understand me?"

I was sitting on a stone. I barely nodded. I felt my nose turn red and my eyes tear up. Mother gazed at me for awhile, then turned around and disappeared.

My thirst was unsatisfied, but I had to drag myself away.

Leaving Gyeonseong-am Behind

As she had promised, Mother came down after the evening meal, and she asked me some troubling questions.

"Did you tell Master Idang that you were coming here? I couldn't say anything.

"You came here without telling anyone?"

I answered in a small voice, "Idang went out sketching, so he is not home."

"Then, you should have told someone else in the family."

Seu-nim Mangong said, "Tsk, they must be very worried." He asked Seu-nim Byeokcho to call the house of Idang. The result of the call was that there was more of a fuss than I had expected. They had worried that I had an accident, and they even notified Idang Father. He almost cancelled everything and went home, but, after he found out that I was at Sudeok-sa, he decided to stay on. Mother was frowning.

"From now on, act so as not to give worry to adults, and tomorrow at day break, go back to Seoul."

I could say nothing. Mother had some power over me which I could not resist.

She continued, "Do not come to the Gyeonseong-am tomorrow. Now, at this moment, let us say goodbye."

"…"

"Why are you not answering?"

"I understand."

Mother gazed at me in silence. She was sending me away sternly, but I am sure her heart was aching. After a while, when she spoke, her tone was a little softer.

"Be careful, go well. The only thing I can tell you is to become a good man. When you grow up, I hope that you will be able to understand me."

After she spoke, she stood up. I followed her out, but the night was so dark that she quickly disappeared, and I was left staring at the darkness behind her. I couldn't sleep at all that night because of my flowing tears.

Next morning, I said good-bye to the two Seu-nims. The head monk gave me an envelope with money in it to use if I needed to. I came out of the Chodang and looked up toward the Gyeonseong-am several times, but never saw my mother. I felt like there was a hole in my heart through which a cold wind blew. I passed the Sudeok-sa temple and got to Deok-san mountain still harboring the hope that Mother might follow me, but that hope was a forlorn one. Going back, every step felt as heavy as if I were in chains. When I arrived at Waryong-dong it was night. Grandmother and Mother were as happy to see me as if I had risen from the dead. But Idang Father, who returned from his drawing trip a few days later, was very different. He asked first for the switch to be brought.

"If you don't tell me the truth, your legs are going to be sore. Understand? Who told you that Ilyeop Seu-nim was in Sudeok-sa?"

"Master Simhyang…."

"What? Simhyang? I cannot believe it! Where did you get the money then?"

"Sincheon Father gave it to me when I left there."

Idang confiscated the money which I had received from my Sincheon father, as well as that given to me by the Seu-nim at Sudeok-sa, and I had to make a promise, which I was not confident I could keep, that I wouldn't go to Sudeok-sa any more.

"I forgive you this time with only a whipping, but if it happens again, I will not forgive you at all."

When he switched my legs, I counted one, two, three ... and silently endured ten blows. When I look back upon this beating, I feel as though it was not a punishment for going to see my mother; rather it was a means of severing me from my mother's love. But the pain of that switching could not cut away the love that had already blossomed in my heart.

In contrast with that beating, Idang Father was more warm and loving than ever. Always, on the table shared by Idang and me, were dishes I liked, and I was always encouraged to eat my fill. We, father and son, went to the public baths as we had before, and he washed my back with loving care.

After a while, Master Simhyang came to visit. Father then announced that he was cutting off his relationship with him. But, in reality, they could not end their relationship because of me, and later on, Simhyang visited that house again.

Going to Tokyo

Despite the cold treatment by my mother, the grudge I had carried against her had disappeared. The yearning for her had returned, and I longed to hear her voice, even if it were stern. But if I acted on these feelings, not only would I disappoint Idang, I could well get my mother into trouble. There was a painful struggle between my longing and my reason.

In this way a whole year passed, and when 1937 arrived, I became fifteen years old. A few days after New Years, Father called me.

"Drawing studies are important, but you cannot omit other subjects, because they are important, too. You need to concentrate on those for a while, so I am going to send you to middle school in Tokyo. You are already a year behind the other students, so you will need to study harder to catch up. If you do well, it may be possible to skip a year."

The mother in Gyeonseong-am had already told me to become a good person, and I did not want to disappoint her. Becoming a good person would mean to become a son who would be helpful rather than harmful.

We got the Tokyo train schedule, and, when everything was ready, Idang handed me a letter.

"Give this letter to Shindo Araki. You are to be staying with him."

"Am I to go to Tokyo alone then?"

Idang had telegraphed Mr. Araki, and he would be at the station to meet me, so I had nothing to worry about. Still, I showed my worry. Father made an identification tag, showing my name and destination, to hang around my neck.

"Don't be shy about wearing this; it is better than getting lost."

I said good-bye to the family, and went with Idang to the Seoul station. Idang got on the Busan train with me, and put my trunk up on the shelf.

"Take care of yourself, and study hard."

When Father heard the departure signal, he stepped off the train. He waved his hand, and I waved back. Maybe separations always come with tears. Idang Father wiped his eyes with his handkerchief, and I felt tears in my own eyes.

I put my ID card in my bag. I had thought of throwing it away, but then I realized that that might be the way Mr. Araki would recognize me.

A Japanese woman was sitting beside me, and tried to give me pointers for getting around in Tokyo.

"How is it that a Korean student can speak Japanese so fluently?"

"I was educated in the Japanese way. But how did you know I was Korean?"

She said that it was because of Idang's outfit, and asked if he was my father. I saw that I was viewed by the Japanese as a Korean; that was a confirmation of my identity. My real father was clearly Japanese, but my mother was Korean. I determined to be a person of my mother's country. This determination didn't change while I studied in Japan, or later, when I was a recognized painter there.

The train trip took all night, and we arrived in Busan in the morning. With the Japanese woman's help, I got on the ferryboat. At the Shimonoseki station, I took an express train to Tokyo. Because of her directions, I had no difficulty, even though it was my first trip. When I got off the train, I put the ID tag around my neck, and followed the Japanese woman into the station lobby. She met her family, so we said good-bye and separated.

From then on, my problems started. Mr. Araki, who was to meet me, did not seem to be in the crowd. I made sure that the tag was showing, but I could not find him. I felt something must be wrong, and started to worry. Finally, the lobby was empty, and my tired body sank into a chair. I felt abandoned again, this time in a waiting room in a foreign land.

4

The Suffering of Love

The Middle-School Uniform

I woke up to someone shaking my arm. It was the janitor.

"You cannot sleep here. You have to go outside. After the last train, and when we finish cleaning, we lock the door."

I took my trunk, and went outside. In front of the train station was a plaza.

Since I had nowhere to go, I found a corner where I could lean against the wall, and put a newspaper down to sit on. I soon drifted into sleep again, but wakened when someone kicked my trunk. I jumped to my feet. It was a newspaper boy.

"Why did you kick the trunk?" I said angrily.

The newsboy was startled, and backed off.

"Where did you come from?" he asked.

"From Korea."

"Alone?"

"Yes."

He gazed at me in admiration, and asked me why I was sitting there. I explained to him what had happened, and he suggested that I go to the police station.

"Thank you."

Right away, I went to the police station and showed them the envelope that Idang Father had given to me. In there, was the address of Shindo Araki. The policeman called a rickshaww and asked him to take me to that address.

The rickshaw passed Shinjuku Park, and continued on for an hour before arriving at Shindo Araki's house. The rickshaw man knocked at the front door, and a woman looked out. He asked whether she knew Masao from Korea, and her face brightened. When I saw that, I felt such relief that I could breathe again. I found out that Shindo Araki was waiting at the south gate of the Tokyo station, while I was waiting at the north gate, because of having followed the Japanese woman out. It was common sense for someone going to Nakano-ku Goenji, where Shindo Araki's house was located, to go the south gate, but I had no way of knowing that.

Shindo Araki and his wife greeted me from the bottom of their hearts. From birth to three years I had been raised in their house, and I was special to them. Since they had no children of their own, I had been like their child.

The next day the wife showed me the way to Honko Middle School, which I was to attend. She took me several times back and forth from the house to the school, until she was absolutely sure I could find my own way. Then we went back home.

In this way, I started my middle school career. Mr. Shindo Araki bought me the middle school uniform and cap, and his wife bought me a commuter pass for the train. After class, when I came out of the gate, she would often be waiting for me, and we would go home together. She would buy me a snack of noodles or sweet rice cake. I felt very grateful, but also a bit guilty that they were doing so much for me.

The cherry blossoms in Shinjuku Park bloomed and then faded; a few months passed by in a flash. In Tokyo, I got my first summer vacation, for which I had been counting the days. I thought that my mother in the Gyeonseong-am would be very pleased to see me in my middle school uniform.

The Arakis were very reluctant to let me go to Korea, but since I insisted so strongly, they finally gave in, and told me to come back quickly.

Unlike my trip to Tokyo, I had no trouble getting to the Seoul station. When I went into the house of Idang Father, he greeted me happily, uniform and all.

When I went into their area of the house, Grandmother and mother embraced me with joy. When I told them all about my night in the Tokyo station plaza, Idang laughed heartily, and clapped his hands.

The pleasure didn't last long, however, because my mind soon wandered to the Gyeonseong-am. I left the house without telling anyone. I took a slow train to Sapgyo; my mind was racing so that I felt that I was going slower than the train. At the Sapgyo station, I paid for a wagon ride to Deok-san, but from there to Sudeok-sa I had to walk. The red western sky turned to darkness, but the moon showed the path clearly. The moon was so bright that I was not afraid on Deok-san mountain. I climbed fast, following the faint path. I passed the Chodang, where Seu-nim Mangong lived, and passed the stone wall of Junghei-sa, and finally arrived at Gyeonseong-am.

The moon, when I looked at it from the courtyard at Gyeonseong-am, was especially big and bright. The moonlight on the leaves was like waves in the water. The breeze cooled my sweat. As I paced up and down, listening to the wind-chimes, a female monk appeared. I told her that I had come to see Seu-nim Ilyeop, and she went away.

After a while, my mother came out. Our eyes met in the space that separated us. I saluted her proudly. I saw a slight smile on her lips, and also tears which sparkled in the moonlight. Mother took me to her own room. I took off my cap, and bowed low to her in greeting. Mother touched my shoulder approvingly.

"Oh, you have become a middle school student."

"Yes."

"You had no problem adjusting to life in Tokyo?"

I told her all about my experiences. When I told her about sleeping in the station plaza on my first day there, she had tears in her eyes. What a contrast with Idang, who had laughed uproariously!

"You must be hungry after such a long trip."

Mother gave me rice cakes and fruit.

"Eat slowly. This is an offering for service."

After I ate, Mother took me to the Chodang to see Seu-nim Mangong, like she did last year.

On the way, she asked me, "Did you talk to Master Idang before you came here?"

"No. If I had, he would not have let me...."

Mother sighed. "Even so, if you do that, will he not worry?"

Idang, who was an elder in the church, had not been pleased by my going to the temple. He wanted me to become a Christian, cut ties with my birth parents, and become his son. Of course, if I had told him, he would not have permitted me to come to see Mother.

"Do not do things of which Idang disapproves. Understand?"

"...."

Mother told me, since I was already there, that I could stay two days. I said in a low voice that I understood.

Seu-nim Mangong and Seu-nim Byeokcho were happy to see me. On the day of my return to Seoul, they gave me another envelope with money, like they had the year before.

Explosions of Resentment

After my return to Japan for the second semester, my mind felt confused and dissatisfied.

I felt resentful, and got angry over small things. Maybe people thought my crankiness was a sign of puberty, but, in fact, it was the result of my visit to Sudeok-sa.

Before leaving for Japan, in the name of saying good-bye, I went again to see my mother. Again, I didn't tell Idang Father. This time, Mother's reaction was completely different than before; she was very cold.

"How could you continue to make trouble? You do not listen to what others are telling you. Don't you know how much you have disappointed Idang Father, as well as the other people around you? Go back tomorrow morning."

I had started out with great determination for that round trip of so many miles, but I got only the cold shoulder, and a scolding. But that suffering was not the end of it. I had arrived at Waryong-dong in the middle of the night. Nobody opened the door for me even though I banged on it. Traveling secretly twice without telling him had made Idang very angry.

I should have stayed there that night and begged forgiveness, but at that age, having already been deeply wounded by my mother, I was feeling sad and tired. It was a short summer night; I could have slept anywhere, but I just turned around and left. My steps were so heavy with weariness and hunger that I went only to nearby Daegak-sa. There, I met Seu-nim Baek Yongseong for the first time.

"Please let me stay here for one night."

A young boy coming to the temple and wanting to stay the night—he was puzzled. I reluctantly told him that I was the stepson of Idang, and that I had gone to Sudeok-sa without telling him, and so had been kicked out of the house.

That made him even more interested in me.

"What made you go to Sudeok-sa?"

I hesitated to answer. If I didn't make him understand, he might throw me out, too; I had to tell him the truth. Seu-nim Mangong had said not to tell anyone, but now I was the first one to disobey his order.

"So, you are the son of Ilyeop?" I could see that he was shocked.

"Please keep this a secret."

The Seu-nim nodded, and asked another Seu-nim to prepare dinner for me. I satisfied my hunger, and slept. The next morning, I ate breakfast, thanked the Seu-nim, and left.

My mind was made up: if they didn't open the door this time, I would go back to the temple and become a monk. But, the gate was already open. I kneeled down in front of Idang Father.

"Where did you sleep last night? I couldn't find you. You couldn't even wait for ten minutes? Where did you go?"

Had I left that fast?

"I slept in Daegak-sa."

Father's anger was extreme. "Do you want to grow up to be a monk? Is that why you visited the temple?"

From then on, until I left for Tokyo, I was always within Idang's sight. Of course, I couldn't go out. If I had something to do I was always accompanied by someone, or by Father himself. This kind of life was very uncomfortable for me.

I found a way to discharge all my pent-up feelings. One of my classmates, Bunda, was a hand-span taller than I was, and was husky as well. He was a gang leader, and a pretty bad boy. He asked me where I had been over vacation, and then tried to start a fight with me.

"Oh, I visited in Korea."

"Korea? Aha! You are one of those garlic-breath Koreans."

"What?" My anger exploded, and I abruptly butted him in the forehead. He was caught off-guard and staggered, and the next butt knocked him flat on the ground. I pulled him up by his collar, and pounded him in the stomach. He screamed and doubled over clutching his belly, and I gave him a kick in the rear.

He fell down on his face; his arms and legs spread out like a frog.

In that instant, I became a hero. All of the classmates, who had been beaten up by Bunda in the past, cheered me, and I became to them a very intimidating Korean. About a month later, Bunda came to me and asked for my help. The members of his gang had been beaten by a gang from another school. Not only did Bunda ask me very courteously, but I couldn't stand the thought that our school should have been beaten out by students from somewhere else. I assented to his request.

The two gangs confronted one another in a vacant lot, which was secluded and away from residences. The leader from the other school apparently underestimated me because I was so short. He was a sophomore, and I could have been, too, had I gone to middle school on time. I attacked first, butting, and, while he was unsteady, I kicked him in the pants. He screamed and fell down. Right away, I took out my knife, and bluffed him by brandishing it over my head.

"If you don't want me to ruin your face, you'd better put it in the dirt."

The other gang was impressed by my vigor, and one by one, began to fall down in the dirt. I whacked each one on the bottom with a stick. This was an absolute victory for Hongo School. This made me a hero again, but the aftereffects were humongous. The parents from the other school protested strongly, and I was called to the teacher's office again and again. I was in danger of being suspended, but Mr. Araki came to the school and begged, and I was allowed to stay. "Masao, do not fight anymore. That kind of thing does you no good."

I already felt as though my pent-up emotions had been settled down, and I decided not to fight anymore, and to study hard. My music, art, and physical education were excellent, but in other subjects I was mediocre. In that way, the second semester passed, winter vacation arrived, and I went to Korea without hesitation.

Night of Heavy Snow

In the Waryong-dong house, there was another student. His name was Kim Gichang, and his penname was Wunbo. He tended to stammer. He was wearing a white Korean coat, and appeared neat and gentle. Father told me to treat him like my brother, and I called him Brother Wunbo.

He asked me, with his stutter, "You ... came ... from ... Tokyo?"

I nodded, and I could see envy in his eyes, but his smile was simple and friendly, and he said that he hoped we would get along well. Even though he couldn't speak fluently, he was very easygoing and pleasant to know.

On Christmas Eve, I went to church with the family. Waryong-dong Mother gave me a sweater as a Christmas gift that she had knitted herself. But the holidays are a time for family love, and I missed my birth mother. Though I knew the family loved me warmly, I could not help but feel lonely.

I left home before all of my repressed yearning could explode like a volcano. This time, I told Brother Wunbo of my destination. I could obey everything else, but I could not accept being told that I could not see my birthmother. What is a mother? Why is it that the longing for her never dies, but continues to well-up forever?

The sky was darkly overcast, and just as I got on the train, snow began falling past the windows. The flakes were big, and in no time, the world outside was all white. When I got off at the Sapgyo station, everything was covered in white, and the snowstorm continued. I hesitated for a while, but finally determined to move on. The snow was over my ankles, but I struggled on. Soon, I couldn't tell right from left. I would slip and fall and get up again, as though I were surfing through waves of water. I couldn't see even the shadow of a person. My sneaker came off, and I had to rummage in the snow to find it. My foot was frozen—I couldn't feel anything.

Finally, the snow stopped, about the time I got to Deok-san. The short winter day had passed west, and it was beginning to get dark. The snow stopped, but now the wind blew so hard that it looked like a blizzard. The snow was blowing hard into my face; tears and snot together ran down my cheeks. My ears and cheeks were stinging as though they were raw. The cold penetrated to the bone, and numbed my whole body. I must have appeared extremely miserable, but I was thankful still to be alive. It was such a hard trek, that when I finally arrived at Gyeonseong-am, I shouted, "I made it!" But I could let no one know about my suffering, because, on such a snowy night, all of the doors were locked tight, and no Seu-nim emerged.

I staggered toward my mother's room. I was shivering, and called in a low voice, "Seu-nim Ilyeop! Seu-nim Ilyeop …!" After a while, Mother came out, and her face showed great astonishment.

"Masao.… you? Here? On such a day, how.…?."

Mother whispered, "Wait a minute. I will get ready to go to Seu-nim Mangong."

She went inside, and came out again right away.

As soon we got away from Gyeonseong-am, Mother took my frozen hands.

"Merciful Buddha!"

Mangong and Byeokcho couldn't believe that I was there. Seu-nim Mangong massaged my legs to get the circulation going, and worried about frost-bite. Mother, counting her prayer beads, was at a loss for words.

What kind of child was I, that I could almost enjoy her suffering? In the eyes of a child, the parent's suffering over children is a sign of love. Maybe that is why children are so likely to give their parents a hard time.

The wind was so strong that even the door-lock was rattling. After Mother went back to Gyeonseong-am, Seu-nim Mangong pulled out his wide pants to their full expansion, and told me to get in with him. I hesitated, but he drew me in, and I was finally able to warm up. We looked like a kangaroo and its baby. Seu-nim Mangong's warmth thawed both my frozen body and my mind. It was not very comfortable, and I wriggled around until Seu-nim Mangong gave me a swat and told me to calm down. As soon as I relaxed, my whole body melted, and I fell into a deep sleep. This strange sleeping place is my most precious memory of Seu-nim Mangong.

My Father

The day I left Deokseung-san Mountain, Mother brought me surprising news: unexpectedly, she asked me to meet with my birth father. Sudeok-sa temple was old, and the roof was leaking, but, because of the cost and technical problems, they could not get it fixed.

"So, I would like you to meet your father and ask him to get it repaired."

"Are you talking about my birth father?"

Mother nodded without saying anything. I knew I had a birth father, but I didn't know of any way I could meet him. I became very tense, but Seu-nim Mangong shook his head.

"We cannot ask a Japanese to repair one of our traditional Buddhist temples."

"If we don't do something, the roof might fall in. We cannot let that happen."

Because of this conversation, I discovered that my father was working for the Japanese governor-general. When I got back to Waryong-dong, Idang Father said something I didn't expect.

"Relax for a few days, then make a visit to Sincheon to see your step-parents and the monk, Kanegio, of the Nishihongan-ji temple. Kanegio will show you something."

Idang said nothing about my Sudeok-sa trip. Maybe he had given up trying to change me with scolding.

The next morning, I visited the office of the governor general in Seoul. High on the flag-pole, a Japanese flag billowed in the wind. It was difficult to accept that place without resentment, because it represented the Japanese control of Korea. I grew up in Korea, the land of my mother, and I was determined to live my life as a Korean, but now I felt confused and guilty.

I was guided to a huge and luxurious room. Because of the décor, I could tell that my father held a high rank. The moment I saw him, I was in no doubt that he was my father. I had met him once in Sincheon, but had been frustrated later at not being able to picture what he looked like. Now, looking at him, I perceived a face exactly like my own. Between Father and me there was silence. Maybe because he was Japanese, I thought, the feeling I had toward him was so different from what I had felt upon seeing my mother.

"What kind of work do you do here, Father?"

"That can't be explained very easily."

"No doubt you are doing something to oppress the Koreans."

Instead of getting angry, Father smiled. "You are no longer a child." I kept on asking difficult questions which pushed him into a corner. "You can't be proud of what you are doing!"

"I'm not proud of it. In the future the Japanese government might have to be judged regarding its big mistake, but this is not what I studied. My job is to investigate Japanese mistreatment of Koreans so that such things may not happen again."

"You're just trying to put a good face on it!"

"I loved your mother, who is Korean, so I became a person who also loves your mother's land. You might not believe it, but I have tried to find a way to apologize for Japanese mistakes, and that is why I have taken this job."

Even now, at eighty years old, I do not know exactly what kind of work my father did, but it was clear that Oda Seizo was one of the Japanese who had the welfare of Korea at heart. Father had many Korean friends, including Song Gisu, who raised me, and Master Idang. In later days, I learned that he had rescued many Koreans who were in danger or unjustly oppressed. Even so, I feel no inclination to beautify my father. What I want to convey is, whether good or bad, whatever my father did had nothing to do with my will or intention. Father lived alone all of his life and died alone as well; he chose his loneliness himself.

I told Father the reason for my visit. "Mother, who is in Sudeok-sa, told me to ask whether you might be able to help with repair of the temple."

As soon as he heard Mother's words coming out of my mouth, he stared into space, his eyes glistening.

"Are you willing to help with that?"

"That is your mother's request, and also your own, so you don't have to worry."

"Thank you. Then I'll go back home."

"Wait a minute." Father hurriedly called me back before I could go out the door.

"A few days ago I met with Master Idang. You are visiting Sudeok-sa without letting anyone know …?"

"If I told him, he would not allow me to go there."

"In the future, he will permit you to go; I asked him especially. But, please, promise me not to go too often, and, when you get there, try not to stay too long. Your mother is a monk, who is committed to live in religious austerity."

"Yes, I understand."

Father continued, "Did Master Idang ask you to visit Sincheon? I bought land in your name in Sincheon. That is your land, so visit there and make sure about it. Also, greet Song Gisu and Monk Kanegio."

I was awed by the realization that Father always had me in his mind, but still I asked in a stern voice, "The land—did you steal it from a Korean?"

"Son! I saved my salary, and bought it for you! I paid generously, too, so you don't have to feel any reluctance."

With a softer voice, I said, "Thank you."

"Rather than holding a grievance, I hope that someday you will understand Mother and me. If we could only have lived together.... but, it could not have been done then, so, it is better to be understanding rather than resentful."

"..."

"Until now, I had tried intentionally not to meet you. I hoped you could learn to stand alone. But, as long as I live, I will always be behind you."

Father was true to his word. He always took care of me like a shadow in the background. But I couldn't say anything except, "Thank you."

As I left, I looked back at the government building, and thought it looked so big and solid that it would not be destroyed easily.

My Hometown, Sincheon

When I arrived at Sincheon station, Monk Kanegio was already waiting for me.

"Oh, you are so big that I almost couldn't recognize you!"

He was glad to see me, and looked at me proudly. I wanted to show the middle school-me to my Mujeong-ri family as soon as possible, but Kanegio took me to stay at the temple, and my luggage was opened there.

The next day the monk took me to the house of the tenant who farmed my land. The land was in Duri-myeon in Sincheon-gun, where the tenant farmer bowed down to me unnecessarily. I became the landlord of a huge amount of land at a young age.

I said, "Take good care of things." The farmer told me that I had his word on it, and he seemed to be grateful to me. I had a huge lunch at the farmer's house, then told Kanegio that I wanted to visit my step-parents in Mujeong-ri.

"Well, yes, you must visit the people who raised you."

After separating from Kanegio, I went toward Mujeong-ri. My hometown looked just the same; the rice fields, the vegetable fields, the path—everything was familiar to me. When I spotted my house, I started to run without thinking.

It was the middle of winter, so I could not hear the familiar mill machines. I banged open the gate and shouted, "Father, Mother!"

When I yelled, the house door flew open, and everyone came running out.

"Yeongeop!"

It had been a long time since I had heard that name. I ran to Mother's arms.

She had tears in her eyes, and I, too, found my voice hoarse with emotion. I bowed deeply to Father and Mother.

"You have really become a dignified middle school student. It is so remarkable, and I am so proud of you."

Father could not stop laughing. Mother worked hard to make a good dinner, and every food was what I had eaten as I grew up. I agree that what we learn to like at age three we still enjoy at age eighty; I still like North Korean-style cold noodles, and pickled flat-fish. I ate a full lunch, but could still enjoy my dinner.

My old friends all came to my house when they heard I was there. They were envious that I had become a Tokyo middle school student. After all that time, I became the leader again quickly, and we shared our thoughts, little realizing how fast the time was passing. While I was there, Mother made all of my favorite desserts.

When I had to go back to Seoul, she made rice cakes, which she packed in a bag for me to take. She said, "This is for Master Idang's household. Please give it to them."

Father gave me a large amount of money, which a big middle school student would be able to handle.

"Use this for what you need, stationery, and so on. And remember that this is your hometown, and come to visit often."

I agreed with him; when I close my eyes even now, the scenery of Sincheon is clear in my mind. The eyes of a child, and of the leader of the gang, saw that mountain and those fields....

When I got back to Waryong-dong, there was another student there, who was very tall. His name was Kim Jaebae, and his penname was Hwadang.

The Painter Na Hyeseok

It was spring vacation, the end of my first year of middle school. I went to Korea during the break, despite Mr. Araki's opposition. It had bothered me that I had not had a chance to tell Mother about Father's willingness to help repair Sudeok-sa.

I was sure that when I brought that news to her, she would be very happy, and pleased to see me.

The most difficult part of the trip was from Sapgyo station to Sudeok-sa, a seven mile walk. It was the end of February, and everything was still frozen. I ran and ran through the cold wind; the sun went down, and still I ran, until, finally, I could stand before Mother. That region was extremely cold.

"You are still a child! It is not yet time for you to become a brave man! You have to learn patience. Did you really want to see me that much?"

I didn't want to hear cold words after I came all the way from Tokyo to the Shimonoseki station, over the Sea of Japan on the ferryboat. My heart twisted miserably.

"Father told me he would repair the temple. I came here to let you know that.

"You could have written a letter for that matter. Anyhow, you've come all this way—go to Seu-nim Mangong and sleep there. You can go by yourself to the Chodang—Mangong will take care of you."

I had to go out of Mother's room.

The biting wind made the trees in the forest cry. When I looked up, the frozen stars looked back at me. Cold tears ran down my cheeks. While I was walking, I heard sounds, and looked back. I thought Mother might have changed her mind and followed me, but that was an illusion. Cold wind shook the branches.

Seu-nim Mangong greeted me warmly. There was one little boy monk there. His name was Mongsul; later, as a monk, he became known as Wondam. Mongsul was a disciple of Seu-nim Byeokcho, and was helping Seu-nim Mangong.

The next morning, after the meal, Mother arrived.

"I hope this child did not disturb your sleep," she said to Mangong.

"Don't worry about that, Ilyeop."

"My friend Na Hyeseok is still in the hotel in Sudeok."

Seu-nim Mangong grimaced. "What? She didn't go back to Seoul yet? It takes a special person to become a monk. Tell her not to think about cutting her hair, and to go back to Seoul right away."

"Yes.... Masao, follow me."

Mother took me to the Sudeok Hotel. On the way, she said, "Na Hyeseok has been my friend since I studied in Japan. A few days ago, she came here saying she wanted to become a monk, but I discouraged her. But, she is still staying here.

So, you stay with her a couple of days in the hotel, then go back home. Do you understand?"

I said yes.

Na Hyeseok had a western face, and was a graceful, beautiful woman. While she was speaking with Mother, she was observing me carefully, and nodded her head.

"Blood will tell."

Mother said, "Don't say those things."

Mother took the room next to that of Hyeseok, then she left.

Hyeseok was very pleased with me. She asked me about this and that, in a gentle way, smiling warmly. At that moment, I felt a sad regret that Mother did not smile at me in that way.

"I heard that you are a good painter. Do you want to see my paintings?"

She showed me unframed paintings done in a western style.

"Oh, are you a western-style painter, Teacher?"

She looked at me with her round eyes, and showed her rather bitter smile.

"Yes.... by the way.... Masao, do not call me Teacher, call me Aunt. I am your mother's friend, so you can address me informally."

"Oh, may I do that?"

"Of course. That is more comfortable for me."

She said that she knew my birth father, too. I asked her how my parents had met.

"I don't know in detail, but I heard that in the train between Shimonoseki and Tokyo they sat side by side."

She told me what she knew, and then told me about my mother.

"Your mother is a very talented person. She is a famous poet, with special writing skills. She has so much talent.... but—how shall I say it?—she is very clear and ruthless about things."

I could understand well enough, in light of her attitude toward me.

"Compared to most people, she is very passionate and hot-blooded."

Na Hyeseok saw my mother that way, but she didn't expand upon that opinion.

I was thirsty to know more about her, but I changed the subject of the conversation.

"Why did you want to be a monk, Auntie?"

She didn't give me any answer.

We went to the Sudeok-sa Temple and prayed, and walked around the temple garden. In the evening, we ate dinner together. She was a warm and pleasant person to be with. I didn't want to back to my own room. As though she had read my mind, she said, "Let's sleep in this room tonight."

We made up two bedding sets side by side.

"Masao, what do you want to be in the future?"

"I ... I want to be a monk."

"What? You want to cut your hair off, too?"

"If I became a monk, I could be beside my mother all the time."

Hyeseok made the same grimace as had Mangong, then she hugged me tightly. Her bosom was big and warm and comfortable. I felt like I was in Mother's arms. After a while, she said softly, "Masao, you didn't drink your mother's milk, and you have not touched your mother's breast?"

"..."

Then, she heard my unspoken answer. She took my hand and put it on her own breast. I felt comfortable and cozy. Maybe she was trying to make me feel what a mother's love would be like.

"Masao ... shall I teach you a children's song or a nursery rhyme?"
Then she started singing softly:

> "In the blue sky is the milky way,
> And one little white boat.
> In the boat there is a cinnamon tree,
> And under the tree a bunny."

I sang along, but she, who had started the song, lost her voice. I thought that she must have had some sad reasons.

Hurriedly, I asked her, "Auntie, are you crying?"

She wiped her tears away. "It reminds me of something sad."

Between us there was silence. Finally, she said, "As a matter of fact, I have a son your age. I left that son, and I left home."

I didn't ask the reason, but I could perceive the mother's yearning for her child.

Na Hyeseok embraced me tightly. Mother had told me to stay two days, but I stayed in Sudeok-sa for five days.

Going to Jikji-sa to Find Mother

I have mentioned that my mother's original name was Kim Wonju. Chunwon, Lee Gwangsu, when he was dating Heo Yeongsuk, had received many beautiful letters from her, and they later married. Afterward, Chunwon discovered that the letters had actually been written by Kim Wonju. When he met her, he told her, "You are as good a writer as the famous Japanese novelist, Higuchi Ichiyo. You should have the penname Ilyeop, since you are the Korean Ichiyo." (Ichiyo means in Japanese the same as Ilyeop does in Korean.)

My mother had writing skills equal to Ichiyo! That mother became the single withered leaf, dedicating herself to Buddhism, and I followed her like a sunflower, so I may, myself, become a dried leaf blowing in the wind.

> The green summer shade has disappeared;
> So soon has the world turned golden.
> My mind is hazy, aimless.
> Like a leaf, swirling in the wind,
> My heart seems solitary, too.
>
> *Autumn Recollection,* by Ilyeop

After the first semester of the second year of middle school, during summer vacation, I went to Sudeok-sa, but Mother was not there. She had gone to the Jikji-sa temple in Gimcheon to study. We were far apart, and I was overcome by loneliness.

It was already getting dark, and I could see the lights of the Chodang where Mangong lived. I thought about staying there, but, instead ran on past to the Sudeok Hotel. Na Hyeseok had told me I could visit her for the summer vacation.

I wasn't sure whether she was still there, but if not, I was going to pay to stay in the hotel.

Luckily, Na Hyeseok was there. As soon as she saw me she asked what had happened; she was very pleased that I was there. After I had told her my experience, she clucked her tongue: What is the feeling of the child for the mother in the middle of the night …? Then she ordered dinner. I was hungry, but I could not swallow.

Like before, we lay down together and conversed. My head rested on her arm, and we again sang the nursery song together, while I comforted myself about not seeing Mother.

After breakfast the next morning, she invited me to stay for a few more days, and I decided to stay one more night. Na Hyeseok treated me very nicely; she was sentimental, kindhearted, and warm.

We went to Sudeok-sa together. As we went up the old stone steps, I looked up at the eaves, and marveled at the bright colors there. There was a dragon holding a magic pearl in his mouth. The name Sudeok-sa means withdrawing from the sufferings of life, discovering one's own path of virtue, and becoming a guide to that path for the rest of mankind. On the grounds, there is a stone tower five stories high, as well as the main temple.

In the front of the temple, carpenters were working. Some were smoothing the wood, while some were removing tiles from the roof. All were very busy. I realized that they were taking care of the repair work; Father had kept his promise.

These were professional carpenters from Japan, who had been specially selected.

The next day, I left there. Auntie gave me an envelope with twenty won inside.

I stayed a few days in Waryong-dong before leaving home to find my mother.

I took a train from Seoul to Busan, and came to Gimcheon where I stayed one night in a hotel near the station. The next day, I went to Hwangak-san, where Jikji-sa temple is located. I arrived about ten o'clock in the morning.

I passed the Ilju-mun door, the Gumgang-mun door, and the Cheonan-mun door, finally reaching the main temple. I had no idea where to find my mother so for a while I just roamed around. I looked inside of the main temple, but Mother was not there. Then, I met a Seu-nim who told me that my mother was in the west temple. I started walking toward the one she had pointed out. The persimmon trees were huge and dignified, but the hanging fruits were no bigger than chestnuts. A locust was singing loudly. When I passed the persimmon trees, there was a brook, which I crossed carefully by a wooden bridge. On the other side, I could see the west temple through the trees and heavy vegetation.

This time, too, she seemed upset and flustered rather than happy to see me. I had come so far, but seeing her made me very uneasy. Mother didn't say anything, but walked ahead of me, stopping under the persimmon trees.

"Why did you come to this place?"

Her words were like a blow, but I calmed myself down, and greeted her formally.

"Have you been well since I saw you last, Mother?"

"Didn't I tell you not to call me 'mother'?"

Feeling the brunt of her disapproval, I drew into myself. Mother grimaced, and thought for a while.

"You are already here. What can we do? I have to tell the head monk."

At that time the head of Jikji-sa temple was Seu-nim Kim Bongryul. He was neither tall nor short, and had a kindly face. Mother told him about our relationship, and asked for his help.

"Oho, you're in that situation, are you?"

Seu-nim Kim Bongryul looked at me kindly, and told me, "Seu-nim Ilyeop is in the middle of her training, so I will take over her role as Mother. Follow me."

I went with him to his room.

"I'm sure your heart is broken. In the future, not only here, but wherever you go, I will be your father. Call me 'Father."

These were generous words to me, and I could not take offense. "… Father."

Seu-nim Kim Bongryul was a married monk, and had a home in Gimcheon. "As of today, we have made a sacred promise to be father and son," he said, sealing the relationship.

I followed him to his home, and greeted his wife. I was amazed when he introduced me, not as a stepson, but as his birth-son, conceived when he was a student in Tokyo. Because of what he said, his wife believed that I was his son, grown up and coming to visit. This was the cause of another story, which we could not recall without a laugh.

That vacation, staying in Jikji-sa, I met two special persons who greatly influenced my life. One was Seu-nim Tanong, and the other was my respected teacher Gwaneung. Tanong had special talents in the arts. He recited poems in a good voice, and his drawing was excellent. He also had his own opinion regarding portraits of Buddha. He was extremely good to me.

In the Biro-jun temple in Jikji-sa, there were a thousand Buddhas. One day, I almost went crazy contemplating all of those radiant Buddhas; I could not leave that place because of their mysterious and solemn spirit. There was a college student behind me there, who later became Seu-nim Kwaneung.

He was a handsome man, wearing a cape, and, when he found out that I was a middle school student in Japan, he told me that he was, himself, studying at the Ryugoku Buddhist University in Kyoto.

When vacation was almost over, I returned to my home in Waryong-dong.

Who Are You, and Why Are You Here So Much?

When winter vacation came, I went to Korea right away. This time, the Sindos did not try to stop me.

Even now, when I see snow, I shiver, remembering this icy visit to my mother.

This year, too, it was snowing when I went to see her. When I arrived at the Sapgyo station, everything was covered in snow. Cottage roofs, vegetable fields, rice fields, mountains—all were white. I was like a soldier in war, bravely plowing through the drifts. The wind was cutting, and the snow filled my sneakers. My feet were like icicles. I barely made it to Sudeok-sa and struggled to make the slippery climb to Gyeonseong-am.

Mother had returned there from Jikji-sa, but she greeted me with eyes colder than the snow. This time, she scarcely glanced at me, and she didn't even ask if I had eaten.

"Go to the Sudeok Hotel to sleep."

I had missed Mother for the whole semester, but I was told to go away in less that ten minutes! The path down the mountain was so slippery that I kept falling, and I felt hot tears on my cheeks.

Na Hyeseok heard me coming, and ran out the door to embrace me. I couldn't control myself—I burst into tears. Auntie sensed that I had gone to see Mother and had been rejected.

"Your mother is so cold that she would kick her own child out into the storm! I, myself, have often been treated coldly, and it has destroyed my affection for her.

Do not be sad—I'll be your mother!" She held my frozen body, and put my feet under a blanket. She got me a dinner, but I couldn't eat. I was so famished that my feelings of hunger had disappeared, and, after my reception at Sudeok-sa, my throat was too constricted to swallow.

She was warm and comforting, and pillowed my head on her arm. The thought kept running through my mind that it would be wonderful if this person were my mother, and I finally fell into a deep sleep.

When I went to the main temple at Sudeok-sa the next day, I realized that the repair work had not yet been finished. The construction was halted due to the deep snow. I walked to the praying rock, and looked up to the place where my mother was. The clumps of snow on the bare tree branches looked like white blossoms. It was a magnificent view of a different world, but my heart would not let me enjoy the beauty. I saw a person with a light tread coming down from Gyeonseong-am. It was Mongsul, whom I had met at the Chodang where Mangong lived. He recognized me, too.

I greeted him first. "Seu-nim Mangong is well?"

His answer was surprising to me. "Why do you ask that?" He glared at me, and spoke harshly.

"I'm asking if he is well because I know him."

He was sullen. "Who are you, and why do you come here so often?"

His words made me lose my temper. "You bastard! How can you speak to me so rudely?"

I slapped Mongsul's cheek. I was angry that a young person had spoken so roughly, and, moreover, I was releasing all of the pent-up resentment toward Mother that I was feeling. I thought that his rudeness was due to the fact that Mother had treated me so coldly. I gave him a swat, and Mongsul started to cry.

Two days later, Mother came to the hotel, and asked me in a stern voice to leave the following day.

Na Hyeseok said, "It is nice to have Masao here. Could he stay a few more days?"

But Mother ignored her question.

"Tomorrow you have to leave. It displeases me to have you here."

"You don't have to pay attention to him. I can make arrangements for his eating and sleeping."

"It's not a matter of money." Mother was very firm.

> Time flows like a river,
> And life is like a fallen flower.

Before the first bend,
The leaf is crushed,
But the spirit endures,
Even until the ocean.

Fallen Leaf on the River
by Ilyeop

I returned home, having received only ice from my mother, and the thought of Kim Bungyul, the Seu-nim at Jikji-sa in Gimcheon, came to my mind. I remembered how clearly he had said that he was going to be my father.

Aje Aje Bara Aje

I bade farewell to Idang Father, and told him I was going back to Japan. I got off the train at Gimcheon, with the idea of visiting Kim Bongyul. However, when I got to Jikji-sa, I learned that Kim Bongyul had gone to Seoul, and was not there.

Instead, the assistant Seu-nim, Tanong, greeted me warmly. I went to sleep in his room, and was sleeping soundly, when, before three in the morning, Seu-nim Tanong shook me awake.

"Tired? I'm sorry to wake you up."

I was confused at the sight of the Seu-nim, who was regarding me serenely, and he said softly, "I have been thinking, and I realize that you have a relationship with the Buddha which is not small. Seu-nim Mangong is the one who gave the commandments of Buddha to your mother, but I am the one who first cut off your mother's hair. It was my Buddhist writings that had awakened her religiously, and influenced her to become a monk. Cutting off someone's hair makes for a close relationship; anyway, you came here because of that relationship. It would not be a bad thing to learn to worship in front of Buddha, and to make an offering. Wash your face, and follow me."

I thought that it was indeed not a minor matter to have lost my mother to Buddha. I followed the Seu-nim into the room of the thousand Buddhas. There were about twenty monks there already. The Seu-nim in front of the gong hit it three times. with a bamboo stick. The first sound was weak, but it gradually swelled. There was a chant which went with that sound, which, in later days, I knew by heart. The meaning is as follows:

I wish for this ringing to spread throughout the universe.
Hell is deep and dark, surrounded by an iron wall,

But becomes bright when the gong sounds.
It eases the suffering of the hungry ghosts
Who dwell there. Then the barrenness is overcome,
And all can awaken in the righteous spirit.

When the echoing of the gong had faded, another Seu-nim chanted about tea, and then, three times repeated words about incense and truth:

Ohm baarah dobia hum
Ohm baarah dobia hum
Ohm baarah dobia hum

Seu-nim Tanong, in his clear voice, chanted along with the other monks. Lastly, the monks chanted in unison, Maha banya barah milda. Even now, when I think about the meaning of the Sutra, I murmur, "Banyara milda."

Aje aje bara aje bara seung aje mogi sabaha
Aje aje bara aje bara seung aje mogi sabaha
Aje aje bara aje bara seung aje mogi sabaha

We spent about thirty minutes at the morning service. This was my first time attending this kind of ceremony, and I could not understand everything that the monks were saying, but I was overwhelmed by the sacred environment. I was deeply impressed just by watching the monks' world.

The monks' meal was at 5:00 AM. Seu-nim Tanong told me to sleep until then, but I couldn't sleep. The Seu-nim came into the room, sat down cross-legged, and, closing his eyes, went into meditation. While I watched him, I thought about my mother. At that same time Mother also had finished morning services, and she might now be meditating or studying. Faintly, for the first time, I realized what it meant that I was the Rahula who interrupted her religious life. Outside the window, the wind was blowing, and the candle flames were wavering.

This was the first time that I attended the monks' meal. The monks were completely silent. Three times the gong sounded. Four dishes, rice, soup, a side dish, and clear water, were in front of each monk. At a signal, the meal was started. On that day, I learned for the first time that not even one grain of rice could be left on the plate, and, after eating, the water containers had to be filled again with clean water.

Seu-nim Kim Bongyul returned after three days. His wife, my Gimcheon mother, had a suspicious attitude. One minute she was glad to have me there, and the next, she disliked me. She thought that I was the fruit of his affair, so it was natural that she should be uncomfortable with me. But she was the kind of traditional Korean woman who viewed this simply as her fate, instead of a betrayal by her husband. At first, she kept her distance, but later she showed warmth and kindness.

I had come to know Buddha because of my mother; but later, my relationship with Buddha became strong, and belonged to me, alone.

5

Following the Water, the Clouds, the Buddha

Dream Walk on Mount Gumgang

At the start of my third-year summer vacation, Idang Father asked me if I would like to visit Gumgang-san. Of course I was delighted. We traveled in a group of six, including Father, Master Cheongjeon, and me. We took the Seoul-to-Weonsan night train, arriving at Cheolwon station early the next morning. From Cheolwon to the Tamgeori station, inside of Gumgang, we went by electric car. As the trolley was crossing the pass at Danbalryeong, to pass the time, Master Cheongjeon asked whether we were aware of the other history of Danbalryeong.

"Another story?"

"Yes. This is a story from the King Sejo period in the Joseon era. King Sejo dreamed about the widow of King Munjong, who was his sister-in-law. Sejo was then ruling in the place of her son, his young nephew. The angry mother spit at him in his dream, and where the spittle struck him he developed chronic boils.

Surely, you know that story. He tried every possible kind of treatment, but nothing worked. Finally, Sejo, with all of his servants, went to Gumgang mountain to be cured. When the royal carriage arrived at Danbalryeong, the king, looking out at the magnificent scenery of the twelve thousand peaks of Gumgang-san, became dejected, and recognized the futility of life. He regretted his usurpation of the throne. He declared that he wanted to shave his head, and remain in that beautiful place, to work on the improvement of his soul. When his followers heard his words, they discouraged him because they feared losing their own status.

Sejo was in a bad position; once the king has spoken, he cannot take it back, but he could see no prospect of attaining his desire to become a monk. To compromise, he took down his hair-knot, disclosing a good deal of white hair, which he removed. Then he knotted up his hair again, hiding the place that was now bald. He did cut off his hair, so he did not lie, but hid in his hair knot the evidence that he had done so, so he did not become a monk. Danbalryeong became famous as the place where King Sejo cut off his white hair."

The trolley crossed the Danbalryeong pass and arrived at Tamgeori. We climbed to Jangan-sa right away. This temple was built under the rule of King Beopheung, during the Silla period, and reconstructed under King Seongjong in the Goryeo era. It was considered to be in an enchanted land, and the Chinese Empress Ki traveled here to bless King Sunje, and his son, the crown prince, wishing them longevity and health. There was a stone tower fifteen feet high, and the temple on the second level is considered to be a valuable Korean cultural asset. We stayed two days in the hotel down from the Jangan-sa temple.

The Jeongyang-sa temple, a branch of the Pyohun-sa, was built by Goamreuk in the first of year of King Munmu's rule in the Pakjae era, and reconstructed by a great Buddhist, Wonhyo, under King Munmu, in the Silla period. This temple has a six-sided herbarium, and a three-story stone tower. In front of the tower is a pillar on which was inscribed a map of the temple, to assist visitors. There is a famous lookout tower at this temple. In it is an exquisitely executed model of the twelve-thousand peaks of Gumgang Mountain, which one can compare with the view from the look-out point.

On the way to Mahayeon, from Pyohun-sa, we saw the Bodeokgul, a cave temple, built in front of a natural cliff. There was a statue of the Buddhist goddess of mercy, cut from the rock, which was very impressive. We arrived at Yujeom-sa temple, which is in the center of Manpok-dong. This temple is famous for a great Buddhist monk, Samyeong. In a battle with the Japanese in the Imjin year, when he heard that the village down the mountain had been attacked, he armed himself with a single staff, and went to see the leader of the troops.

When the leader learned of the approach of a monk carrying only a staff, he thought he must be no ordinary man. The captain asked Samyeong, "What is the most valuable treasure in Korea?"

"If I let you know, would you want to have it? I will tell you the secret. In Korea, is no special treasure; but, now, if I took your head to the king, he would reward me richly. So, at this moment, your neck is the most valuable treasure in Korea."

The captain was awestruck by Samyeong's words, and treated the monk with respect.

Yujeom-sa temple, where Samyeong-daesa stayed, is one of the thirty-one major temples of Buddhism. It was constructed during the Silla period, even before the formal introduction of Buddhism into Korea. The founder was Nochun, who was a district magistrate in Goseong. The following story is told about the construction of Yujeom-sa:

> *Nochun received notice that a ship had arrived at the port. In that ship were fifty-three images of Buddha. The Buddhas all flew to an elm tree in the mountains, twenty miles away, and one by one landed in the tree. Nochun built a temple near that tree, and named it Yujeom-sa. The fifty-three Buddhas were enshrined there.*
>
> *In Yujeom-sa was a huge gong, which was one foot thick. If this gong was to be struck by an ordinary young man, there would be no sound; but, if Samyeong struck it, the sound would reverberate from the valleys of Gumgang mountain all the way to the sea.*
>
> *From Yujeom-sa, we went to the Biro-bong peak. Biro-bong was the highest peak of Gumgang mountain, and the flower and zenith of Gumgang. It faced another peak, the Yeonglang, and made for a spectacularly majestic sight. From Biro-bong we went to the Singyeo-sa temple, and encountered the Guryong waterfall. That waterfall was located a kilometer west of Onjeong-ri, at the top of the Okryukye valley. It was about one hundred feet high. On the way, there were seven ponds, connected to each other, each one lower than the next. Water flowed from the first to the second, to the third, and so on, looking like a string of rosary beads. These ponds were called Childam, which means "seven ponds," and the final destination of the water was the Guryong Falls.*

Some time ago, I had the experience of seeing Niagara Falls, on the border between Canada and the United States, which is a huge and magnificent falls. Guryong Falls, which I saw in that long-ago summer, was not big and powerful, like Niagara, but there was a rainbow on the falls from the Okryu valley, and the mystical experience was no less than that at Niagara.

The stone formations of Manmulsang were strange and wonderful to see. They looked like human beings, a hermit, the Buddha, all different kinds of animals.

When I think back to that experience, I am frustrated that I cannot remember clearly enough. In my memory, the myriad aspects of Gumgang mountain are dim, and seem like a dream. At that time, to have a camera was not very common, and I was only middle school-age, so it is natural that these memories, like my images of my hometown, should have become dim. Because of that, my frustration and nostalgia are even stronger. During that trip, Idang Father and the other artists made sketches for their future paintings. I have drawn all of Korea's famous mountains, except for the Gumgang, where I went that summer, and that is a circumstance to be lamented.

Nowadays, as a part of the North Korea-South Korea exchange program, the tourism possibilities are developing, so I have hope that I may someday, in the future, come to draw Gumgang. The artist, Jeongseon, has painted Gumgang to high acclaim; if I do it, I will use stone-powder colors, which will last thousands of years …

Not only is Gumgang the most beautiful and famous mountain in Korea, its valleys are home to many big temples, as well as smaller ones, and the cottages of hermits. This beautiful spot has produced many wise and accomplished spiritual leaders. My teacher, Seu-nim Gwaneung, studied there at one time. Mount Gumgang, like the holy land, is sacred ground.

The Young Painter

A few days after we came home to Waryong-dong, I went to Sudeok-sa. Mother greeted me coolly.

"I didn't think you'd come this summer…."

"I went to Gumgang-san with Idang Father, so I am late."

"You went to Gumgang-san? That is a wonderful mountain."

Mother closed her eyes gently, and rolled her meditation beads. She seemed to be recalling Gumgang-san.

After a while, I left Mother, and went to the Sudeok Hotel. Na Hyeseok welcomed me with warm smiles.

"From now on, don't let yourself be greeted with rejection; stop here first, then you can see your mother later…."

I understood her concern, but how could I be this close to Mother, and not want to see her?

The next day, I went up to Sudeok-sa. The roof repair on the main temple was finished, and the Japanese carpenters had left. Inside of the repaired temple, I saw that the wall paintings had been covered up; apparently, they had been careful not to harm one of Korea's cultural assets.

(I have mentioned that these murals were similar to those at the temple at Asuka in Japan. When I returned to Sudeok-sa after the war and the liberation of Korea, the paintings were gone. Mongsul, who had become a monk and taken the name Wondam, told me that Seu-nim Byeokcho had smashed the paintings and used the pieces to fertilize the chestnut trees. The paintings had been done with the stone-powder process, and were very precious. I was devastated to learn what had happened to them.

I went to the Chodang and greeted Seu-nim Mangong and Seu-nim Byeokcho. Monsul, remembering that I had hit him, was hostile at first, but we played together in the valley, and then everything was all right; he was still only a child.

When I returned to the hotel that evening, Na Hyeseok was painting. She was intense and full of passion. I had never seen her that way before. She had always welcomed me warmly, but this time her gesture indicated that she didn't want to be disturbed. Her concentration was driven by a burning focus. I sat down far enough away not to disturb her, but I suddenly had a strong desire to paint.

After I was sure that she had finished her work, I spoke up. "Auntie, I'll be a painter."

She made a naughty face. "Why? You said you wanted to be a monk?"

I answered sincerely, "Even if I became a Seu-nim, I could still draw. I often dream that I become a Seu-nim and a painter."

She advised me very seriously, "In my opinion, becoming a monk is a later matter, but to become an artist is an immediate thing."

Then she lent me her extra easel, some watercolors and a brush, which I could use during the rest of the vacation.

I left Sudeok-sa and went to Onyang, because I wanted to draw there. Once I had gone with Idang to the Onyang Hot Springs Hotel, and had seen their beautiful garden, I was inspired to draw. That hotel was Japanese-run, and I got permission from the manager to set up my easel in the garden, which was a very pretty spot. In the pond, carp were swimming amongst the water plants, and there were many trees around it, attractively arranged. I sketched with a charcoal pencil, and put oil colors onto my palette. Gradually, I fell into a trance. Later, when I regained my senses, I realized that a man of about fifty years was standing behind me.

"Son, do you want to sell this painting to me?"

I was astonished. "I … I have never had occasion to sell a painting; I'm not good enough to sell my work."

"No; that painting gives me a feeling that I want to have. Good painting is that painting which one wants to possess."

He told me that he would give me twenty won for the picture. At that time, my tuition was ten won, so that represented two years' tuition. Room and board was four won per month, so, if I used the money for room and board, twenty won would last me five months. I had learned oriental painting from Idang from time to time, but I had done western-style painting only in my classes.

That evening, the gentleman reserved a hotel room for me, and the following day I finished the painting, and he paid me twenty won for it.

"You are sincere, and you have real talent. I think that someday you will be a famous artist, so I want to have this painting."

As he predicted, I am now a painter. Looking back, I think that he was the first person to recognize me as a real artist. If that picture is still in existence, I would exchange one of my current works, ten times bigger, for it; I would like to have it back.

That summer, I visited Jikji-sa. It had now become important to put visits to Kim Bongyul Father on my schedule. In that place were not only Kim Bongyul, but also Seu-nim Tanong, so I felt like I was at home.

When I arrived at Jikji-sa, Seu-nim Tanong, Seu-nim Park Kobong, and Seu-nim Cheongdam were all in the meditation area. While I was with them, a woman with a young baby on her back, entered, and laid the baby at the feet of Seu-nim Cheongdam. She said to him, "This is your child. Do as you will—raise her or give her to someone else—it is up to you."

I found out that these were the wife and daughter of Cheongdam, prior to his becoming a Seu-nim. Buddha was frustrated by having a son in the secular world, and Cheongdam was undergoing similar frustration because of his prior life. I felt compassion and pity for that baby, because we were both Rahulas. Much later, I learned that both mother and baby became monks; I suppose that was their karma.

Now, let me tell you about the second time I sold a painting. At about that time, I again met Seu-nim Gwaneung, who was a student at a Buddhist university in Japan. He liked a picture of the Buddhist Goddess of Mercy that I had drawn in Jikji-sa.

"That is a good painting; could you give it to me as a gift?"

I gave it to him immediately. Later, I got a letter from him saying that the landlord of his rooming house wanted to have the same picture. I did a careful drawing on silk, and sent it to Kyoto, where he was staying. A few days later, I received thirty won in the mail. This was the second sale of my painting. During that summer, I had earned fifty won, which was big money; but, even more than the money, knowing that someone recognized my talents made me happy.

The Bell at Dasol-sa Temple

While I was in Jikji-sa, Master Choe Yeonghwan, whose pen name was Hyodang, visited there. He was a scholar of religion, a politician, and an educator. He accomplished many things both before and after the liberation of Korea, but we cannot ignore his efforts to spread knowledge of the tea ceremony.

Father Kim Bongyul introduced me to him. He was an open and tolerant person, and immediately invited me to go with him to Dasol-sa.

"It's all right if you want to go for a few days." Father Kim Bongyul gave his permission, so I followed Master Choe Yeonghwan. We went from Gimcheon to Jinju, where we stayed at the home of a friend of Master Choe Yeonghwan, near Namkang. The next day we traveled by bus from Jinju to Dasol-sa, which was in Sacheon in Goyang-myeon. When we got off the bus, Master Choe took me to a house which was down the hill from Dasol-sa; it was isolated from others in the village, and looked like a painting. There, he introduced me to a gentleman of about fifty years.

"This is Master Beombu."

I greeted him. Later, I discovered that he was a famous student of Chinese literature, as well a distinguished scholar of oriental philosophy. He was a brother of the famous Korean novelist, Kim Dongri.

Master Beombu's back yard was an orchard with well cared-for peach trees, and in the garden were sun flowers. Through the open door, I could see a glowing sunset, and a cool breeze was blowing.

Master Beombu asked me to approach him, and he stroked my hands. I felt his warmth. The master said with a gentle smile, "You look smart. You have come so far to my house that we must have had a previous karmic relationship, so make yourself at home."

"Yes."

He lived downhill from Dasol-sa and cultivated fruit trees, but he was not an ordinary person; I felt strongly that he was a sage rather than a farmer. Just to meet him made the trip worthwhile.

We ate a carefully prepared dinner, and then went to the temple. Dasol-sa was about one kilometer up the mountain from the house of Master Beombu. The path led through a forest of pine trees. When we arrived at the temple, Master Choe directed me to my room, "I'm sure you must be tired, so go to sleep early.

Since you are in a temple, it would be a good idea to follow their way of living, but it is your choice. You can sleep late, and do whatever you want to, or follow the schedule of monks. In this temple they get up at four-o'clock and complete their routines, but if you are too tired, sleep in."

I wanted to take part in the monks' life; if I did so, perhaps I could gain a little more understanding of my mother. Why was it that, even if she were a thousand miles away, my mother's face would come to me first in my every decision? To become a dried leaf, blown and finally crumbled by the wind—perhaps that would lead me to my mother and resolve my yearning for her. If I could share meals with Mother and sleep in the same house, perhaps I wouldn't have become such a vacation-vagabond. By now, in Gyeonseong-am, in Sudeok-sa, Mother would have gone to bed. Thinking about that, I closed my eyes.

I woke up at the sound of a gong. I arose, and went to the bell pavilion. In the darkness of early morning, a monk was striking it, and when I approached him, he asked, "Do you want to strike the bell?"

"Yes."

I wished that the gong-sound that I made might echo through the darkness, past time and space, all the way to Mother's ears.

"When I give you the signal, hit the gong hard."

The monk signaled by body language when to hit the gong. I pushed hard at the huge clapper. The sound, reverberating against the eardrum, was very loud at first, but the waves that followed became gradually less intense. Just before it faded away altogether, the monk gave me the signal to hit the bell again. I continued to sound the bell whenever he gave a signal. Surely, the sound was traveling to the village where Beombu lived. The image of Mother flashed in my mind, and I murmured, "Mother, your son is ringing the bell; please, listen!"

After I mastered the techniques of ringing the bell, I displayed my skills at Jikji-sa in the morning, whenever I visited. I came to embrace the simple act of bell-ringing as a form of therapy. Hitting the bell not only helped me physically by allowing me to rid myself of pent-up aggression, the beautiful sound it produced was emotionally soothing to the soul.

Tea Ceremony and Wind in the Pines

That morning, after breakfast, I went with Master Choe into a room that held a fire-pot, and all different kinds of tea utensils.

"Now I will make tea; please savor the taste."

"Thank you."

"Since this is the first time, I will explain it to you. The tea cannot be made heedlessly. Drinking tea has its own rules; that is the tea ceremony."

Master Choe put charcoal onto the kindling fire. As it was getting hot, he put a tripod over the fire, and hung a small pot to boil the tea water. When the sound of boiling started, he asked me if I could hear it.

"This sound, is it like anything else? Maybe you think it is similar to the sound of wind in the pines?"

I listened attentively, and I did hear a sound like I had heard from the pine forest as I walked to Dasol-sa from Master Beombu's house.

"Oh, it really does sound like the wind blowing in the pine trees."

"Right. That is why we call the sound of tea-water boiling, 'pine wind.' You must not wait until that sound is gone. If the water reaches 100 degrees centigrade, there is no boiling sound. When the tea gets that hot, the flavor disappears, and the vitamins are lost. So, when you hear the pine-wind, you must remove the kettle from the fire-pot. The water will then be around 80 degrees Centigrade."

When he heard the proper sound, Master Choe removed the kettle. Then, with a bamboo ladle he dipped the water into the teacups. After he swirled the water around, he poured that water into another container. Next, he put two scoops of green tea powder into each teacup with a bamboo scoop, and stirred it with a tea stick.

"Stirring tea has a rule, too. Stir to the right, and then to the left, with power, so that the bubbles form evenly."

He cradled the teacup in his hands and placed gently it in front of him; put his hands on his knees, and bowed his head. "Drink it, but give thanks first. Put your hands in your lap, as I did, and then bow your head and say 'thank you.' It is the essence of the tea ceremony to drink with appreciation and gratitude. Put your teacup in your left hand, turn it two and one half times with your right hand, to your eye, and finish the tea in two and one half sips. When you have finished, wipe the area your lips have touched with your hand, and set the teacup down. Then, touch your clothing to make sure it is correct."

I followed Master's instructions to the letter.

"You did very well. After you drink, you may ask to see the teacups, to appreciate their beauty. That is another step in the etiquette. While you admire the teacup, you must look at the bottom, because you do not want to miss the name of the ceramic artist, or the year it was created."

He poured water into the cups we had used, stirred with the tea stick, and dried them with a towel before he stored them away. The slightly bitter taste of the tea I had drunk in my first ceremony, stayed on my tongue.

Master continued telling me about the tea ceremony:

"Though it is known as a Japanese custom, the tea ceremony was originally ours. The tea ceremony was already established in the Silla and Baekje periods, and our ancestors were the ones who taught it to the Japanese people. But, while it is flourishing in Japan, in our country the tea ceremony has almost vanished."

When I perceived the depth of his feeling, I couldn't say anything.

"If it does die out, it would be the loss of something important; the Independence Movement means the preservation of our own national traditions."

He didn't go into detail about the Independence Movement to me, but I had the feeling that he was a part of it.

I lived in Japan for a long time, traveled to China, and had the opportunity to visit many European countries. The taste of the water in our country is far superior to that of anywhere else in the world, especially the cold water from the well, and the broth made from bottom-of-the-kettle rice; we need no other drink.

Maybe that is why we lost the tea ceremony, because our water tastes so good, even without boiling the tea.

Some may say that the tea ceremony is useless, but I believe that the ritual makes the tea even more enjoyable. Since the ceremony is a part of our tradition, it has an historical meaning, and should be cherished. Master Choe, who saw the preservation of the tea ceremony as an important part of the conservation of our culture, made a real contribution.

While I was staying at Dasol-sa, I had the chance to meet the novelist, Kim Dongri. We often had dinner at Master Beombu's home, and visited with him.

The time flew by like an arrow. I was to have stayed at Dasol-sa for a few days, but Master Choe treated me well, and I liked Master Beombu, and I liked the pine forest around the temple so much that I just continued to stay there, even after I should have returned to Japan. Once or twice, Master Choe reminded me that I should go back, but I didn't budge. It seemed possible for me just to remain there and eventually become a monk. I was attracted to the idea of becoming a great monk, one who was a scholar, and also had a good personality—one who cultivated his personal development, and artistic skills by his own efforts, rather than by studying in school. I put off leaving day by day, until one day a detective from the Goyang police station came seeking me out. Vacation had long been over, and I hadn't returned to Japan. Finally, Mr. Araki contacted Idang Father in Korea, who looked for me in Sudeok-sa. He was told that I had been there, but left long before. When he heard this, Idang contacted my birth father at the viceroy's office, and he started the search for me. They discovered that I had been in Jikji-sa, and was now staying in Dasol-sa. Father ordered the police in Goyang to send me back to Japan immediately.

I was nabbed by the detective, and left Dasol-sa like a criminal. As we walked down toward Master Beombu's house, I heard the pine-wind blowing. Now, whenever I see a pine forest, I remember the sound of wind through the branches, and the sound of Master Choe's tea-water boiling.

The plain-clothes detective took me to Busan, and didn't leave until he was sure I was on the boat to Simonoseki. I crossed the Sea of Japan with complicated feelings, but the steam-whistle sounded the same as always.

To Mother

The sycamore trees on the campus of my Hongo Middle School were changing as it was autumn. The green leaves were showing spots of red, and the morning and evening winds were chilly.

During that time, I visited many museums, and became more and more ambitious about becoming a painter. My art teacher, Mr. Terauchi encouraged me, after recognizing a talent in me. I had already experienced selling two works of art, which made my determination all the stronger. Becoming a Seu-nim who pursued painting had not panned out, so I decided to go to an art college to study both the practical skills of a painter, and the theories of art. I wrote a letter to Mother at Gyeonseong-am:

To Mother:

I regret making everyone worry about my whereabouts during last summer's vacation, but I got back to Tokyo safely, and I am studying hard, so please don't worry. Mother! I have decided to become a painter. Mr. Terauchi, my art teacher, told me about Sesshu, the famous Japanese painter. He was in the temple when he was young, but he concentrated on drawing instead of memorizing the Sutra. His teacher-monk thought of making him a very noble monk, and tied him to a pole inside the temple. When he heard no sound from him even after many hours, the teacher peeked in through a crack. What he saw shocked him, and he suddenly threw open the door only to witness a big rat trying to bite Sesshu's toes. After he ran in and kicked away the rat, the monk was shocked again: the rat was not a real animal, but only a drawing. Sesshu had drawn with his toes, using his tears. The teacher was very moved, and let him draw as much as he wished. When he was in his twenties, with the help of that monk, Sesshu went to China. When he returned to Japan, he lived in Kyoto, and became a founder of the Japanese school of painting in India ink. He had natural talent, but he worked harder than anyone to become an outstanding Japanese painter. I am determined to follow in Sesshu's footsteps.

Mother! I know that you are a famous poet. In the future, I will put your poems into my pictures, so that the artwork of mother and son will appear together. It is my desire to honor both of our work in the highest possible manner. It will be my sole mission to create works that will be worthy of your poetry.

Dear Mother! Since I now have my goal, I will no longer need to roam around aimlessly and make people worry. I promise that I will honor your name by doing my very best.

When I saw you in Gyeonseong-am, you told me not to call you Mother, and you were not affectionate. Still, you are my mother, and I am your son. It is my destiny to follow you. I will visit you in Gyeonseong-am during winter vacation.

At the palace in Chiyoda-ku, Sinjuku Park, in Tokyo, the leaves are like fire. Before long, the cold wind will blow them down, then winter will be here. Mother, the winter cold at the mountain temple is very severe. Please take care of your health. Stay well until I see you....

Mother did not answer my letter, but, since mine was not returned, I assumed that she received it, which she did. During winter vacation, I returned to Korea. Having left all of my luggage with Idang Father in Waryong-dong, I went to Deokseung-san. After we greeted each other, Mother mentioned my letter.

"I received your letter from Japan. You are determined to become a painter? ..."

"...."

"It's not a bad idea to develop your inborn talent, and become a good painter by making your best efforts."

Mother continued, "I saw in your letter that your writing skill is not bad, but in the future, even in a letter, I must again ask you not to address me as 'Mother.' In case someone should see the letter, what would I say? If you address me as 'Mother' in your letter, I have to tear it up after I read it. Please keep that in mind."

She was not as cold to me as the last time, but still she was very firm. When I came out of her room, the winter wind in Deokseung-san was as cool as her demeanor. I heard it howling as I went down the mountain.

I stopped by the Chodang, and found Seu-nim Mangong scolding Mongsul because he had broken a lamp while he was cleaning the soot from it. I didn't want to remain in that environment, so, as soon as I greeted Mangong, I stood up.

"Why?"

"I am going to sleep at the Sudeok Hotel."

"Is that woman, Na Hyeseok, still there?"

"Yes."

"Huh. As soon as she found out she could not become a monk, she should have gone back to the secular world. Why in the world is she staying here?"

Seu-nim Mangong was muttering with closed eyes. My chest was tight with worry as I walked to the hotel, because I had not returned her art materials last summer. But, as always, generous Na Hyeseok didn't care about that, and made me feel welcome.

I told her last summer's story. She listened wide-eyed, and said, "You hid in Dasol-sa because you wanted to quit school, and they grabbed you?"

"Something like that."

"Oh, my God!...."

"I had to leave the art-tools you lent me in Jikji-sa. Before this vacation is over, I'll get them and give them to you."

One day, Master Goam, Lee Eungro, came to the Sudeok Hotel to see Na Hyeseok. She introduced us. He brought pictures of an exhibition of his art work in Tokyo. These were India-ink paintings, but drawn in contemporary style, and were very impressive. We exchanged telephone numbers in Tokyo, and promised to meet there.

Transporting Funds for the Independence Movement

I greatly desired to visit Dasol-sa before winter vacation was over. I had felt so much at home there; during that summer, I had wanted to stay forever.

I visited first at Master Beombu's home, then went to Dasol-sa. On the way there, the wind through the pines roared louder than I had ever heard before.

The elaborate welcome I received at Master Choe Yeonghwan's mirrored the significant effort I made in traveling so far to get there. He served me mal tea that he brewed himself.

After I had been there three days, Master Choe told me, "I have something to do in Seoul. What would you like to do? Do you want to wait for me here?"

"No, I have to leave, too."

He looked at me for a minute and smiled, then said, "Then, do you want to go with me through Daegu to Seoul? It should be a good trip."

Trip? Trip? Just the thought of it was exciting. I had traveled so much all my life, I had no fear about making a journey. I decided to go with him.

He took off his monk's robe, and put on a western-style suit and fedora hat. He was tall and slim, and looked very nice.

As we had last summer, we stayed one night at the home of Master Choe's friend in Jinju; I regret that I cannot now recall his name. He treated us well. If my recollection is correct, he was responsible for collecting money from all the rich people in the area for the Independence Movement fund.

When we got to Daegu, Master Choe took me to a private dining room in a big gourmet restaurant. This room was typically used only by the owner. His name was Park Gwang, and I met him on several other occasions after that day.

He made enough so much delicious food that the weight of it all made the table legs buckle. From outside the room, I could hear singing accompanied by a kay-agum, a Korean harp-like instrument. Mr. Park was a benefactor from Daegu who donated money to the Independence Fund. Park's motivation for opening the restaurant was not out of a culinary calling, but rather to provide people with a safe meeting place; a haven from Japanese harassment. I didn't realize this at the time, of course, but came to understand later what the situation had been.

The next morning Mr. Park Gwang wrapped many envelopes individually in white rice paper, and layered them in a bag, one by one.

I asked, "How come you have so many letters?"

Master Choe answered, "Korean people are sending letters to their relatives in Manchuria, China. By chance, there is someone going to Manchuria, so we collected all of these letters for him to take in person. It is not very heavy—do you want to carry it?"

"Yes."

I led the way, and Master Choe followed me. On the night train to Seoul were many special detectives, who, if they became suspicious, would search a person and his luggage. Fortunately I did not trigger any alarms since I was wearing the uniform of Hungo Middle School in Tokyo. It helped that I wasn't nervous either, since I believed the bag I carried held nothing but letters.

We arrived safely at the Seoul station the following morning, took a trolley to the third street of Jong-ro, and went to the Waryong-dong home together.

Idang and Master Choe were old acquaintances. Master Choe told Idang Father, "Masao was so smart. I had no trouble this time bringing these letters." That's when I realized that this was not the first time that letters were transported, and that Idang Father was also involved in the process. That was the way I found out that Idang was secretly supporting the Independence Movement. He never spoke to me about it directly, but I was aware, through his conversation, that he was strongly in favor of independence.

After a late breakfast, Master Choe said to me, "I know you must be tired, but let's go one more place." Idang Father agreed. We went to Seongbuk-dong, and stopped at a tall front gate.

"This is the house of Master Manhae, Han Yongun."

Master Han Yongun did not look well. I bowed deeply to him when Master Choe introduced us. Master Choe gave our bag to Master Han Yongun.

"In the future, Masao will be doing this kind of errand often."

I realized then that I could be a helper in this endeavor. "Any time you have one of these errands, ask me."

Master Han Yongun looked at me, and I saw a shadow cross his face. He probably felt guilty using such a young child. In those envelopes were not letters; they all were full of money. Before we left the house, Master Han Yongun gave me five won.

"When you need it, use it." The image of brightly smiling gaunt face is vivid to me even now.

On that day, he met with Seu-nim Jeogeum at the Sun Institute, and then returned to his Waryong-dong home.

Idang Father asked us whether we had a good trip, but I could tell that he had been worrying about the transfer of the letters.

"Yes. I delivered the letters well."

I could see the relief on his face, but immediately he frowned, and murmured to himself, "I hope that independence comes soon. You have to concentrate on your studies."

When I glanced at him, I saw that his eyes were red. I realize now that this was a sign of ambivalence on his part—his uneasiness about putting me in possible danger, in the name of fighting for Korean independence.

The Mansion in Izu

When I became a fourth-year student, I decided that after this term, I would take the required exam to go to Art College. In the school system at that time, it was customary to go to college after five years of middle school, but it was possible to take the college exam after only four years. Since the exam included the fifth year work, I bought all of the textbooks for that year in order to study for the test. I studied fourth year subjects at school, and fifth year subjects alone at home.

I didn't immediately start middle school after elementary school, and pride made me determined to make up for that wasted year. Looking back, I view the fourth year as the most studious of my life. One day, when I returned home from school, a guest was waiting for me. He was an aged gentleman wearing a very expensive kimono, and sporting a handsome mustache. He looked me over carefully.

Mr. Shindo told me, "Masao, this is your grandfather. Please greet him."

I knew that I had a grandfather, but I had never met him. I bowed low to him, as Mr. Shindo asked me to do. Grandfather asked me to come close to him, and, for some reason, this made me glad. I was still young, and the idea of encountering a newfound grandparent was heartwarming. When I got near him, Grandfather stroked my head.

"Oh, you are big! It was my mistake that we didn't meet before."

Grandfather nodded with some strong emotion. Even though we had not met before, he seemed strangely familiar, probably because we were of the same flesh and blood.

"Masao has a talent for drawing. He is going to skip fifth year, and wants to go to Art school. He is studying so hard!"

Grandfather opened his eyes wide when Mr. Shindo spoke. "You want to be a painter? What art school do you want to test for?"

"I'm thinking of going to the national art school."

Grandfather looked proud, and smiled briefly. "I would like to see your work, so I could judge your talent. Can you draw the Buddhist Goddess of Mercy to give to me?"

Grandfather took out his wallet and gave me forty won to buy materials to do the painting. I received this money politely.

"After I finish it, how can I deliver it to you?"

"When you finish the painting, have Mr. Shindo bring you to my home in Izu.

This is my formal invitation to you."

Then Grandfather stood up. "Now that I have met Masao, I must go home."

When he got to the entrance, his driver gave him a deep bow, and opened the car door for him. Grandfather got into the car. At that time, to own a private car was the sign of extremely high rank. After he left, I asked Mr. Shindo,

"What does Grandfather do?"

"Now, he is old and retired, but earlier he was a bank president, and he also inherited a huge fortune."

Shindo Araki told me that Grandfather's name was Oda Hosaku, and that he was a descendant of Oda Token. I realized with surprise just how great the Oda family was. My grandfather and my father were their descendants, but my mother was a Korean, Kim Ilyeop. Since I consciously lived and saw myself as a Korean, I was not overly impressed by the Oda family status; in fact, I actually felt negatively towards them as they were responsible for preventing my mother and father's marriage from happening.

Though part of me wanted to hate him, somehow I couldn't muster a sense of resentment toward Grandfather, maybe because of the blood-tie. I laughed to myself that in my deepest mind I had a two-sided heart.

In any case, I had to make a picture of the Goddess of Mercy to take to Grandfather as a gift. I bought silk at the art store. I drew the picture carefully, then transferred it to the silk. I had often seen Idang Father draw pictures on silk, and had some experience at it myself, so everything went nicely. When they saw the finished painting, both Mr. And Mrs. Shindo Araki were stunned.

"Masao is a genius! His painting is as good as that of the best painter in Japan!"

In my opinion, too, the Goddess of Mercy was drawn very well.

On Saturday, after Mr. Shindo got home from his bank, we took a train to Izu.

"Originally, your grandfather lived in Yamaguchi, but, after he retired, he moved to Izu, near Tokyo."

Izu was in the Adami Hot Springs area, about two hours from Tokyo by train.

At the Adami station, we took a rickshaw, which stopped in front of a mansion as big as a castle. The house was surrounded by a forest of big trees. The landscaped garden, which I guessed to be an acre in size, had a pond with fish leisurely darting from one end to another. We passed the garden and approached the house. Grandfather greeted me with one of his deep smiles. Beside him was seated a graceful lady.

Grandfather said, "This child is Masao."

Grandmother looked at me in disbelief. After a moment, she reached out her hand, saying in a low voice, "Masao, I am your grandmother. Come here so I can touch your hand."

Grandmother's hand was pretty and soft. I saw tear drops in her eyes.

In that mansion was a gallery where important paintings lined the walls, and Grandfather had hung my picture in the same gallery! For a few moments they seemed awe-struck, then Grandfather nodded with satisfaction.

"Great work! I have no objection at all to your plan to study art."

"Thank you."

"The dean of the art school at Tokyo National University is a friend of mine.

I must tell him that my grandson is taking the entrance exam for that school."

Grandfather wanted to use his influence, but I politely refused his assistance.

"Thank you for your willingness to help, but I don't want to get into the school because of your influence. If I pass the test and get admitted, that will be great.

But, if I don't, I can continue with fifth year, and take the exam later, so it won't be too bad."

Grandfather looked at me proudly, and said, "Of course you are right. As a member of the Oda family, you must be admitted on your own abilities. I will watch."

It made me uncomfortable to hear about the family clan, but I was pleased that he understood my thinking.

The most impressive thing in that mansion was the bathtub. When I turned on the faucet, water from the natural hot spring poured out. I took a shower in the water from Adami Hot Springs, and spent one night in that mansion like a palace.

Hometown Before I Got Famous

That year, I did not plan to go to Korea during summer vacation because I thought this would be the best time to study for the entrance exam. However, when summer arrived, I couldn't settle down, so I finally went to Korea. I packed all of my books to study and left.

I went to Sudeok-sa first. This time, I stopped first at the Sudeok Hotel. As usual, Na Hyeseok greeted me warmly. Whenever I went there, of course I wanted to see Mother, but now I felt some excitement about seeing Na Hyeseok as well. I didn't hurry to Gyeonseong-am first—maybe that was a sign I was becoming an adult. That night, I slept with Na Hyeseok in the hotel. The next morning I went to Gyeonseong-am, sweating in the heat, and greeted Mother.

Always before, I had come in the evening, so she thought it strange that I had arrived so early.

"As a matter of fact, I arrived last night, stayed in the Sudeok Hotel, and came up now." Mother didn't express an opinion.

I stopped by the Chodang and greeted Seu-nim Mangong. As I went down the mountain, I saw Mongsul, who was playing in the water of a stream in the valley. I was happy to see him, and took off my clothes and jumped into the water.

"Have you been good?"

I had asked politely, but Mongsul answered quickly and with open hostility, "Who are you? Why do you always show up at vacation time?"

I grabbed his neck and held him under the water. "Who I am has nothing to do with you!"

Mongsul's face was turning blue. He was too young to fight strongly with me, and again he started to cry. Many years later, after Mongsul had become the head monk at Sudeok-sa, he admitted that he had confronted me because he had heard I was a Japanese spy.

"What? I was suspected of being a spy?! …"

"I can't tell you who it was, but he told me that you might be a spy and to be careful."

To hear this was a real shock to me, but I could see how it was possible that I could arouse suspicions, since few people knew of my relationship to my mother, and I had turned up on a regular basis. But—a spy?! This was absurd! At that time, there were often people from the Independence Movement hidden in the temple, so I supposed that it might have been possible for someone to have become concerned about the presence of a spy, but I never imagined that I might have been suspected. Of course, I learned these things at a much later time, when Mongsul was the head of the temple.

After I visited Sudeok-sa, I returned to my Waryong-dong home, and concentrated on my studies. Master Choe Yeonghwan visited, and I accompanied him back to Dasol-sa, bringing my books along. Three days after we arrived there, a guest appeared. He was Seu-nim Im Hwangyeong, from the Haein-sa. He was the teacher of Master Choe, and was a tall, well-built, and handsome man.

"By the way, would you like to visit Haein-sa?"

Of course, I accompanied him to Haein-sa.

That temple was on Gaya-san, a very famous and scenic mountain, at a spot with more strong spiritual qualities than any other place in this hemisphere. The noted monks, Seu-nims Suneung and Ijeong, built the temple during the King Yejang period. The name Haein comes from Haeinsamae in Avatanska Sutra.

The Haein-sa temple subscribes to the ideas of Avatanska, and many famous monks were educated there.

I asked Seu-nim Im Hwangyeong, "What is Haeinsamae?"

"Well, that is difficult to explain.… To understand that, you have to know what Avatanska Sutra is."

The Seu-nim tried to explain in a simple and easy way. "Avatanska Sutra describes Buddha's enlightenment, in the Haeinsamae."

"The world view of the Avatanska Sutra is that of a perfect world of one mind, uncontaminated by that world which we see with our eyes. It is a true world, untouched by suffering. 'One mind' means perfect, true, and pure perception.

"The goal of Haeinsamae is a state of seeing a world outside, of constant change and variation, while our inner perception is changeless and eternal. When we seek truth and meaning, we move toward Haeinsamae. Part of Buddha's wisdom is that, after suffering, we begin to perceive the truth. Haeinsamae is the story of Buddha's enlightenment, and of the real self who exists in our deep mind, the home to which we have to return."

I could not understand all of Seu-nim Im Hwangyeong's explanation, but I realized that Haein-sa was an historically rich temple, which had developed many famous disciples.

At Haein-sa was housed an 80,000 volume complete collection of Buddhist scripture, called *Palman Daejang Gyeong of Goryeo.* This collection represents a treasure, not only of Korea, but of the world, of Buddhist teachings, covering theory, world view, ethical principles.

After visiting Haein-sa, I realized that Buddhism had provided Korea with a rich tradition of art and architecture, as well as more esoteric spiritual values.

In Haein-sa, in front of the temple, was a stone tower with a pagoda-roof on each of three levels, and a stone lantern. About fifty meters from the main gate was another stone tower, showing typical Silla architecture. At the top of a cliff was a stone statue of Buddha (Ma Ae Bul), as well as another Buddha statue (Seokjo Yeoryae Ipsang), both considered national treasures.

In a separate temple building, employed as a museum, were displayed many valuable art objects relating to the temple, including Nahandosagyeong.

We often refer to a Seu-nim as "unsunapja," which means that the Seu-nim is not attached to any specific place, but rather moves like smoke or vapor across the land, concentrating the devotion. In Haein-sa, many high priests have stayed for a while, then left, and the register showed countless scholars who have visited there. In the Silla dynasty, Choe, Chiwon, and in the Goryeo, the most reverent priest Uicheon, and Master Samyeong were included among the visitors. In the Yi dynasty, the high priest Hoeun, Yuji left a collection of his writings called Hoeun, that tell the story of the everyday life of a priest. One such example:

At sunset, human love is disbursed.
The old year is relinquished, the new one accepted.
The carrier of the book-bag is seeking a teacher,
Across the mountain, over the water—
The journey is long, and also short.
Maintain the body with two meals, rice and porridge,
And, in the middle of the night, light the lantern,
And pray with spiritual discipline, for the nation.
With karma, life is lived without attachment.
My life is spent reciting and interpreting Buddhist scripture,
Trying to understand its meaning.

As I look back over the eighty years of my life, I see that I did not do enough reciting and interpreting Buddhist scripture, but I did succeed in living without attachment, in the way of "unsunapja." In my middle school years, moving from place to place like meandering clouds in the sky was in fact my first important religious training. Surely no other young person would have had the opportunity to visit as many famous temples; nor to have had received the love of so many great monks. I'm sure that it was no accident that these experiences led me into the direction of becoming a monk myself.

While I was in Haein-sa temple, I met the artist Jeong Jongyeo, and was fortunate to learn more about dessin and sketching.

When I returned to Seoul, it was nighttime. I went directly to the Daegag-sa temple, but could not meet with Seu-nim Baek Yongseong. I learned from the monk that greeted me that he was sick in bed. I slept in Daegag-sa, in the fragrance of brewing medicinal herbs.

The next day I returned to the Waryong-dong home, where I stayed a few days before traveling to Jikji-sa. There was no Tanong, or Kyoto Buddhist college student, but Father Kim Bongyul greeted me. I was busy coming and going between Jikji-sa and his home in Seongnae-dong in Gimcheon. The Gimcheon mother was no longer suspicious, and greeted me like her own son.

One day, Kim Bongyul asked me seriously, "I heard that during the last vacation you delivered letters. If you are not too busy this year, could you help us again?"

"Oh, I'm not too busy—I can help you to do that."

Kim Bongyul took me to the home of Park Gwang in Daegu. The next day we took the briefcase full of rice paper bundles which had been left at the Daegu teacher's home. In the same way as last year, we took the night train from Daegu station, but this time two detectives came to our seats.

One of the detectives asked Father Kim Bongyul, "What is your destination?"

"I am on my way to the Buddhist research center in Seoul."

"May I see your luggage?"

Father Kim Bongyul gave him the suitcase that contained his personal items. The detectives inspected the contents, then returned the bag and apologized. They paid no attention to me, and went on to another seat. Kim Bongyul had a tense expression, and his face was white.

When we arrived at the Seoul station, we headed to the Buddhist research center.

There we found Seu-nim Tanong and Seu-nim Jeogeum, and another Seu-nim Ha Dongsan, from the Beomeo-sa temple. This was the first time I had met him. Dongsan told me, "Every time you go to and from Japan, you have to pass through Busan. Next time, please come to visit Beomeo-sa."

We had breakfast at the research center, and then visited Master Han Yongun in Seongbuk-dong. He was very happy to see me.

"Wow, you have become so grown-up since last year."

I delivered letters twice more, but I never could have imagined that I was really shuttling money for the Independence Movement. I thought that I was carrying family letters to the independence fighters in Manchuria and Shanghai, and as such was worried that if the letters were found, the location of the fighters might be compromised.

I don't think that Master Choe Yeonghwan or Father Kim Bongyul used me, nor do I think that they were kind to me only so that I would agree to the tasks. They were kind, and we were close, so that it was natural for me to do those errands. Even from the beginning, if I had been told the truth, I would have done it anyway. In that, they were good to me.

6

Toward the Two Forbidden Gates

The Flower Blooms and I Draw

After I returned to Tokyo from Korea, I concentrated on preparing for the college entrance exam. Mr. and Mrs. Shindo were proud of me, having watched me stay up late and wake up early to study. Mrs. Shindo never forgot to provide snacks at night, and always paid close attention to my nutritional needs. The house was as quiet as a temple, with Mr. and Mrs. Shindo walking around on tiptoe so as to not break my concentration. I told myself that I absolutely had to pass the exam in order to show my gratitude towards them.

Even after school, Mr. Terauchi trained me intensively in drawing from still life and from plaster casts. He thought that, even though I might be behind in subject-studies, I could perhaps make up for it with good practical skills.

Honestly, I didn't even notice as the autumn came and went. Winter arrived, but I couldn't even think about going back to Korea. I experienced nosebleeds, and Mrs. Shindo began to tell me that if I didn't make it this time, I could try again next year. Finally, the New Year came, and soon thereafter was the day of the entrance exam. In February, the weather in Tokyo was still very cold and blustery.

"Masao, please eat this, and pass the exam." Mrs. Shindo made me sticky rice, she told me, so that I would stick to the school. This was typical of her care and love.

Luckily, the questions turned out to be what I had studied, so I knew most of the answers. The skills-test was in two sections, one the sketching of a plaster cast, and the other the drawing and coloring of a still life. Much later, I found out that I got a perfect score on the skills-test.

It was the date when those who had passed the test were to be announced. Mr. Shindo went to the bank, but then called home. As soon as he had arrived at work, he had called the school to find out the results.

"You made it, you made it! Not only did you pass, but you got a very high score. Congratulations!"

I felt happiness circulate through my body like my blood. I wanted to see it with my own eyes. Mrs. Shindo accompanied me, so that two people could verify the test results posted on the wall of the Tokyo National University. She was weeping with joy.

"You made it, Masao. I'm so proud of you."

This is how I became a student of the Tokyo National Art School. People get pleasure in many ways, but the great pleasure of accomplishment I now experienced for the first time.

A few days after I received notice of my acceptance at Tokyo National Art School, my birth father arrived. Mr. Shindo had informed him of the good news. Father couldn't hide his happiness.

"Masao, I am so proud of you. People who applied after five years could not get in, but you succeeded in only four years…."

The first time I saw him, I had gone to him to ask for help in rebuilding Sudeok-sa; now, this was the second time we met. I had not often seen him in person, but I had always knew that he was behind me, and now I felt it more than ever. I realized that my admission into the university gave my father deep emotional satisfaction.

"You are so grown up. Soon you will be the age I was when I met your mother."

Father's eyes misted as he looked back into his memories.

Father took me to a tailor for a college uniform and hat, and paid my tuition, and bought many drawing materials, all of the highest quality. He gave me two pairs of shoes, and plenty of pocket money. This was the first and the last time I roamed around Tokyo with my father.

The entrance ceremony was in March, 1941; I was nineteen years old. The Art School was on a hillside in Gichiyoji. The campus was huge, filled with trees, and melting snow made the brooks run fast. Like every new student, I was filled with hope, and I still remember the first lecture that I attended. The professor of aesthetics was Gimbara Shogo. He spoke in a gentle voice.

"The flower blooms. It blooms whether we notice or not. I draw. Whether anyone notices or not, I draw."

His sentences were like a poem. Their rhythm, and his gentle voice gave me a strange sensation. After that, his words became to me like a magical incantation, to be called upon when needed to solve a problem. After that, when I drew, I could lose myself in my work. I could draw without expecting attention or recognition, just for the satisfaction of doing it. The magic spell that Professor Gimbara Shogo gave me, remains with me to this day.

At the end of March, I was invited, with Mr. And Mrs. Shindo, to my grandfather's house in Izu. That was my college-entrance congratulatory party in Grandfather's big house. Dozens of people, politically and financially well known, had been invited, including Tokotomi Soho, a very famous politician and literary scholar. Grandfather introduced me to all of his close friends.

"This is my grandson. After four years of middle school, he was accepted to the National Art School. He is an exceptional person."

People clapped in congratulation, but I could not really feel that I was the First Son of the Oda family. A few days later, I was asked unexpectedly to visit the office of the dean.

"So ... your grandfather is Oda Hosaku."

"Yes."

"I saw him a few days ago, and he could talk about nothing else than how proud he was of you."

I felt uncomfortable and began to blush. He watched my red face, and smiled, and then said something that I had never thought of.

"Why didn't you tell us about that at the interview? If we had known that you were the grandson of the Oda family, you would not have had to go through that complicated process...."

"What? What complicated process?"

The dean suddenly looked uneasy. "Well ... your test scores were way above average, but there were some problems in the interview." He didn't explain further, but I guessed that my mixed-blood status had been the problem. In any case, Grandfather's influence, which had weight in politics, even in the palace, was beginning to affect my life. He had kept his promise not to use his power to get me admitted, but now my success was giving him pleasure.

It was a beautiful spring day, and the campus was filled with flowers. I wrote a letter to Idang Father and to Kim Bongyul Father to tell them I was now a college student, but I did not write to my mother in Gyeonseong-am. I wanted to show up at her door in my college uniform to see what kind of reaction she would have.

With the Uniform

The first vacation after I entered art school, I went to Korea without hesitation. When I arrived at the Waryong-dong home, everyone was excited, and there was a congratulatory party. Idang Father smiled all the time.

"I had heard that you passed the exam, but I really appreciated your letter. I am so proud of you!"

Brother Wunbo gave me a thumbs-up, and said, stuttering, "You are on your way!" Of course, he meant that I would become a number-one artist. Wunbo put on my college hat, and said, "Do I look like a college student?…." I realized that his expression was of both congratulations and envy.

Sukdang, Bae Jeongrye, Idang's only female student, suggested that we go to Changgyeong Palace to observe and to draw, which we did.

I spent a few days at Waryong-dong, then went to Sincheon. Usually I went immediately to see Mother upon arriving in Korea, but not this time. Maybe that meant that I was growing up. Usually on vacation I scurried like a squirrel from Sudeok-sa to Jikji-sa to Dasol-sa, but I had visited Sincheon only once since I had left there, and felt sorry about that.

Going to Sincheon proved to be a very good decision. When Father and Mother saw me in a college hat, they were so happy that they cheered.

"You a college student! It is like a dream."

Mother could scarcely let go of my hand. By that time, Brother was married, and helping Father. He also welcomed me warmly. I was the only one of my grade school friends who had gone to college, and everyone envied me.

While I was there, I visited the local temple, Nishihongan-ji, and visited Kanegio. He welcomed me warmly as well, happy to see I was a college student.

Father said, "Since you are here, you should visit your tenant farmer. You don't have to worry about sharecropping. I saw that it was sold and the money put where it will grow. In the future, it will be a big asset for you."

I had never given any thought to my property or my assets, but when I saw the crops on my land, growing so well in the sunshine, I was filled with satisfaction.

From Sincheon, I returned to Waryong-dong, then immediately set off for Sudeok-sa. When I arrived at the gate of the Sudeok Hotel, the sun was setting. Na Hyeseok was still there. When she saw me in my college hat, her eyes popped.

"Masao, have you become a college student?"

"As you see!"

She half believed and was half suspicious, so I explained all that had happened to me. She congratulated me, and shook my hand warmly.

The next morning, I started to Gyeonseong-am with a light step. I was imagining how happily Mother would greet me as a college student. Of course, her expression showed her complete surprise.

"What's going on? What has happened?"

I couldn't stop smiling, but I tried to be dignified. "I have become a college student."

"You didn't even finish your middle school?...."

"I took the entrance exam after four years."

"So you passed the exam?"

"That's why I am wearing this uniform."

Even though she tried to maintain her stone face, Mother couldn't hide her happiness. "Let's go tell Seu-nim Mangong about it."

I led the way. As she followed, she came up to me to brush the dust from my shoulders, then stepped back and regarded me proudly. Every time I had visited my mother, I had felt like I had failed her in some way, but this time I was a source of pride to her, and that made me happy. In the Chodang were Seu-nim Mangong and Mongsul.

"Masao has become a college student. He didn't graduate from middle school; he skipped a whole year and took the exam."

"Oh! Masao must be a genius!"

I bowed down to Seu-nim Mangong. He asked Mongsul to bring an envelope, into which Mangong put some money and gave it to me.

"You are now in college, so I'm sure you will have many places for your money to go, so take this."

I tried to refuse, but, after he insisted, I put it in my pocket. Mongsul couldn't take his eyes off my uniform. For the first time, he didn't show me any hostility.

Na Hyeseok showed me her paintings, and I looked them over carefully.

"What do you think about my work?"

"Well, overall the color is not pure and bright, and it is all very dull. Could you brighten it up a little bit?"

"You are so conceited! How can you criticize a more experienced person?...." She slapped my head lightly.

"Well, I'm a good art-school student"

"Hey, kid, you have only been going for a few months."

"Then, why did you ask me to judge your paintings?"

"I gave you the opportunity to learn from my work."

Of course, I didn't back down. "The artist that won't accept criticism cannot make progress."

"You are so over-confident that it scares me." She was laughing as she left. "I can see how fast you are growing. In a few years, maybe, I'll have to look up to you."

We spent a few days together, without any awkwardness, then I returned to Seoul. But that vacation was not filled only with happiness. When I visited Dae-gag-sa, I learned that Baek Yongseong had passed away. I was sure that he was now among the famous dead Buddhist priests, but I felt lost that he was gone from this life.

I burned incense before Seu-nim Baek Yongseong's portrait, and prayed.

Seu-nim Baek Yongseong was one of thirty-three people who had joined in an independence movement against Japan in 1919, and he was imprisoned for a year and a half. That was important, but even more so was the fact that he had been in the forefront of the Buddhist reformation in Korea. He revived traditional Zen Buddhism, and taught the real meaning of Buddhism. He reformed the system and the management as well. This is one of his poems:

On Owon Mountain was a man seeking a cow;
He sat alone in the empty house under the moonlight.
No one can say what is long or what is short;
what round or what is sharp.
Only one small flame could burn the universe.

He also sang a song of praise for Buddha's goodness;

On Geumo Mountain, the moon always rises unchanged.
In the Nakdong River are endless waves,
But where is the fishing boat?
As before, sleeping under the reeds.

This song extols Buddha's basic principles when he established the Daegak worship. Seu-nim Baek Yongseong taught that the principle of truth comes from an awakening. What does that mean? We are endowed with senses that afford a viewpoint creating harmony, and the wisdom of harmony is bright and shines everywhere. If the origin of truth is awakening, the alternate origin of the universe also lies there.

Master Heo Baekryeon in Mudeung-san

I stayed home for a few more days, then went to Gimcheon, since Father Kim Bongyul lived not far from the Gimcheon station. Often, when I went to Gimcheon, I would run into a girl student who was the daughter of the owner of a department store. She was interested in me because I was a middle school student in Tokyo. This time, she was surprised to see me wearing a college uniform.

"Wow! What happened to you?"

"Oh, I started to college."

We exchanged a few words of greeting, but I just kept walking along. However, she kept following me, along with her two friends. She was a young lady of big build, and I would not have said she was pretty, but she was a modern woman.

When I arrived at the Seongnae-dong home, Mother came out, surprised to see me in my college uniform. She was also surprised to see the girls coming behind me.

"Who are they? Why is this girl, who is big as a horse, following you?"

"She is the daughter of the owner of the department store, and I guess those are her friends. But I didn't bring them; they just followed me home."

Mother clicked her tongue. "Really!.... The whole world is changed. All of the girls nowadays are too bold. Jeongung [Korean for 'Masao'], you are too young to be going out with girls."

Then Mother scolded the girls, and sent them on their way. They were probably just excited to see someone in a college uniform.

I greeted Mother formally, and told her what had been happening in my life.

She showered me with admiration and pride. Let me introduce my family there.

In Seongnae-dong, I had two younger brothers, Gwanggyun, a middle school student, and Gwanggi, who was in grade school. There were also two sisters, younger than Gwanggi, Songja, who was three or four years old, and Jukja, who was just a toddler. I was the big brother to them, and therefore very popular with them. Gwanggyun and Gwanggi were proud of their college student brother, Songja would not leave me alone, and I changed Jukja's diapers.

That evening, Father Kim Bongyul came home, and we, father and son, had a warm reunion. One day, Kim Bungyul said to me, "Why don't you go visit Master Choe Yeonghwan in Dasol-sa, and then come back here before you return to Japan. Meanwhile, I'll get the money ready which you will need in Japan."

"I don't need the money."

"Hey, I don't want to be a father in name only, but a real father to you. So make sure to come back."

"O.K."

Before I went to Dasol-sa, I stopped by Master Beumbu's house. He, also, congratulated me sincerely. In Dasol-sa, Master Choe Yeonghwan proudly patted me on the back and gave a big laugh.

"Ah, you have become an art student. I must do a favor for you. I will introduce you to Master Heo Baekryeon."

Master Heo and Master Choe were as close as brothers. His home was set against Mudeung Mountain, with a stream running beside the house, like a picture postcard. He also cultivated tea, and his love for it was extreme.

Master Heo asked me, "Your name?...."

"I'm Masao."

"I can call you Jeongung, then. You are a student of the Tokyo National Art School.... The painters in our country can draw well, but they are behind in theory, and you must become a painter who has both skill and theoretical knowledge."

"I'll keep that in mind."

When Master Choe took me to Mudeung-san, it was not only to introduce me to someone; he had another purpose. I realized that Kim Bongyul also had a purpose in sending me to Master Choe.

Master Heo gave us an envelope wrapped in rice paper. It contained the independence movement funds which had been raised in Gwangju. We put it in a bag and took it to Master Park Gwang's home in Taegu.

At Master Park Gwang's, I went to sleep right after dinner, tired from the trip.

About midnight, I opened my eyes, and saw, in the next room, Master Park Gwang, Master Choe, and others whom I did not know, altogether five or six people, sitting around the table. I crept in through the slightly open door, and found them, in a smoky haze, playing dominoes, but talking about something else.

Master Choe said, "The funds from Master Heo are a lot more than we expected." Someone answered, "Even so, it is not enough for our big purpose, so you must work harder to raise money."

I finally realized that the bundles of letters were really the funds for support of the independence movement. But, I still didn't feel that I was unfairly used by others, nor did I realize that this was an activity opposed to Japan.

I asked myself, "Are you Japanese?" and I shook my head. "Then, are you Korean?" From one corner of my mind came the answer, "Yes, I am a Korean."

Then I felt a strong pain, like part of my heart had been cut off.

The Japanese thought of me as Korean, and kept me at a distance. Koreans regarded me as Japanese, so I was treated as neither and both; I wanted to be a person understanding and loving both countries, but if the situation arose when I had to choose only one, I was raised in Korea and had Korean culture in my blood. Not only as one Korean, but to pay back all of the people who had loved and helped me, I had to do this work. The next morning, Master Park Gwang laid out the whole bunch of envelopes, all wrapped in rice paper. We put them in the suitcase and took the night train to Seoul.

Seu-nim Jeogeum in the Buddhism Institute was the same as last year. We ate breakfast there, and then went to the home of the poet Han Yongun in Seong-buk-dong.

"You have changed from a middle school student. Now you look like an adult."

The Master looked at me proudly, then gave me thirty won. After I became a college student, the idea of pocket money had apparently changed a lot; thirty won was enough to supply a student for half a year.

On the way back to Japan, I stopped at Gimcheon, and Kim Bongyul also gave me big money. My first vacation from college, and people had given me so much money that I was walking on air.

Military Training

At the beginning of the second semester, the school's military training started. The training officer was in the active service, and the training was, not once or twice a week, but two hours every single day. More than learning rules about rifles and swords, it was intensive military training to prepare one to fight in a war. We wore complete military outfits, did field marching, and practiced with live ammunition.

But the officer could not overcome my mental reservations. Despite the training, I remained skeptical regarding the subjects of killing and injury. I hadn't come there to learn how to kill people.

The officer emphasized that you must be willing to give up your life without hesitation for the greater glory of Japan; but, if life is gone, what does glory mean?

I was thinking about quitting the school, and going to Jikji-sa or Haein-sa and drawing and painting there.

One day my knee was skinned and bloody from field marching and crawling on the ground, and when I got home I spoke seriously, "I.... quit my school."

Mr. and Mrs. Shindo were shocked. That was natural, since I had skipped a year, and tried with all my might to get accepted.

Very concerned, Mr. Shindo asked me the reason.

"The military training is too severe. I can't stand it."

"What? Military training?"

Even Mrs. Shindo opened her eyes wide in surprise. I showed them my bloodied knee.

"Oh, my God!.... We cannot let this happen. Masao is too weak for military training."

But, Mr. Shindo remained frowning for a few moments without saying anything.

Then he said, "Do not quit school. Think of how hard you have worked.

Just stick with it. Instead, let us try to find a way for you not to have to go through that severe training."

A few days later, the training officer quietly called me in.

"Masao, you have a weak heart....? So, from now on you will be participating in training only once a week, and the rest of the time you can use as you wish."

I realized right away that this was the result of Mr. Shindo's efforts. "Thank you."

"By the way, Mr. Seizo is your father?"

"Yes."

"Your father told me that you have a weak heart, and asked me to take the appropriate action."

In short, Mr. Shindo had reported to my father, and my father had taken the action. I felt that my father was near me even though he was far away. I could be sure of my father's love, even at a distance, and I was freed from that horrible training because of him.

The Girl in Gimcheon

Mother and I came out from Gyeonseong-am, and walked toward the Chodang where Seu-nim Mangong was.

"Have you had an opportunity to visit Master Han Yongun?"

It was such a sudden question that my heart jumped. "Yes, I went there with Master Kim Bongyul and Master Choe Yeonghwan to deliver a bunch of letters ..."

"Lord save us!...."

Mother closed her eyes, clearly struggling with the conflict between her love for her own son and for the worthy cause. Finally, she spoke in a low voice, "Listen carefully to what I'm going to say. I wish for you to take care of yourself. A person who is honest and doesn't lie is one who has integrity. Attain that first, then be one who does good for other people and for society."

"I understand."

"There can be a sacrifice involved in working for society, but to sacrifice one person for the good of all can be a holy thing."

Mother stopped speaking when we arrived at the Chodang. Seu-nim Mangong and Seu-nim Byeokcho greeted me happily. "My, you look so grown-up! You'll have to get married soon."

"Oh, I have to graduate from college first." This is the first time I had heard anything about marriage. Then Na Hyeseok at the Sudeok Hotel said a similar thing to me.

"Oh, who will be the bride of Masao?"

Marriage.... At that time, that was not a real concept to me.

While I was staying in the Sudeok Hotel, Seu-nim Yun Seoho asked me to draw a picture. He was from Sincheon in Hwanghei-do, and he liked me because we were from the same hometown. When I gave him the picture, he was very pleased and satisfied.

After Sudeok-sa, I went to Gimcheon. When I got off the train, I walked toward Seongnae-dong. I was wearing my college uniform and a cape, and walked along proudly. The girl from the department store came jumping out, just like last time.

"Oh, Mr. Masao! How are you? I was thinking that this was the time of year you usually come."

She was blushing, but, in contrast to her gladness, I didn't have anything to say. I greeted her simply, and returned to my walking without a warm expression. The family in Seongnae-dong was happy to see me. After Mother took my hand, she said something unexpected. "Jeongung, I will be selecting your bride, so don't you dare to date anyone."

"Marriage? It is far too early!"

"Too early? When a man gets to be twenty, that is the time to marry."

I didn't want to argue with her about my marriage, and I understood her feeling of wanting to choose my bride. "Please, Mother, select one for me."

The next morning, I went to Jikji-sa. I greeted Seu-nim Tanong, and we had lunch together. The daughter of the department store owner visited me there, bringing a man and three other girls.

"What are you doing here....?"

"This is a gift of congratulation for your becoming a college student."

She gave me a package in which were underwear, socks and gloves.

"I was wondering if you just picked these up at the department store."

"I told them about it already, so it is O.K."

That night we had a congratulatory party. We invited the son of the blind man beside the temple entrance, and Jonggap, one of my friends, so we would have an equal number of men and women. We had fruits, cookies and dried octopus, and Korean rice wine to drink, and sang popular songs. After having a little wine, we all felt relaxed and went outside to play games.

I needed to go to the bathroom, so I left the crowd. There was a full moon that I appreciated even after some wine. When I turned to go back to the others, to my surprise, there was the department store girl.

"Mr. Masao, may I ask one thing?"

"Yes...."

"What do you think about me, Mr. Masao?"

I was perplexed by the sudden question. "I want to thank you in many ways for giving me the gifts...."

"I asked you what you think about me."

"I think you are nice."

Her eyes sparkled. "You don't think I'm too bold?"

"Oh, no, not bold. You are a very open person."

She looked relieved, and laughed. Then, in an unsteady voice, she said, "I respect you, Mr. Masao. I'm so, so happy to get a chance to talk with you."

She was liberated and headstrong, but I felt no attraction to her. But, even now, when I think about my youth, her face comes to me, though I don't recall her name. Our hands never touched, but I could tell from her eyes that she really loved me.

Master Juknong and Master Manhae

It was a snowy night and Master Beumbu was inside reading a book, so my visit made him happy. I ate dinner with him, then went to Dasol-sa. The snow made walking on the mountain path difficult. Master Choe Yeonghwan greeted me warmly, and said, "Actually, I thought it was time for you to come, so I was waiting for you. We would like you to deliver the letters again this year."

"I understand."

The next morning, Master Choe and I went to Jinju. We stayed over night at Hojuk-sa, near Chokseokru, at the home of a friend of Master Choe, who was not connected with a temple. When we left Hojuk-sa we had many of the letter bundles in our luggage. Then we went to the home of Master Park Gwang in Taegu. There, to my surprise, was Father Kim Bongyul.

"Father, what brings you here?"

"Welcome, welcome—I was waiting for you."

"For me?"

"Yes. This time, come to Seoul with me."

We didn't leave Taegu right away, because, I guessed, the funds were not yet ready.

Not far from Master Park Gwang's home there was a famous calligraphy expert called Juknong, whose real name was Seo Donggyun, and Master Park Gwang introduced me to him. He was a handsome and intelligent man, of character as straight as a bamboo stalk. His penname, Juknong, referred to bamboo, and he drew bamboo exceptionally well.

Master Juknong closed his eyes and then said, "Bamboo is the symbol of an honorable scholar, and of integrity and fealty ..."

"How can I draw the bamboo that well?"

"The importance does not lie in the technique; of course to make the ink, hold the brush and make the line requires technique, but that alone does not give life to the picture.

"Then how?"

"Do not concentrate only on accuracy. First of all you must have a sublime spirit and a flexible mind." I was quiet and listened carefully to his words.

"Once you have drawn something well, you can never reproduce it exactly.

This is because the second time you have a different mindset."

That whole day I drew bamboo, until I became intoxicated with the India ink in Juknong's studio. The next day, I went there again.

"Oh, you didn't go to Seoul yet today?"

"We plan to leave tomorrow, so I want to learn some more today."

"Ha—what a man!"

Master Juknong did not refuse me, and taught me one more day.

The next day Kim Bongyul and I took the night train to Seoul. When we arrived at the house of Master Han Yongun in Seongbuk-dong it was lunchtime.

Master Han Yongun's health appeared to me to have gotten worse.

"Masao, you have been a great help to us this year, too."

I could see that he led a simple life; we ate only homemade noodles. When we left his house, he tried to slip some money in my pocket even though I refused it.

This was the last time I delivered funds for the independence movement. The following vacation time, when I came to Korea, neither Father Kim Bongyul nor

Master Choe asked me to do so. I guessed that this was because they thought my luck might have run out. Or perhaps it was because of rumors about problems in the temporary Korean government in Shanghai, which caused people in Korea to stop raising the funds. If that wasn't it, it may have been because the health of Manhae, Han Yongun, the central figure of the movement, was extremely bad, depriving the movement of its focal point.

Mister Lee Wunheo described him by saying that Manhae was a great Zen master, who brought Buddhism from the mountain to the big city where it could be spread, and that he was a great leader who rescued the nation, and tried to create a democratic society. He was knowledgeable about both Zen Buddhism and other religions. He knew well both spiritual and secular truths. Mister Park Gwang said about him, "Manhae had great dignity and patriotism, as well as love for his people. He was an absolutely pure and fair person, with unchangeable integrity, genius in art and literature, and he was a pioneer of Buddhist reformation."

Among Manhae's poetry, which was originally written in Chinese, was "Our Eulogy:"

Wherever man goes, there is his home,
Though some may grow homesick and nostalgic;
Fashion a loud eulogy to wake the nation.
Peach flowers, dropping, make pink stains on the snow.

Another poem was titled, "If It Is a Dream:"

If restraint of love is a dream, then successful freedom is also a dream.
If laughing and tears are dreams, then serenity is also a dream.
If the world is a dream, we know eternity from our dream of love.

From restriction find emancipation, from pleasure and sadness find the absence of desire, from Buddhist law find eternity. This is an expression of pantheism.

The Daughter of the Village Chief

My advisor, Kawasaki Godora, emphasized the importance of sketching by saying,

"To the painter, the ability to sketch is like his lifeblood."

In my second year, we began sketching from a human model. The woman would remove her clothes and take a pose. Before this class, Professor Kawasaki told us, "Sketching the nude as well as the still life much improves your ability to draw well. As you draw the lines of a living person you endeavor to make the image breathe."

It was the first time I had ever seen a woman without a stitch of clothing. She would pose for twenty minutes nude, then rest for ten minutes covered with her robe. This would be repeated four times in two hours. We had a chance, as well, to draw from a male nude model. The professor instructed us before we sketched the male nude, "We cannot describe the sexual organs for the female, but we can do so for the male model. To draw that organ will help to improve your drawing ability."

To the students, however, drawing skills were a distant second to their interest in the female model. It was exciting to reproduce the flesh of her breasts and nipples, and the curve of her waistline. At the end of the class, the model could choose the picture which she liked the most. Her choice would reflect the quality of the work, and we recognized that she had good artistic judgment. She often selected my work.

One day, around that time, I went with my classmate Ide Goro to the Akaki Mountain in Gunma-ken. He was the son of the wealthiest family in the country, but a simple and honest person, and we were very close friends. We left Tokyo on a Saturday morning, and arrived at the mountain an hour later. We concentrated on sketching the whole day, and didn't even realize that the sun had set.

We hurried down the mountain, but there were no hotels nearby. We met a farmer working in the fields, and Ide asked him, "Do you know of a house near here where we could stay overnight?"

The farmer looked us over, and said, "I don't know where you came from, but there is no place here where you can stay. To me, you look like students. Maybe if you go to the house of the village chief he would let you stay there."

We walked toward the tile-roofed house the farmer had pointed out to us. It was already getting dark, and rain was beginning to fall from cloudy skies. We worried about what we would do if he would not let us stay, but, luckily, when he heard we were Tokyo University students, the chief kindly gave us a room.

We were guided to a guesthouse in the back yard. He warmed bath water for us, as we were wet with rain. In the bathroom were two clean and ironed robes.

While we were bathing, dinner was prepared.

"While dinner is cooking, you can drink this." He gave us warmed rice wine.

"Oh, thank you. To be able to stay overnight is something we are really thankful for...."

We very much enjoyed our dinner, complete with wine. When we returned to our room, two beds had been laid out under mosquito netting. "They are so kind! Maybe this is what the hearts of country people are like."

We were tired and lay down on the beds, but continued to talk late into the night.

It was very late when we suddenly heard something outside our door. A female voice said, "Excuse me."

"Who is it?"

Ide stood up and opened the door, to find the daughter of the village chief.

She was wearing a neat kimono.

"Excuse me," she said again, and then stepped into the room.

We were flustered to have a woman visit in the middle of the night. "Please have a seat" was the only thing we could think of to say. But then, she came under the mosquito net. The three of us sat under the net.

"Father said that guests should be offered hospitality, so I came."

"Oh.... What is your name....?"

"I'm Yoshiko." Yoshiko was a beautiful girl; our age or a year younger.

"What is your school....?"

"I didn't go to college. My parents wanted me to have training to be a bride and get married."

"Is that so?"

Now she was curious about us, and asked, "When you graduate from Art College will you become a painter?"

"Yes, that's right."

"So, you came to sketch. Can you show me your drawings?"

I was confused about what was going on. Did I have to show my drawings to a woman who came in the middle of the night? But we couldn't kick her out, because her father had sent her to us. We showed our drawings to her, and she examined them carefully, and finally expressed her appreciation of them.

I couldn't take any more, and said, "It's too late. Why don't you go back now? We can talk tomorrow."

But her answer, which I could not even imagine, was, "Father told me that I could have a good time with the two of you, and that I could sleep with you."

"What?!?" My eyes became big. What kind of father would send his own daughter to sleep with a strange man? Even if he had done so, what kind of a girl would carry out such a request? I thought that behavior was not even human.

But, she apparently had no intention of leaving. There seemed to be no choice but to lie down on our beds. She lay down between me and Ide.

In the quiet darkness I could hear the sound of a woman's breathing close to me. Suddenly, I recalled the body of our nude model. My breathing became shorter. She was leaning close to me, and if I just reached out my hand I could hold her soft body. The daughter of the village chief, the nude model—I was confused by these two images blending into one another. Even so, I felt strongly that I could not accept that blended image. I felt that something was wrong with the situation.

It was only a few hours since we had met. To have a relationship with another person in the room—I was not that brave. Also, though I was old enough, I had never had sexual relations; I was only an innocent child.

Finally, I turned my back to her, and pretended to be asleep and snoring. She realized that I was not going to have relations with her, and she turned toward Ide. Right away, Ide began taking off her clothes, and I began hearing his rough panting. I could hear her making a sound of moaning, and the bedding began moving violently. I don't know how I could have gotten to sleep, or how I slept, but when I opened my eyes in the morning, Yoshiko was already gone. I shook Ide awake.

"You bum! You alone had fun, and now you are sleeping late.… You didn't get only a pumpkin, you got the whole vine.…" Ide's face was red, perhaps with shame.

"Of course it was fun. And Yoshiko was a virgin."

"In any case, I cannot understand the kind of parents who would send their unmarried daughter to sleep with the guests." Ide tried to appear sophisticated. "That is a Japanese custom. Before marriage, if there is a guest who is a good man, the father sends the daughter to sleep with him. Do you know why?"

"…?"

"That is sex education for the daughter. If she knows nothing about sex, she would not be able to please her husband."

"This is very different from Korea. The point is not to keep her innocence, but to practice how to satisfy her husband. That is the one who is considered a good wife?" Ide nodded. That is a strange custom to a Korean, to whom chastity and faithfulness are of primary importance. Ide explained further that the custom had almost disappeared, but could still be found in the countryside.

"So you do not have any responsibility to Yoshiko?"

"Oh, if I wanted to I could propose, but if I don't propose to her nobody would blame me."

"Still, that is a barbaric custom."

As Ide said, that custom had almost died out by that time. Now, it has completely disappeared in Japan. These days, the Japanese man still does not care if the woman has had sex before, which may be due to that past tradition. Japanese people are generous about sexual freedom before marriage, but after marriage a woman must be faithful to her husband. Whatever the sexual custom may have been, the breakfast table the next morning was spread like a feast. During the meal, the village chief asked Ide,

"During summer vacation, could you visit us for a few days?"

"I'll think about it," Ide answered.

Later, the village chief wrote a letter to me and Ide. I answered him, inviting him to visit us in Tokyo. He did indeed come to Tokyo, and stayed one night. As he was leaving, he asked me to help arrange a marriage between Ide and Yoshiko. Ide didn't seem much interested in Yoshiko at the beginning, but, as time went on, he began to show sincerity toward her.

The Marriage Meeting

During the summer vacation of my second year of college, when I arrived at the Waryong-dong home, Idang Father told me, "I have a girl student about whom I have been thinking. Would you please meet her once?" I was not interested in marriage, but I could not refuse Idang's sincere request. The woman in the picture he showed me was very pretty. She had a good background, being the daughter of a wealthy family.

I went with Idang Father to the girl's house in Hyewha-dong. The tile-roofed house, as large as a palace, gave evidence of the wealth of the family. I greeted the girl's parents first, and in a little while the girl came in with a tray of tea and cookies. After we greeted each other by shaking hands, the others left, leaving the girl and me alone. She was even prettier than her picture. I felt that I should start talking, and cleared my throat.

"May I ask your school....?"

"I attend Ehwa Women's University."

"Your major....?"

"I major in voice."

"You must have musical talent." This time, the girl asked me, "I understand that you attend the Tokyo National Art School?"

"Yes. I major in Oriental Art." There was no further conversation. They served us a good dinner, and we returned to Waryong-dong. Mother was curious.

"She is from a good family, and, most of all, she is a very respectable lady.

Let's us promise now and marry later."

"I'll think about it."

I soothed her with those words, and a few days later went to Sudeok-sa. I didn't tell my mother in Gyeonseong-am about the marriage meeting, but Na Hyeseok clapped her hands with joy when I told her.

"So, you had a marriage meeting?"

"Yes, I told you."

"Did you like her?"

"It doesn't matter whether I like her or not. This is not the time to think about marriage."

"You could start dating now, and marry much later."

"If I did that, what would I do if something went wrong?"

"If so, you still would know that you had at least fallen in love once."

"I don't want to date irresponsibly. I don't intend to date her without plans to marry. I like her, but this is not the time for me to marry, so I am not going to start dating."

"Ah, now I see! Masao is a very conservative man."

"Auntie, I have heard stories about how easily my mother fell in love, and how you would always talk about being a modern woman and act freely." I didn't realize that my voice had raised and that it held traces of anger.

"Masao!"

"See what has resulted from irresponsible and improper behavior? Mother became a Buddhist monk, and you, Auntie, were kicked out of your home and have lived alone for many years. I won't act irresponsibly."

"Oh, Masao, have you become a philosopher?"

"To live a single life like my father, and to become a monk. That is my wish." She opened her eyes wide and grabbed my hand.

"Are you an impotent man?"

"Of course not."

"Then why?"

"Free dating involves irresponsible and self-indulgent behavior, and I won't do it. That's all."

My words were strong, but she was not a person who could sulk for long.This vacation-time, she gave me as a gift a large landscape that she had painted in oils.

"Receive it as a remembrance." I gave her a sample of my work as well.

A few days later, Master Goam, Lee Eungro came to visit Na Hyeseok. I had met him the previous fall when he had an exhibition in the Ueno Art Gallery in Tokyo. At that time, I already had the ability, as a painter, to judge the quality of the art work of others. Now, meeting him again at the Sudeok Hotel, I had the opportunity to share my opinions with him.

"I'm sorry to tell you, Master Goam, but in painting in the southern style, you must rethink a lot of things."

"What do you mean....?"

"Those who paint in the southern style, try to imitate their teacher, but do not sketch from life. You have to converse with the spirit of the mountain and the waterfall. If you carefully observe the landscape, then you can create something worthwhile. That is my opinion." Na Hyeseok agreed with me.

"When the artist Tiuna in Germany sketches even one blade of grass, he does so from the real thing as a model. Michelangelo and Da Vinci have produced great examples of sketching ability, but the painters in our country have neglected sketching, which is the basis of art-education."

Master Goam nodded. "I partially agree with you. But, don't assume that I don't sketch at all."

Master Goam was a student of Matzbayasi Gaigetsu. He had tried to find a new style of drawing to make his own, but my impression, when I saw his exhibition, was that he still imitated his teacher.

"Ah, Masao can already criticize my painting! Before long, you will be well known for your own accomplishments."

When I returned to Gimcheon from Sudeok-sa, the Seongnae-dong mother had arranged another marriage meeting. This time, the girl was a grade school teacher. We met in a tea room, and were much freer than had been the meeting in Hyewha-dong. We talked a lot, but, still, it was not the time to marry, and I did not show my interest.

The Change in Seu-nim Gyeongheo

Around the end of the summer vacation of my second year in college, I visited Beomeo-sa Temple on the way to Japan. Seu-nim Dongsan, who greeted me there, asked me to stay overnight, and I did so. Every other time I had visited there I had been in a hurry to get to Japan, and had not taken the time to look around.

Beomeo-sa is at the Gumjeong-san mountain. This is not a very high mountain, and is characterized by big rocks and boulders in strangely shaped formations. It is a beautiful spot, and is one of the more famous mountains of the country. The Nakdong River runs along the mountain, and, when I climbed to the top, I could see the blue Pacific Ocean, like a picture.

About five miles north of the village Dongrae, there was a huge, bizarrely shaped rock on a mountain ridge, on top of which was a well. Golden fishes swam in that well, and that is why the mountain was named Gumjeong-san.

Here a temple had been built, and that was Beomeo-sa. In the book of Eastern Buddhism, it is mentioned that good omens have been recorded in Gumjeong-san.

In front of the gate of Beomeo-sa ran a very clean and cold stream, coming from the top of Gumjeong-san, and when I dipped my hands into that water, and drank, it seemed to purify my insides. Passing the first gate, and arriving at the Cheonwang gate, I noticed a shrine with Buddha's picture with four devas, the heavenly guardians. At the pillar of the Buli gate, there was writing by Seu-nim Dongsan. "Buli" means truth, and if one passes this gate and goes inside, he can see a display of the truths of Buddhism. God's light is so mysterious that there is no way to comprehend it with our worldly knowledge, and the writing on the pillar helps us gain the insight and discipline necessary to approach this light.

Beomeo-sa is a spectacularly beautiful sight because of it location on the mountain. It is a place famous for producing many excellent high priests. The great Seu-nim, Gyeongheo, was from Beomeo-sa, and he built an education institute where young scholars were trained. One day, I asked Seu-nim Dongsan,

"What kind of person was Seu-nim Gyeongheo?" Dongsan did not answer right away, but rather closed his eyes and rolled his beads. After a bit, he opened his eyes and said, "Seu-nim Gyeongheo entered Buddhism when he was thirteen years old, at Cheongkei-sa in Suwon. He transferred his ascetic practice to Donghak-sa, and learned from the great master Manhae. When he was twenty-three, he was already able to teach acolytes in Manhae's place."

Then Seu-nim Dongsan told me a story about Gyeongheo while he was in Donghak-sa:

> One day Seu-nim Gyeongheo went away from the temple, and, on his way back, was overtaken by darkness and a rain storm. He hoped to stay in one of the houses in the countryside, but at each one he was turned away. He was told that there was an epidemic, and that they feared admitting him. He noticed that every house seemed to be in mourning, and to hold a dead body.
>
> Seu-nim Gyeongheo trembled, and felt horror at the thought that he might be about to die. He sat all night under a big tree out of the storm, and sank into deep thought. He had taught, and had been very sure, that there was no difference between life and death, but now he realized that he had not understood the problem at all, and blamed himself for this lapse.

When he returned to Donghak-sa, he sent away all of his students, telling them he was not qualified to teach them, and went into seclusion to pursue the study of his own faith. He made a small opening in his window to receive only a handful of rice, and searched day and night for the answer to the problem of life and death. In one hand he held a knife, and he put his chin against a nail-studded board so that if he nodded off to sleep he would be awakened.

The Seu-nim who was the assistant to Seu-nim Gyeongheo went down to the village one day, and, meeting one of the Buddhist devotees, said, "Do you realize that since the Seu-nim went into seclusion in his little room we have had all kinds of problems in Donghak-sa. People don't know what to do, so they are just playing around."

"How can a Seu-nim who is just playing around eat of our offering of valuable rice? What will happen to him after he dies?"

"Well, I don't think he could be more than a cow, do you?"

"As a Seu-nim, how could you give me such an answer?"

"Then, what kind of answer do you expect?"

"Even if he comes back as a cow, he would have to be a cow without nostrils. If the cow doesn't have nostrils, there would be no place to put the ring to control it."

The young assistant couldn't understand what he was getting at, so he returned to the temple and asked Seu-nim Gyeongheo what it all meant. As soon as Gyeongheo began to hear his story, he realized what was going on, stood up, and emerged from his seclusion. When he did so, it was as if his doubts had disappeared, and he returned to his original nature. He was awakened from his suffering and from the reason for his suffering. Seu-nim Gyeongheo composed chants in praise of the enlightenment of awakening:

> The moon of the mind is isolated and round, but its moonlight covers everything. When I had forgotten the light, I had also forgotten the world that it covered, until it came back to me.

After that, Gyeongheo left Donghak-sa, and didn't have his own place. Sometimes he taught, and performed Buddhist ceremonies, wandering the world like wind or clouds. During that time, he built the educational institute at Beomeo-sa, and taught the young scholars.

Seu-nim Dongsan continued,

"In recent years, there has been no one who has inspired as many anecdotes as has Gyeongheo. In person, he seemed like a monk who had broken many of his vows. Sometimes he drank, sometimes he enjoyed the company of women, sometimes he was seen with unsavory companions ..."

"Those are clearly broken vows."

"No, those are acts that he no longer considered important, though it is easy to confuse that with the breaking of vows." Seu-nim Dongsan was worried that I had confused breaking vows with the ability of the great Seu-nim to focus on important things rather than petty rules.

"Many monks who never reached the greatness of Seu-nim Gyeongheo saw only his actions and took them as permission to break the temple restrictions, eating forbidden food, and so on. I feel sorry that such individuals have been confused in that way. In that sense, Seu-nim Gyeongheo must take some responsibility for clouding the atmosphere. Lord have mercy!"

Then Seu-nim Dongsan explained in detail the concept of religious discipline.

"The scholar-monk must have a clear routine of religious practice. Some people take rules too lightly, and do not pay attention to the words of the teacher. But, Buddha never acted in that way, and his followers must not do so either. So, understanding and behavior must be in accord with the discipline. Lord have mercy!"

Seu-nim Dongsan emphasized that to follow a religious commitment in this way is to provide an example to others. I thought that I had made a good decision in staying overnight at Beomeo-sa, and I agreed that those that did not have a full understanding of Gyeongheo and only imitated his actions were mistaken. In the beginning, it is correct to follow the rules. That applies not only to the teachings of Buddha, but also to the study of painting. I was always mistrustful of the one who proclaimed himself an expert artist without having mastered the basic skills.

I arrived at my current status by respecting tradition, working hard, and putting great effort into mastering each step. Probably, I was influenced by the good example of Dongsan.

Now, in my honored status as a monk, I believe that I entered through the gate of truth. I remember that I had a fine youth, filled with many pleasures, but I also made many mistakes, and a shadow of sorrow clung to me. The experience of that light and shadow was the process which led to the attainment of enlightenment.

Discovering Stone Colors

In the fall of that year, there was an exhibition of art by Korean artists who were working in Tokyo. Among those, I found Mr. Jeong Maljo unforgettable. He had graduated from Osaka Art School, and had developed his own technique to express traditional mannerist subjects. His work was exhibited in a gallery in Ueno, and, I when I saw it, I thought that he was bound to be famous in the near future. In this, I was right; soon, he received an award from the prime minister, and became an honored and prolific artist.

At that time, female Korean artists like Cheon Gyeongja, Park Naehyeon, and Bae Jeongrae were active in Japan. Lee Eungro and Cheong Jongyu were there, too. Chang Ukjin and Lee Chunggeum were graduates from my university, but were somewhat older than I. I had a close relationship with this circle of people, my sisters, mentors and seniors.

I concentrated on listening to lectures about theory, and worked hard to attain special colors for myself. The colors I could buy were not sufficient to my needs. On Sundays, I would go to the river and pick up stones of black, white, blue and red. These I would crush into a fine powder, which I mixed with glue for my use in painting. Through experience, I learned that, while it is difficult to reach the right color, it is not impossible. In fact, natural stone colors were used in many ancient Korean mural paintings. If vegetable or animal dyes had been used, they would have changed over time, but stone powder colors used in those murals have stayed the same for thousands of years.

Some Koreans revile stone powder painting, under the impression that it is of Japanese origin, but stone powder colors originated in Korea. A thousand years ago, in the Goguryeo period, this technique was used in many temple murals, and in their architecture. I read that in Japan stone color was first used in 1916. Think about it! It is obvious that stone powder painting first began in Korea.

Let me repeat: stone color is not a characteristic of traditional Japanese art. I regret that the technique of stone powder painting was so little taught in Korea that it has nearly died out. In Japan, on the contrary, they started only in 1916, but the technique has continued to thrive. Perhaps it is indiscreet, but I cannot help but look down on an artist who criticizes stone color as a Japanese technique. During my college years, I was very attracted to the stone powder method, and did many experiments combining the various colors. People even called me the magician of color, due to the energy and passion I invested in that pursuit.

Creativity comes from perceiving the phenomena of the universe, and being able to express them. Michelangelo, Da Vinci, Millet, all are great artists because they affect us emotionally. When we view the *Evening Bell* of Millet or the *Mona Lisa,* for example, we feel comforted and calmed. I am not as great an artist as they were; still, my hope is that viewing my work may impart that same feeling of serenity. In reality, some who saw it were awakened to something within them and changed their religion; and some who were very ill became empowered by the experience. Perhaps, then, something of my wish has come true.

In any case, I determined that I wanted to become a painter who portrayed Korean mountains. Mountains were where my mother was; when I thought of my mother, I drew the mountain; in drawing the mountain, I could forget my mother. The bosom of the mountain was my mother's bosom, and in that bosom I could draw the mountain. To me, the process of drawing the mountain was a conversation with my mother, even more than a means of encountering nature. In every painting, I endeavored to express that serenity and holiness.

7

The Hopeless Years

Japanese Military in Mangwol-sa Temple

During the second-year winter vacation I went to the Zen Institute, as in other years, and met Seu-nim Geumchu, who was the acting master-monk in Mangwolsa.

After we greeted one another, he invited me to visit Mangwol-sa. I had been there many times before, and hesitated before agreeing, but Seu-nim Jeogeum encouraged me to go. Mangwol-sa had been built nearly two thousand years ago, during the Queen Seondeok period, in Silla.

It is located on Dobong-san Mountain, in Gyeonggi-do, Yangju-gun, and is rich in history. The first master monk was Master Haeho, and, during the King Munjong period in Goryeo, the temple was rebuilt by Master Hyegeo. When I went to Mangwol-sa I was planning to stay only a few days, but it didn't turn out that way. A unusually big snow storm occurred two days after my arrival, and no one could get into or out of the temple. We were snow-bound for one week. During the time we were isolated, something happened we were not anticipating: a division of army men arrived on the mountain. I was the one who first noticed them, while I was sketching the beautiful scenery of Dobong-san. When they got to where I was sketching, they appeared to be undergoing training in mountain-climbing, and they took over our area. They were all wearing parkas, but I thought that they were a military unit because of their youth and their disciplined marching.

"Where are you from and why are you here?" I asked in Japanese. They were surprised, and scrutinized me and my college uniform.

"We are special military police, based at Yong-san in Seoul. I didn't expect to see a student of the great National University here."

"Military police? Why are you here on this rock?"

"We are on special duty. How about you, Student?"

"I know the master Seu-nim here, so I came to spend a few days during my vacation." At that moment, the wooden gong from the temple sounded, indicating the lunch hour. I asked the MP, who seemed to be the leader, "Shall we go to lunch?"

"No. We have our own lunch." I took him to the room where I was staying. Seu-nim Geumchu came, and asked me in a low voice, "Where are they from?"

"They are military police."

"Wow! They have come to inspect the temple. That is a big problem."

"Why would they inspect the temple?"

"Maybe they got information that some dissident is hiding in this temple."

"Then, is someone hiding in this temple?"

"Not really. But if they insist, we are helpless."

"You haven't done anything wrong. What could they possibly do?"

"That's true, but it is very complicated. Could you please help us? Just talk nicely to them." When I saw how worried he was, I became very calm.

"I understand. Please don't worry too much." When he mentioned the word "dissident" he meant someone who was participating in the independence movement. Members of that movement who were noticed by the police would just cut their hair and become temporary monks. Also, there were many real monks who were taking part in the movement. When I saw how many MPs had come, I was sure they had received lots of information about this temple. If so, I was sure they were planning to investigate intensively. I realized that Mangwol-sa was in danger. As they were finishing up their meal, I served tea.

"When you said you were on special duty, did that mean you are going to search the temple?" The captain was lighting a cigarette, and didn't say no; Seu-nim Geumchu's guess must have been right.

"My name is Oda Masao, and I am a student of Tokyo National Art School. Of course, I am not involved in any political activism. This place is for the teaching and meditation of Buddhist monks, and is no place where suspicious people could hide."

"How can I believe that?" He spoke sharply, and was obviously not about to take my word for it.

"I can't help it if you don't believe me, but I am telling you the truth." Still, he looked at me with suspicion in his eyes.

"Even though you may be honest, we must assure ourselves of it."

They had come purposely on a snowy day so that no one could escape in any direction without their awareness. I continued trying to appease them.

"If you came here to find political dissidents, you are bound to fail. There is no one like that in this temple."

"If that is true, can you help us?"

"What do you mean?"

"We have to interrogate all of the Seu-nims here. Can you translate for us?"

I realized that my word alone would not send them away. "If you really have to do that, would you please handle them politely? You have already shown a lack of courtesy by disturbing their meditation."

"I understand."

After a while, the MP requested that everyone assemble in one place. The captain asked the Seu-nims, one by one, about themselves, and I translated. As he had promised, he behaved politely. If he had just continued his questioning I would not have mentioned my father's name, but he ordered his subordinates to search the temple. Of course, they were searching for a dissident Seu-nim or for incriminating documents. That was a dangerous moment, and I had to come up with emergency measures. I confronted the captain.

"Wouldn't it be against the law to search the temple without the proper warrant?"

"We are special investigators, and can search without a warrant." His attitude was authoritarian.

"Even if you are a special investigator, I will need to ascertain from the viceroy whether or not it is legal to search a holy place. Please write down your position and affiliation."

"Are you threatening us?"

"Of course not. But I do not believe that is the correct way to proceed, and I want to find out for sure what the legal process should be. The viceroy, Oda Seizo, is my father, so I don't have to go through a complicated procedure to find out."

"Are you his son?" His voice was surprised.

"Yes. Didn't I tell you my name was Oda Masao?"

The MP captain's attitude changed drastically when he heard my father's name. He stopped the search immediately, and his interrogation of the Seu-nims dwindled. From the change in their attitudes on hearing his name, I realized how powerful a position my father held. The leader of the squad told me, "My name is Sato, and I graduated from Waseda University. I hope you understand what difficulties we experience in our work for Great Japan."

After a while, they went down the mountain in the snow. I recognized that they had not singled out Mangwol-sa for searching, but rather that it was part of a wider and more general program. As seen from the Korean viewpoint, they were ugly persons who disobeyed the law, but they saw it as their only way to root out workers for the independence of Korea. By my action, Mangwol-sa avoided the danger.

I now became more aware than ever how determined Japan was to destroy the independence movement, and I developed more skepticism than ever about my father. The Sato group retreated upon hearing my father's name, in their effort to please his son. Father had said that he worked in the office of the viceroy in order to help Korea, but it bothered me that he was of such a high rank. I hoped with all my heart that Father would stand up for Korea, but that was the dream of a young man unfamiliar with the practicalities. That much I loved Korea. The relationship between Sato and me was not ended by that incident. Much later, I met him again in a very unexpected place, when he took an important action which affected me. This kind of meeting is very mysterious.

"Masao, without you we could have been seriously damaged. Thank you, thank you!" Many Seu-nims, not only Geumchu, expressed their relief and gratitude. After things got back to normal, there was another occurrence which kept me at the temple. The master monk, for whom Geumchu had been filling in, was sick. Shortly after the MP incident, he suddenly passed away. It was sad that he had slipped away from us. It was now necessary to obtain a doctor's certificate in order to have a cremation, and there was no one to handle the matter. At that time all government business was handled by the Japanese, and involved endless red tape. I was the only one who might be able to take care of it. I went down the snowy mountain road and visited the Japanese doctor who had treated the Seu-nim. He was already aware that he had not had long to live, and granted me the certificate without much hassle. Next, I took the certificate to the police station. I showed my student ID to the policeman, and asked for permission to cremate the Seu-nim at Mangwol-sa. In those days, there were few college students around, especially ones who studied in Tokyo, and the policeman gave me the permission after only a few questions. The next step was to locate some petroleum. There was a shortage of all fuel, and to find petroleum was as difficult as picking a star from the sky. I explained my difficulty to the policeman who gave me the certificate.

"I'm so sorry to ask, but could I have some gasoline for the cremation? At the temple, there is not a single drop." The policeman was regretful at first, as he had no petroleum either. But he searched until he found some, and gave it to me.

"Thank you!" That was the first time I had experienced the funeral procedure within a temple.

The second semester of my third year of school, Ide Goro told me that he was going to marry Yoshiko. I knew they had been dating, but I didn't understand why they were in such a hurry to marry, even before graduation.

"Why? Is she pregnant?"

"No, no such thing. Yoshiko is such a good person, and so pretty, that I think I could find no one better, and this spring I am going to marry her."

"You are going to have a wedding ceremony before graduation?" I couldn't understand, so I asked, "How will you make a living?"

"Her parents are going to help us out, and if that is not enough, Yoshiko could always work. We won't starve."

Ide spoke calmly, but I could detect a shadow of worry on his face. "Why are you in such a hurry? You could wait to have the ceremony until you are established." Ide answered uneasily, "Hey! Right after graduation we all have to go to war. There is no guarantee that any of us will come back. We at least have to plant a seed before we die."

Now I could understand why he spoke of his intention to marry with such a worried look. But, if that was the case, I felt sorry for Yoshiko.

"Think again about it. Yoshiko could become a young widow."

"Yoshiko wants it too, Masao. We do not have a tomorrow. We might die very soon, but we must love each other in the meantime. You are the one who should think about it." Then Ide disappeared.

Ide's words were not mistaken: *For us, there is no tomorrow.* That fear was widespread among all of the college students. We had no faith in the future. We all tried to follow our dreams, but when we thought about death, we became scared. Among young people, many were very patriotic, but not my school friends who wanted to become artists. We were more egoistic, and almost none of us wanted to die for our country. One moment we were thinking about becoming great artists, creating masterpieces, and the next moment the thought of death haunted us. Most of my friends were sunk in depression and nihilism, and tended toward decadence. As he said, Ide married in May of that year. Cherry trees were blooming, the new bride looked very happy, and Ide enjoyed his newlywed status until he was dragged off to war.

In that year, I had an important meeting with the Japanese teacher, Ito Shinsui.

He was the Japanese equivalent of Master Kim Eunho, Idang in Korea, in that he was as noted an artist. Master Shinsui lectured in the university about color.

When he found out that I was a foster-son of Idang, he paid special attention to me. He invited me to his home, and I became his protégé.

"Study hard. If I am not mistaken, you will be a great painter in the near future." Master Shinsui praised and encouraged me, but I was one of those who did not believe in tomorrow.

Incident in Haein-sa Temple

I spent my third-year summer vacation at Haein-sa. Seu-nim Im Hwangyeong was a calligrapher, too. One day, he called me in and showed me two pieces of art work on which the ink was not yet dry.

"Could you do an errand for me?"

"Tell me what you would like me to do."

"Can you deliver this to the chief at the police station in Hapcheon instead of me? The other one is my gift to you."

"I'd be glad to do it; you don't have to give me anything."

"Boy, I want to give it to you in remembrance of me. Please keep it."

"Thank you.'

The chief of police in Hapcheon was so surprised to receive this art work that his chin dropped in amazement and he could not close his mouth.

"I never saw anything like this. He is a famous calligrapher. Please tell him how much I appreciate it." After he served tea to me, I left the station. I went to the bus terminal waiting room to go back to Haein-sa. At that moment, many Japanese police inspectors entered, searched the luggage of all of the passengers, and questioned each one. After searching the belongings of a man of about forty, they slapped handcuffs on him without asking whether it was right or wrong. He struggled against them, and they hit him with their truncheons. Their savagery continued: he fell to the floor and they kicked him again and again. Then they dragged him out like a dog, and disappeared somewhere.

I felt like a big grinding stone was sinking in my chest, and an ashen-faced old man was trembling at what he had seen. It was then 1943. The Japanese government was becoming more and more outraged, and, it seemed to me, more desperate as time went on, and all of Korea was becoming a crucible of fear because of their tyranny. My prediction was that Japan would ultimately fail. If someone oppresses the innocent, there is no way that he can be saved. I was on the side of Korea because I saw that the actions of the Japanese were not right, and because I felt so sorry for the Korean people who were oppressed.

I returned to Haein-sa deeply depressed. I was walking with my head down when I was confronted by a policeman. At that time there was a police post at

Haein-sa so the authorities could keep tabs on the Seu-nims and their followers. This was because they had information that patriots sometimes hid out in the temples.

"What's the matter? My boss wants to see you." I followed the policeman, puzzled about why this should be so. When I got into the boss's office, he smiled.

"I heard that Masao is an art student."

"How did you find that out?"

"It is my job to find out about the people who go in and out of this place." He smiled a cunning smile, and I was disgusted.

"So you secretly investigated my background?"

"Don't take it so hard. I know you are not doing anything improper. I didn't call you in for questioning. I just want to help if you feel uncomfortable about anything."

"The only way you can help me is by leaving me alone."

"What is your relationship with the master monk, Im Hwangyeong?"

"He is nice enough to let me visit during every vacation, how and when I can."

"Let me give you some advice. It would be better, in my opinion, not to get too close to the Seu-nim."

"Don't worry; I can decide what to do. If there is nothing further, I will go now."

If they had searched my background, surely they would know that I could not be a bad person. I was the son of Oda Seizo; clearly, the chief was trying too hard to be kind to me. Still, I could not get rid of my apprehension, because they kept following me.

As I had feared, right after the start of the second semester in Tokyo, I got a telegram from Haein-sa. It said that Seu-nim Im Hwangyeong was very ill, and implored me to come quickly. I was shocked—only a few days earlier he had been healthy. I couldn't believe that he had fallen so seriously ill. I knew it was no joke, and I hurried back to Korea. Haein-sa looked like it had been plundered by a gang of vandals. One Seu-nim told me, "At three AM, during meditation, the police came and took dozens of us, including the master Seu-nim, to the station.

Master Seu-nim Choe Yeonghwan from Dasol-sa was also taken."

I hurried to the police post in Haein-sa, and talked to the chief there.

"What was the reason you arrested the Seu-nims?"

"They are political criminals."

"How is it possible for the disciples of Buddha to be political criminals? Don't talk nonsense!"

"They were arrested because we received information that they were helping the Korean Independence Movement." He was pretending to be busy, and spoke coldly. "Where are the Seu-nims?" I asked.

"They will be in the Hapcheon police station. You had better not involve yourself in this matter, Mr. Masao." I let his words go in one ear and out the other, and ran to the police station. I asked to see the Chief of Police. He was the one to whom Seu-nim Im Hwangyeong had given the calligraphy the previous summer.

"Chief, the Seu-nim you are holding, Im Hwangyeong, is the one who gave you the gift of his art work. He is only a Seu-nim who does calligraphy, not a member of the independence movement."

"We are in the middle of our investigation; soon we will have the results."

"Please take steps to see that he is not harmed. He could not stand to be tortured by hanging upside down or having water forced into his nose." He answered gently, "We are not using severe measures; please do not worry too much."

"Seu-nim Choe Yeonghwan, whom you also arrested, is innocent as well. Please give me the privilege of providing the two Seu-nims with a private meal."

"I can give you a permit for Im Hwangyeong, but not for Choe Yeonghwan."

I didn't know why he was allowing a special treat for one but not the other. Perhaps it was because Im Hwangyeong was older than Choe Yeonghwan, or perhaps it was that he had made a gift of his art work. I served a private meal to Im Hwangyeong, then left for Seoul immediately. I realized that this was a very important matter which could not be resolved by the local authorities, so I went to see my father at the office of the viceroy.

Father was surprised by my sudden arrival, since I should have been in Tokyo studying. Without preamble, I spoke directly.

"I'm sure you know that Seu-nims have been arrested by the Hapcheon police."

"That is not my territory, but I heard about it."

"Please release Seu-nim Im Hwangyeong and Seu-nim Choe Yeonghwan immediately."

"What is that you are throwing at me?"

"They are innocent!"

"We got information that the Korean Independence Group based in Shanghai, dispatched an important person to encourage and coordinate a concerted action in Korea. We were informed that the ones raising the funds to support this action were Im Hwangyeong and Choe Yeonghwan, and that they were providing liaison with that agent. They were the main planners of the proposed uprising."

"Father!"

"OK, go on."

"Father, this is only the fourth time I have seen you. You came to Sincheon when I didn't know you were my father, then I went to ask you for the means to repair Sudeok-sa, and then I met you in Tokyo when I was admitted to college, isn't that right?"

"...."

"But Seu-nim Im Hwangyeong and Choe Yeonghwan I saw every vacation; they provided me with food, a place to sleep, and pocket money, too."

Father's face turned red. Perhaps he didn't like to be blamed by his son, or perhaps he was embarrassed by the situation.

"I don't see you often, but through Mr. Sindo, I provided you with tuition and money to live on, too. You didn't realize that?"

"I know."

"Then how can you say what you did?"

I could tell that Father's voice was trembling.

"Moneywise, you treated me very well; but they are the ones who gave me the affection which you did not give me. They gave me a special education and a special love."

"...."

"They are innocent. Please release them right away!"

"Masao!"

"I received benefits from them which, as a father, you have a duty to pay back. If you refuse, I could not help hating you."

Father's face became distorted. I knew how he felt, but that was not the time to consider his feelings. I had to insist or risk losing two very important people.

"As I told you, I am not directly involved in that matter."

"If I go out this door, I will be in Hapcheon tomorrow. I won't go back to Tokyo until I see them freed." I threw out my last threat, and left the office of the viceroy. I went to my Waryong-dong home to talk to Idang Father, and he was worried, too.

"I hope that they get out soon. Otherwise, they will have a hard time in prison. Please help them as much as you can."

On the way to Hapcheon, I was grateful my father was not involved directly, and I trusted that he would consider my request. I had complained that I didn't see him often, but I knew that he truly loved me. The evidence for that was that Father had remained single all this time.

My expectations were not wrong. Father could not get everyone out of prison, but he did obtain the release of Seu-nim Im Hwangyeong and Master Choe Yeonghwan, which I had requested. When I arrived at the Hapcheon police station, two people were delivered to me.

Seu-nim Im Hwangyeong did not look too bad, but Master Choe bore many marks of torture. When I observed his condition, my anger boiled up. When they saw me, Im Hwangyeong and Choe Yeonghwan embraced me so tightly that we made one person, and we all cried. In the history of rebellion against Japan, the incident at Haein-sa played a big role. At that time, all of the Seu-nims of Haein-sa and its branch, Dasol-sa, as well as their fellow supporters of the independence movement, were arrested by the Japanese, and underwent severe tortures.

Funeral at Izu

In December of my third year of college, I received a message that my grandmother had passed away. I went to Izu in Adami with Mr. and Mrs. Shindo. Many relatives and friends were there, but Father didn't come. I met my uncle who lived in Yamaguchi-ken, which was Grandfather's hometown, and I shared greetings with cousins.

My father was the first-born son of my grandfather, so, according to the genealogical table, I would be the eldest grandson of the family. But, since I was born of a Korean woman, they did not treat me as the eldest grandson. If Father had been there, perhaps the situation would have been different, but Father never visited his parents after he left home. I could guess another reason why I was not treated as the eldest grandson. As I have mentioned, my grandfather was a very wealthy man, and, if I had been accepted by the relatives as the eldest grandson, I would have been in line to inherit that wealth. I never considered the inheritance, but I'm sure that they did. Even then, I knew in my gut that money can make people ugly. I endured that cold reception not only because I was not interested in the inheritance, but also because I had no intention of living as a Japanese. But, I would be lying if I said I didn't feel a sense of estrangement.

The funeral took place three days after the death. Following the traditional Japanese procedure, the body was cremated and the ashes gathered up with bamboo sticks and placed into an urn. The urn was placed in the Oda family graveyard in Oyama, Kanagawa-ken.

I was like oil in water at Grandmother's funeral, and I made up my mind that I would never again attend an Oda family ceremony, big or small. I knew in my bones how deeply feelings of alienation cause people suffering and sadness, and I was more determined than ever to live as a Korean, and to never again experience that alienation from the Japanese.

Amita Scripture

When vacation started, I immediately hurried to Korea. I left my luggage at my home in Waryong-dong, and went to the Zen Institute. Seu-nim Jeogeum greeted me warmly.

"A few days ago we had a meeting of high priests here. Your mother, Seu-nim Ilyeop, was one who attended. The meeting included Mangong, Tanong and Hodongsan, as well as many other priests whom I know."

At that time, Japan required that even monks change their names to the Japanese style, and serve in the army. Some monks rebelled against this requirement, and were further oppressed by the Japanese. The purpose of the meeting had been to devise a plan to respond to this crisis.

In my travels from temple to temple I had become acquainted with many seu-nims. I knew that, as a group, they were intelligent, and more concerned with principles than the average person. This led them to join the fight for Korean independence, and to help the movement both openly and secretly.

Japan tried to completely destroy the culture of Korea, and this led them to attempt to take over the temples, ordering that Master Monks be appointed by the office of the viceroy. They tried to force the believers to practice Japanese style Buddhism. This was the first time that the temples had been run by married monks, who were under the protection of the Japanese government, and gained almost total control over the religious practices. These monks, concerned only about their own well-being, almost obliterated the traditional temple-ways.

Those whose duty it was to guide and teach religious principles to the mundane world, were instead occupied with gaining their own foothold in power. The monks who built and participated in the Zen Institute were attempting to reform these practices, and preserve the honored traditions. The Institute was the place where monks could get training, and where they could go to cleanse themselves spiritually. On March 13, 1941, many famous monks gathered at the Zen Institute for a meeting. They studied original Buddhist teachings, and reached the determination that there should be no married monks, in order to protect the Buddhist law. At that time, the preacher was Seu-nim Dongsan.

The Japanese had regarded that meeting as an unlawful assembly, and forced them to destroy their statement of principles. The next meeting was the recent one dedicated to fighting the drafting of monks into the army. The Japanese were persistent and vicious in their efforts to strangle Korean Buddhism. It seemed to me that the Japanese were willing to destroy themselves in order to destroy it. Despite their efforts, however, the Korean spirit and religion were not even shaken. Even some of the married monks who appeared to the outside world to be cooperating with the Japanese, were secretly supporting the independence movement. These monks were often vilified by the Korean people, who perceived them as traitors, but they prevented the total destruction of the traditional temple practices. Kim Bongyul Father, and Master Choe Yeonghwan were typical of these brave monks. These people should be recognized for their importance in gaining the independence of Korea.

Of course, the presence of married monks made for an unsettled atmosphere, and there was continual conflict between the married and the unmarried monks. To resolve this issue was to require much sacrifice, but that was the legacy left by the Japanese occupation. In any case, the Japanese made every effort to weaken the power of the unmarried monks, who were endeavoring to protect their own traditions. My mother in Gyeonseong-am recognized the difficulties of the times, and urged me to take care of myself.

"Nobody knows what this world will be; this is a confusing time. So, at this time, try to avoid hasty or imprudent actions. Also, it is better not to travel here and there so much anymore."

"I understand perfectly." When I went to the Sudeok Hotel I found Master Lee Eungro there visiting Na Hyeseok. They were both artists, but, it seemed to me, they had a special relationship as well. I could not tell whether that relationship was a simple friendship, or one of love between a man and a woman. Whenever I stopped by the Sudeok Hotel, I would often find Master Lee Eungro there, but the nature of the friendship was their own business, and I never tried to figure it out. Later, I heard rumors that Lee Eungro had bought the Sudeok Hotel. I am sure he had special memories of that place, and so do I. Much later, on the way to Sudeok-sa, I stopped there, only to find the hotel fallen into decay, and I felt anxious that the whole thing would be swept away. However, the hotel was designated as a cultural asset, which was good news for me.

I traveled to Jikji-sa, visited my Waryong-dong home, and then went to Sincheon in Hwanghae-do. When the train stopped at the Sincheon station, I walked through the waiting room out into the public square. I stopped in amazement. The square was crowded with army draftees and their families, and with patriotic women whipping up enthusiasm. The demonstration continued all night.

The departure of the soldiers means that there is almost no chance that they will be returning. Despite the efforts of the patriotic women, the faces of the soldiers and their families were lost in shadow. Their anxiety penetrated my heart.

That anxiety followed me to my Sincheon home, and I did not find my older brother there. He had been drafted a few months before. There was no liveliness in the household, and my father, mother and sister-in-law were heavy with worry.

I tried to consol my parents.

"Do not have only bad thoughts; Brother will return for sure."

"If it does turn out that way, it would be wonderful."

Even though I said it, I was not at all sure that he would return safely.

Kanegio, the master monk at the Nishihongan-ji, was so busy that he couldn't even spare the time to have tea with me. Every day, he received at Sincheon five or six dead bodies from the battle field. Most bodies were given to their families, but bodies of unmarried soldiers were cremated and saved in the mortuary of the temple. Monk Kanegio was kept busy arranging and presenting the memorial ceremonies, and attending to the mortuary. Between his duties of hitting the wooden gong and reciting the scriptures, he scarcely had time to blink.

"Masao, please help me."

Kanegio asked for my help, and I wore the monk's robe and cap which he gave to me, and followed him as his assistant. After cremations, memorial services were held either in the school yard or in the temple, and, if Kanegio was busy, I would recite the Amitagyeong Scripture, and hit the gong.

In Seoul, I hadn't been aware of what was going on, but in Sincheon I saw how many young people were being victimized. Dead bodies came from as far away as Manchuria, or from even more distant small islands. During that time I was half-monk. The smell of incense, the mournful crying of the families, and the sadness of young men killed in battles which belonged to countries other than their own, returns to me clearly through my nose, eyes and ears even now.

Please Come Back Alive

In 1944, I became a member of the graduation class of Tokyo National Art School. It was one year before the end of World War II, and Korean independence.

In April of that year, the government sponsored an exhibition of the art work of the college students, and I won an excellent award. But art had lost its importance in my life. Immediately after graduation, all students were to be sent to the battlefield, so we underwent severe military training. Enduring that training left me half dead. The training was to become high ranking officers, and I received no special treatment. The school no longer offered art classes except in the basics of drawing. Often, students from middle school to college age, were sent in a group to rural areas, to help in farming land from which all of the men had been drafted into the army.

That happened, as I remember, in the early part of July of that same year. I heard that Lee Gwangsu was to give a speech in Hibiya Park, and I decided to attend. He insisted that Japan and Korea were one nation, and that college students should be glad to fight for their country. To hear a writer so eminent and respected in Korea take this position made my blood boil. On the way home, I made the decision that I would absolutely not go into the army.

I went to Korea during summer vacation, and determined to take action. I visited Idang Father, Mother in Gyeonseong-am, Seu-nim Mangong, and Na Hyeseok.

I shared my heart with them, and then went to Sincheon. I greeted my parents there, and stayed a few days in Nishihongan-ji. Then I traveled to Kuwol-san Mountain, my destination being Paeyeop-sa Temple. I knew no one there, but if I had stayed at Jikji-sa, Dasol-sa, or Haein-sa, where I was known, the Japanese police would have found me easily. The head monk thought it strange to see me, a student, deep in the mountains.

"What made the student come here?" I disclosed everything to him, thinking that that way I could get help from him.

"As a matter of fact.... please give me a place to hide. I was to be forced to go into the army, but I don't want to die in a cause I don't believe in. Please."

"Even here, we cannot guarantee your safety."

"I will hide here as long as I can. I will pay for my room and board. Please let me stay."

Actually, I had prepared for this by saving quite a bit of money. But the head monk at Paeyeop-sa would not let me pay. I was so relieved: there was to be no more military training or fear of death, and I sketched Kuwol Mountain, and hiked around and read books. I memorized Buddhist scripture and often withdrew for prayer and meditation. I needed no other heaven.

At the end of September, two detectives came looking for me at Kuwol-san. I had to return to Tokyo for school and military training, but I had already missed a whole month.

"Are you really Oda Masao?"

The inspector, satisfying himself that I was me, persuaded me to go with them. Like the last time I hadn't shown up in Japan after vacation, Mr. Shindo had contacted my father, and he had been trying to find me for a month.

The two inspectors escorted me to Busan, and put me on the ship to Japan, where I was accompanied by another inspector. At Shimonoseki, I was handed off to still another inspector who took me to Mr. Shindo's home. Mr. Shindo berated me in a high voice, so that he would be heard by the inspector.

"Masao, aren't you ashamed of yourself? Other people are volunteering for the army to protect the nation, but you, who are graded highest in your class in our great empire, refuse to do your duty. I am deeply grieved. If you hadn't turned up at the last minute, I was going to commit suicide because I hadn't guided you well."

"...."

"To gain forgiveness for you temporary misjudgment, you must faithfully participate in training."

"I understand," I said reluctantly. Mr. Shindo told the inspector, "Sorry to have caused you all this trouble. From now on, I will take responsibility for him, and you can return to your duties."

My plan had failed. It was not easy to avoid army service, and, as bad as I felt, I had to give up the attempt. I went back to school, and attended the military training as well. In December of that year, I graduated. The graduation ceremony was scheduled for February of the following year, but because of the national emergency, it was held two months early. That means that there was lots of ceremony preparatory to going onto the battle field. Nobody was proud or happy about their graduation.

Graduates from the college were given two weeks leave before having to report for duty. This gave them time to visit their relatives. At the graduation ceremony, each person filled out an enlistment paper, signed with a thumb-print, and was given a student-volunteer army arm band.

"For two weeks you must wear this."

After receiving the arm band, and with a heavy heart, I visited Grandfather in Izu. He had aged a lot since Grandmother's death, but was still his courteous self. He said,

"Depart as a proud Japanese, and be willing to die as an honorable soldier."

That was the traditional Japanese attitude, but one for which I had no sympathy. That was the last time I saw my grandfather. Before going to the battle field, I had to say goodbye to my fathers in Korea, but Mr. Shindo was worried.

"When you go to Korea, are you going to hide out somewhere?"

"I'm going there to say goodbye. Don't worry, I'll be back."

From the moment of affixing a thumb print to the enlistment document, each student was treated like a real soldier. As students, if we went AWOL we were accepted back without question, but, after receiving the armband, if we did so we would be treated as deserters. That was why Mr. Shindo was so worried. As a matter of fact, I was thinking about that, myself, but as soon as I got to Busan I was followed by a high-ranking policeman. He took the same train to Seoul, and followed me to Idang Father's home in Waryong-dong, then switched with another policeman.

I went to the Zen Institute to say farewell to Seu-nim Jeogeum, and then to Daegak-sa, and, of course, on the way down, I went to Sudeok-sa. When my mother in Gyeonseong-am saw my armband she closed her eyes.

"Namukwanseumbosal ..."

She spoke in a low voice, which, I thought, I might never hear again.

"Mother.... I'm being drafted right away." Mother didn't speak for a while, and she didn't scold me for calling her "mother." After a bit she said quietly,

"Come back alive. I'll pray to Buddha that I will see you again."

Mother was continuously rolling her prayer beads. I was flooded by feelings of love for her. I said goodbye, and left.

Seu-nim Mangong, Seu-nim Byeokcho, and Mongsul were also sad to see me go. When I said goodbye to Seu-nim Mangong, for the last time he gave me pocket money. I couldn't pay back the money he gave to me. By the time I came into control of my funds, Seu-nim Mangong, who had loved me so much, had already passed away. We meet and separate continuously though out our lives, and who can tell when the final farewell occurs.

That night I spent with Na Hyeseok in the Sudeok Hotel. Looking back now, I realize how precious and distressing that night was. That was the last time I ever saw Na Hyeseok. She had been the one who helped me understand and control my passionate longing for a mother's love. If she hadn't been there, my misery might have led me to suicide. She embraced me, who was starved and wounded, with a mother's love.

"Loss can be very painful. Sometimes, I, too, have wanted to die. But life is a blessing. Even though it means suffering, it means, sometimes, pleasure, too." From that night, when she spoke about the blessings of life, Na Hyeseok lived less than two years. Maybe she was already expecting her death. She died in 1946, at the age of 50. For an artist, that is the age of maturity and ripeness, and that thought makes me very sad.

Last, I visited Kim Bongyul Father. My four younger sisters and brothers were all sad to see me go the army. Mother's eyes were red. I felt the importance of this relationship, even though we were not connected by blood.

"Do whatever you can to stay alive. Run away if you have to. Come to me and I will hide you. Japan will be destroyed very soon." While he was speaking, he slipped money into my pocket. The inspector had his eyes on us from a distance. After I got to Busan, I went to Beomeo-sa, and the inspector made an exasperated face. I bade farewell to Seu-nim Hadongsan, and then took the ship from Busan to Shimonoseki.

Hurrah for Korea

Luckily, I was assigned to the army headquarters at Nagoya instead of to the battlefield. There had been twenty graduates of the Tokyo National Art School majoring in oriental art, and all were sent to the battlefield except me. I felt that I was working at the army headquarters because of my father. I was his only child, and he could not send me into battle, not knowing if I would live or die. At least, that is my guess.

Anyhow, I did work in Nagoya. I served as an army artist, and, as a specialist, did not have to wear any insignia. If it was because of my father, I truly appreciated him for it.

Later, I learned that all of my classmates who went to the South Sea Islands were killed, except for one, whose name was Ide. My closest friend, Ide Goro, who married in our junior year, was killed, leaving his wife, Yoshiko. It was so sad: a young man in his twenties died.

For Whom? For What?

It was lucky to have remained alive. Most of all, I was blessed that I could survive without having to kill anyone who was as innocent of any crime as I was myself. I felt guilty about my classmates, and that I could survive just because of my father. But any amount of shame could not equate with death. Any means should be used to avoid becoming a victim of the emperor.

I was proud of being a Korean, and I loved Korea. I felt lucky that I was involved in support services, and did not have to participate directly in the trampling of the Koreans. Eight months after I went into the army, the Showa Emperor publicly declared the surrender of Japan. I stayed in the army one more month after the August 15 liberation. At that time, there were 200 Korean prisoners of war being held in the Nagoya army supply center. The lieutenant who was responsible for them did not know what to do. If he freed them, they might turn into rioters who would lynch him, but he could not keep them locked up for no reason. I told him, "Free them right away!"

"I am not against freeing them, but, if they turn into rioters, I cannot shoot them. What shall I do?"

"Even so, you cannot detain them."

"So. You speak Korean well. Can you pacify them, and take them to Korea and free them there? That was a good chance to get back to Korea.

"I see. I will do that on one condition."

"What is it?"

"They are prisoners who have been confined and abused. To appease them, we need some sort of soothing policy."

"Soothing policy?"

"Yes. My condition is that the supplies we have in storage be given to them."

"Nonsense! The army supplies of Great Japan be given to Korean people?!...."

"Japan is defeated. There is no need for army supplies anymore. How much can 200 people carry anyway? At least, we should give this gift to people returning home. That would be good etiquette, and, besides, would prevent a riot."

The lieutenant agreed reluctantly. I went to the prison where the Koreans were being held, but they hadn't yet heard about the Japanese surrender.

"Oh, gentlemen, Korea is independent! The emperor has surrendered."

I delivered this news in Korean. They cheered and shouted, "Long live Korea!" until my eardrums almost burst. I had to calm them down.

"Gentlemen, please calm down. Korea is independent, but you are not in Korea. You are in Nagoya, Japan, now. If you want to get back safely, there will be lots of difficulties to face. You might get shot by a Japanese soldier who could not accept Japan's defeat." They became quiet immediately.

"If you want to get to Korea alive, you have to follow directions."

I asked them not to go off half-cocked, and they trusted me because I spoke in Korean. Then I took them to the supply center.

"Now, you can take as much as you can carry. This is a going-home gift for you."

They were ecstatic. They gathered up blankets, flashlights, shoes, etc., and one man took, by my calculations, around a hundred pounds of rice. I thought he must be poor as a church mouse at home.

They were carrying such heavy loads that, even had they wanted to riot, they would not have been able to do it. I took them to Maizuru Harbor in Nagoya, and then to Busan. When we arrived at Busan, I shouted at them, "Gentlemen, you are free! Go home to your families!"

They again shouted and cheered, "Long live Korea!" I also was happy that the war was over. That was September 22, 1945.

I left the group, and immediately went to Seoul. Idang Father jumped out of the house and embraced me.

"You did well! You came back alive!...."

I saw tears in his eyes. I took off my army uniform. I was happy now to have the hope of living as an artist in liberated Korea. I didn't have to go back to school, and there was no reason to go back to the army either. I was determined to live in Korea. The war was over. I rejoiced that I did not have to live in danger any longer. As it turned out, I was mistaken: Behind the joy of liberation perils awaited that would threaten my life.

Volume 2

1

Escape

To the Hometown

I left Nagoya Army Headquarters for Busan with 200 Korean prisoners. That was September 22, 1945. After I arrived at my Waryong-dong home, I sent a letter to the Nagoya headquarters letting them know that I had completed my mission, and that I was not going to return, in view of the fact that the Japanese army had been disbanded. I stayed at Waryong-dong for a while, and went to Gyeonseong-am. I wanted to let my mother know as soon as possible that I was safe. Mother was speechless, and her eyes were wet for a moment before she went back to her normal expression. Finally, in her low voice, she said, "You came back safely; I know that is because you were in Buddha's care."

"Yes." I was very happy to see her, as well, but managed to control myself.

"How are you going to live from now on?"

"Since I've graduated, I don't have to go back to Japan anymore. I plan to live in Seoul and do art work." Until that moment, I had not thought about what my future might be like, and I began feeling a bit anxious about it.

"You haven't had any problems living in Korea?"

"What kind of problems exactly do you mean?"

"For example, how about your family registration."

My birth records show me as Song Yeongeop, a son of Song Gisu, in Sincheon, in Hwanghae-do, but in school, I had been registered by my Japanese name, Oda Masao. I had a dual identity, one in Japan and one in Korea. From now on, I had no need to return to Japan, and the Korean citizenship was enough for me.

"In the future, you must marry, and you will face a lot of government red tape. Won't it be necessary to clarify your citizenship?" Mother was calmer than I had ever seen her, and her voice was strong. What she said made sense.

"Now you have become an adult, and I know that you are able to decide the best thing to do. I am telling you this from my wisdom as an elder: Think carefully about what you want to do, and don't make enemies."

"Yes."

For the first time, I felt like an adult. Even though I was more than twenty, I had not fully emerged from childhood.

On the way back to Seoul, I thought seriously about my future, and, for two reasons, I had to visit Sincheon, Hwanghae-do. First, I needed to reclaim my birth identity as Song Yeongeop. I had left Sincheon and became a foster-son of Idang Father, but that relationship had never been legally recorded. As mother said, to live in Korea, I had to clear my birth records. In addition, I was worried about the safety of my parents in the North. After the liberation of Korea, the American army was stationed in the South and the Russian army in the North. If a communist government was instituted by the people of the North, it would be difficult to live there, and I felt a responsibility to try to move my parents to the South as soon as possible.

My second reason was to sell the land which my father had bought for me. If a communist government came to power, it was obvious that it would be confiscated. I could not lose the land for which my father had saved to provide for me. Suddenly, I felt a strong attachment to that land, perhaps because of my fears for my father's safety. I had no way of knowing what had happened to him after Japan's surrender. I hoped that the officials of the viceroy's office had been evacuated to Japan. My father had been in a strong position as assistant to the viceroy, and I had always figured that he was well able to take care of himself. But, since the fall of Japan, the situation was very different, and he was not in a good position any more. He might have been in some sort of accident during evacuation, so I worried about him, and I felt drawn to the land he had given me. I told my plan to Idang, but he counseled strongly against it.

"Don't do it! Now, in the North, they are clearing out the landlords as well as the people who were close to Japan. If you go there, you would have a hard time getting out alive. Forget that land! Just pretend you never had it. If you need money for your future marriage expenses, I'll give it to you. With your artistic skills, you will soon become a rich man."

If my only problem was the land, I would have listened, but I had to get my birth records straightened out.

"Don't worry too much. It'll still be OK."

"I said, listen to me!"

"I'll visit, and then come back."

Then I left home. I went to Gaeseong by train, and there I met three people going to North Korea. Two of them were merchants selling gum, chocolate and other American-made items. If they were traveling freely back and forth over the thirty-eighth parallel, perhaps it wasn't so dangerous after all. Luckily, they were willing to guide me. The third man was like me. He wanted to sell his assets in his hometown, and move with his family to the South.

We climbed up the mountain, and walked across the thirty-eighth parallel. It was the early part of November. The mountain was covered with colorful leaves, as red as if the trees were ablaze. Squirrels, leisurely opening acorns, heard our voices and scampered away. The sky was absolutely blue, and as clean as an eyeball. There was no indication anywhere I looked, of any kind of disaster. I felt like a mountain climber. The sun disappeared red in the west, and we ate our rice rolled in sea-weed, and went to sleep wrapped in our blankets. I watched the stars until I fell deeply asleep. When I awoke, my body felt as heavy as cotton soaked with water, and my calf muscles were tense and bulging.

After we passed the thirty-eighth parallel, we separated. In three days, I arrived in Haeju, my weariness worsening day by day. I could scarcely put one foot ahead of the other, my throat was sore, and my shoulders ached as though I was carrying heavy luggage. I was clammy from fatigue. My first thought was to find a warm hotel room and lie down. I went into the first one I saw, and when I got to my room I fell like a log. I felt lonely and despairing, like I had fallen into a deep lake. I had barely fallen asleep when someone knocked at my door. My heart fell.

When I didn't answer, the pounding grew in intensity.

"Who is it?" I pretended to be perfectly calm.

"This is an inspection. Open the door, Comrade!"

The use of the word "comrade" was like a thorn stuck in my throat. I thought for a moment about escaping out the window, but, my body being in no condition for that, I gave up. Maybe if I made no mistakes, they wouldn't do anything to me. I pulled open my door lock. In the hallway were two strong young men, and my eye fell on their public-security armbands.

"Comrade, what is your name?"

"I am Song Yeongeop."

I didn't mention Oda Masao or Kim Seolcheon because Song Yeongeop was the person who lived in Shincheon in Hwanghae-do. I thought that was natural, but I found out later that was my second mistake, the first being to cross over the thirty-eighth parallel.

"Address?"

"Mujeong-ri, Sincheon-eup, in Sincheon-gun."

"Where are you heading for?"

"...."

"I asked you, where are you heading, Comrade?"

"I'm going home."

"Aren't you running away to the South?" Their eyes were red with suspicion.

"If you aren't telling the truth, you will be in serious trouble. Do you know that?"

Even so, I could not tell the truth. They were suspicious because I had not answered right away, and they looked at my rough and dirty appearance. I regretted that I hadn't at least shaved.

"Comrade, you must come with us."

"Where are we going.?"

"You'll find out when you get there."

"Are you forcing me to go to the police station?"

"We're not forcing you. We are just inviting you to come with us. After some questions, if we find out you are what you say, you will be released soon. Just follow us."

I had no choice but to go, but I had the feeling of walking into a bottomless darkness. I knew I had committed no crime, so, surely, I would be released, but that was just my hope. They delayed my questioning, behaving with deliberate slowness. After they put me in a cell, they didn't even talk to me until the next morning. I realized at last that I had walked into the jaws of the tiger.

Comrade, You are the Son of a Wicked Collaborator

I was jailed in the Heiju police station, which had been used as a prison during the Japanese occupation. All of the murals had deteriorated, and the iron bars were rusted. The worst thing was the chill from the concrete floor. There was no heating system, and I shivered sleeplessly all night from the cold. There were a few people already in the jail. A man of about forty years appeared to be the head of the prisoners, and he asked me to make a report of myself.

"I am Song Yeongyeop from Sincheon in Hwanghae-do, and studied in Tokyo. After liberation, I stayed in Seoul, and was now on the way to my hometown."

"Stop for a minute." He stopped me in the middle of my speech.

"Did you say you studied in Tokyo?"

"Yes. I graduated from the National Art School of Japan."

"But, Comrade, what did your parents do?" He talked like one of the public security officers.

"They have a rice polishing business, an orchard, and also do foreign trading."

"Foreign trading? …"

"They exported rice to Japan." Suddenly he shouted,

"Oho, Comrade, you are the son of pro-Japanese persons! In those days you had good food and clothing based on the blood of the people. Now it is your turn to suffer."

It was just play-acting for the prisoners. But, perhaps, he was predicting my immediate future, and I felt very uneasy. After taking an hour for that make-believe report, the real inquiry started. I was guided to an interrogation room by a prison officer. A man was waiting for me in a corner of the darkened room. When I got close to him, I felt that I had seen him somewhere before. He asked me the same questions that the officers who had taken me from the hotel had asked.

"Comrade, name?"

"Song Yeongeop."

"Address?"

"Mujeong-ri, Sincheon-eup, Sincheon-gun, in Hwanghae-do."

Then, he asked an unexpected question. "If your name is Song Yeongeop.… do you know someone named Song Gisu?"

I was shocked to hear my father's name. How could he have known that? I looked at him more closely, and was shocked again. He had been a policeman in the Sincheon police station under Japanese occupation. When I was a college student, he had come to see the head monk, Kanegio, and I met him there. A little hope entered my mind that, since we were from the same hometown, he might release me.

"Don't you recognize me? We met each other at the Nishihongan-ji temple with the monk Kanegio, before liberation. I'm Masao, who attended the Tokyo National Art School."

I could tell by his face that he recognized me, but my bubble of hope burst immediately. He shouted at me.

"Comrade, do not ask useless questions. Just answer what I ask." He added in a strong tone,

"I never met you before." We really had met before, but there was no way to prove it. He asked again, "Do you know Song Gisu?"

"He is my father." He looked at me sharply.

"Now I can see that the comrade is the son of a wicked pro-Japanese. By trampling the people's blood, you could live well and strut around. For that, you now have to live a hard life." He used the exact words that the chief prisoner had used.

Oh, boy, that didn't bode well. Clearly, mentioning the name of Song Gisu in the North would lead only to disaster. Still, this seemed like an injustice, and I protested.

"Up to this day, I have never cheated anyone, or done anything wrong. I have never damaged any person. Why must I be treated as a criminal?" Then, he started swearing at me.

"Didn't I tell you to shut up and answer my questions? You are too cocky, Comrade!"

"You just keep calling me 'Comrade, Comrade,' but, what makes me your comrade?"

"After you get a taste of our treatment, perhaps then you will know the meaning of the word, Comrade!" I was extremely provoked, and answered back, determined not to give in.

"I didn't commit any crime. Rather, you are the one who is a criminal. I remember that you were the cop who collaborated with the Japanese. You tortured Korean people, and treated them cruelly. You were a traitor to your country! I don't understand how you could have become my interrogator." He clenched his fists and leapt to his feet, his face turned blue and he was spluttering with rage. He banged his truncheon on the table, and, then, without hesitating, on my head.

"You son of a bitch! Where do you get off talking to me like that?" He was so angry he was gasping for breath. "Everybody knows that Song Gisu was pro-Japanese, and, while the rest of us got only gruel or went hungry, you had good rice to eat. You are the son of someone like that, and you think you can call me a traitor?"

"My father always helped his neighbors; he never turned anyone away. Also, he supplied funds for the independence movement. But, you! You were the one trying to apprehend the workers for independence, with sharper, redder eyes than even the Japanese had. Let us ask the other people who is the greater traitor!" My head was hurting from the blow from his nightstick, but I could not help defending my innocent father. The policeman kept strongly denying the facts.

"Comrade, you must be in a conspiracy against me! I was not a policeman!"

"No matter how you lie, the truth remains the truth."

"Song Yeongeop, you will get the right response to your falsehoods, so be ready for it!"

My first interrogation was over. When I returned to the cell, everyone looked at me with worry and curiosity.

"You'll have a hard time living in here, you...." The chief of the prisoners spoke in a sympathetic tone of voice.

After liberation from Japan, in order to correct the spirit and thinking of the people, an effort was made to erase any trace of Japanese influence. To me, it seemed to have been less an effort to do away with Japanese power than an effort to expand communist power. Often, those who were powerful under the Japanese seemed to have undergone a rapid change of heart, and were now powerful under the communists.

At that time, the process of land reformation and doing away with the landlord class, had not yet been completed. However, already "the people" were sitting in judgment, but that whole concept is nonsense. It was called a court of judgment, but in reality it was the mob crying, "Confiscate his property!" with the response being, "Justice!" Then that person was gone. It was like a game, but people's lives were in the hands of the powerful. "The People" were put on a pedestal, but they were being used by the communists to get rid of their enemies.

This was not a revolution, it was a process of retaliation for private feelings of hatred or favoritism, resulting in massacres such that the smell of blood was everywhere.

A Dream

I regretted not listening to Idang Father's advice. Trying to find my family had resulted in being imprisoned as the son of a Japanese collaborator, and I was in danger of being disposed of at any minute. I couldn't sleep. I was nauseated by the toilet smell in the cell, and I caught cold which made my body feel heavy and feverish. Most of all, I was afraid that I might never get out of that place, and my sleep ran away from me. My eyes were wide all night, until I fell into a half sleep as dawn approached. I wandered in a dream, searching for a temple in order to become a monk. I was walking on a path through a pine forest. I could hear the sound of pine wind, like I had heard on the way to Dasol-sa, but that did not seem to be where I was. Neither was it Sudeok-sa or Jikji-sa. My steps had taken me to the Iljumun of a temple which I had never seen. The mountain was huge and beautiful and mysterious. It seemed like that temple could not be in this world. As I approached the main room of the temple, the daeung-jeon, there was an old Seu-nim with white hair, wearing monk's robes, and holding long sticks. His white hair was blowing in the breeze. I could tell at first glance that he was a great Seu-nim in this temple. I approached him.

"Seu-nim, I came here to be a monk. Please accept me." The old Seu-nim regarded me carefully, and nodded his head.

"Truly, I knew that you were coming."

I followed the old Seu-nim into the Daeung-jeon. Inside the room was a mysterious atmosphere, and the golden Buddha had a gentle and welcoming expression. I bowed three times to Buddha, then I woke up from my dream.

The dream was so vivid that I couldn't fall back to sleep. Then, the next night, the dream continued. That time, I woke up in the middle of receiving religious precepts and having my head shaved. The dream was like a serial drama, and the third part was also connected. The old Seu-nim commanded me, "Come back after you study more."

"What? Where and to whom should I go to study?"

"If you go behind this temple and climb up, you will be able to see the Buddhist Goddess of Mercy."

"I understand."

As the Seu-nim instructed me, I went back of the temple and climbed the mountain. I climbed for a long time before I came upon the Buddhist Goddess far up the mountain. The Goddess was sitting cross-legged on a big rock beside a waterfall which fell with a roar into a deep valley. The sunshine made a rainbow in the mist from the waterfall, and the rainbow arched behind the smiling Goddess.

"Welcome!"

The Goddess's voice reverberated mysteriously. I joined my hands together and bowed.

"I came here to study." The Goddess nodded.

"First, sit beside me and meditate." I did as she suggested, crossing my legs in her same posture. The Goddess's soft voice echoed again.

"Who are you?"

"Yes.... I am...." The Goddess was smiling and, because I was hesitating, said,

"From now on think about who you are."

I closed my eyes quietly. Who was I? My past life moved before me in a panorama. Born between Japan and Korea, raised by Shindo Araki in Tokyo, then becoming a son of Song Gisu in Sincheon, Hwanghae-do, adopted by Master Idang Kim Eunho, studying in Japan and getting a Japanese family history I became Masao, meeting Mother in Gyeonseong-am—all of this passed like a movie film. Many people's faces came to me: Father Kim Bongyul in Jikji-sa, Shindo Araki, Na Hyeseok, and professors and my college friends ... Within my portion of life I tried to find my self, and continued my meditation, but I could not find the answer. Who was I? Was I a sinner or not? I felt pain in my heart, but continued to meditate.

Had I been a collaborator with Japan? When this question occurred to me, my heart ached even more. Clearly, I had done nothing for the Japanese; I had done nothing against Korea. Rather, as a Korean, I had hoped to be able to help my country. Even so, I was not comfortable with myself. Something was making me uneasy.

Right. Even though I, myself, had done nothing against Korea, my father was Japanese, trampling down Korea. Because of him, I could eat well, have good clothes, and attend college, while most Koreans could do none of those things. When I reached that point in my thinking, I could sense some light coming into my eyes. I had a feeling of relief, like a barrier had been removed. My thinking began to soar like an airplane taking off.

Yes, of course, I was a sinner. My life's purpose must be to clear away my sinful acts. Japan could attain redemption for sinful actions toward Korea, and my efforts must go toward redeeming my part of that sinfulness. That is my fate.

Suddenly, I could no longer hear the roar of the waterfall. What had happened? I opened my eyes a little bit. I was still sitting cross-legged by the waterfall, and I saw an incense burner beside the Goddess, emitting smoke. At that moment, the ash fell from the burning incense with a tremendous crash. I was astonished; the sound was louder than that made by the fall of an old tree.

"Why can I not hear the waterfall, but I can hear the falling ash make such a huge noise?" The Goddess smiled inwardly,

"Is that so? Then you have finished your study. Go back down the mountain." I was confused.

"I still didn't discover who I am."

"You have already realized it." As I rose from my position of meditation to follow the command of the Goddess, I woke up from my dream.

This three part dream is still as vivid to me as if I had it last night. Even though it was a dream, I was determined to devote my life to atonement for what Japan had done to Korea. The pledge I made on that day became my life-goal, and Korea became more to me than the place where I grew up, or the country of my mother. The dream did not change my current situation. I was still in a prison cell, and I might well be condemned to death the next day by the judgment of "The People." But, after I told him about my dream, the chief of the prisoners looked at me wide-eyed.

"Wow! That is a good dream. You might get out of this place."

"How nice if that were to happen!"

"Just wait! I'm sure you will get out of here soon."

I had a slight hope about my unpredictable future: that I might get out and go back to South Korea.

The Portrait of Kim Ilseong

"Hey, Song Yeongeop!"

It was still the middle of the night when the prison guard called me unexpectedly. When I opened my eyes, it was about one o'clock in the morning. I had been moaning on the concrete floor with only one blanket. I followed the guard to the interrogation room. There, a man I had never seen was waiting, rather than the interrogator who had been there before. This man was dressed in expensive clothing, and had a degree of dignity, so I could tell that he was not a person of ordinary rank.

"I am from central headquarters in Pyeongyang."

He introduced himself briefly, but I had no idea what central headquarters might be or what kind of position he might hold. I guessed that he must be a high ranking official in the communist party.

"I looked at the comrade's interrogation record. Is it true that the comrade was graduated from the Tokyo National Art School?" He looked me with both suspicion and curiosity.

"Yes."

"Then, are you a painter?"

"I'm not yet a professional, but I am thinking of making my living by drawing and painting, so, yes, I am a painter." He listened to me and nodded his head.

"Do you want to smoke?" The cigarette pack which he offered me had been made in Russia. I took a cigarette and put it between my lips. When I inhaled the smoke deep into my lungs, my head became filled with fog and the room began to spin. I was thinking that this man had my future in his hands. His decisions could mean the difference between life and death for me. He asked no further questions. After that, there was no interrogation for three days, and I was left in the cell with nothing to do but be angry. On the fourth day the prison guard called me. Waiting for me were the high-ranking person I had seen before, and a Russian man. The first man asked me,

"The comrade is a painter; then, can you draw portraits?"

"Yes."

"Then, let's test the comrade's skill."

The high-ranking person said something to the Russian which I could not understand, and the Russian gave me drawing materials along with two photographs. One was of a Russian person and one was of a Korean. Much later I realized that one was a picture of Stalin and one was of Kim Ilseong. I started drawing Stalin. Both of these men had very individual characteristics, so getting a likeness was not difficult. While I was drawing, the two men in the room drank coffee, smoked, and watched me. They were astonished even before I had finished the work. When I was done, the Russian man made a sound of admiration. If I had done a commonplace or sloppy portrait, they might have laughed at me, but, using the characteristics of the two subjects, I easily produced good likenesses. The high-ranking official offered to shake my hand. "You have had a hard time. It was my mistake not recognizing the comrade as a genius. Now your suffering is over, and you will have an honorable revolutionary assignment."

There was no way I could find out what that revolutionary assignment might be, but I was relieved that the prospect of an early death had apparently passed.

"Now, let's introduce ourselves formally. This is Syamsyulin, who is a painter, so you can exchange ideas." I took Syamsyulin's hand, which was very hairy. He was a head taller than I, and his whole body was covered with fur.

"Syamsyulin is an artist whom I invited from Russia to help find a painter who could make portraits."

"Glad to see you."

He greeted me awkwardly and seemed to know only a few words of Korean. After shaking hands, the official ordered the guard,

"Bring this comrade's luggage." I wasn't sure what had happened to my bag, but the guard brought it. When I saw my bag, I was as happy as if I had met a family member whom I thought I'd said goodbye to forever. The good feeling was short lived, however, as the official rushed me on my way.

"Let us go to Pyeongyang, Comrade." I was pushed out of the building without time to say goodbye to my fellow prisoners. In front of the gate a shiny black sedan was waiting for us. It had been hell in the prison, and, departing so quickly, I felt compassion for those I was leaving behind. As I was getting into the car, I looked back. Unexpectedly, the Japanese-collaborator policeman came into my sight. He was looking at me strangely. I thought he was uncomfortable about letting me out alive, since I knew about his previous career. But I erased that opportunist from my mind when I left Haeju. Mother had told me not to make enemies; to retaliate might make things worse in many ways.

Meeting with Kim Ilseong

I had been apprehended near Sincheon, and was taken to Pyeongyang without the opportunity to visit my family. We stayed in Yeongmyeong-sa near Moranbong in Pyeongyang.

"A great responsibility will be given to you, Comrade." The high official patted me vigorously on the back.

"What kind of responsibility are you talking about?" Inside of myself, I was relieved that I had been saved, but I felt uneasy as well. What kind of job could they be talking about? Is it something I could handle? If it was connected to bloodshed, I wanted to reject it. They had praised me as a painter, though, so maybe it was not something I would have to refuse. I didn't know exactly what to expect, but now I found out that my job was not connected to bloodshed. As before, Syamsyulin and I were given photographs of Stalin and Kim Ilseong.

"This is the revolutionary project for you comrades."

"What?"

"We are on the first step of a huge project New constructions are starting everywhere. We need many more portraits than those we have available. That is why we need your help."

My revolutionary project with Syamsyulin was to draw portraits of Kim Ilseung and Stalin. That was not to be for one or two, but a great volume of portraits, as if printed out from a factory, that could be used across the whole nation. We shouldn't laugh; if photography had been more advanced, the project would not have been necessary at all, but, in that case, I would not have been able to save my life either. Every government office had a bare wall with space for huge portraits of the leaders, and every other kind of office was required to have one, too. It was obvious why they needed more help; thus, my life could be saved, even though I was the son of a Japanese collaborator and a wicked bourgeoisie.

I drew Kim Ilseong, Syamsyulin drew Stalin, and every day we toiled like laborers at painting portraits. I was bored doing such simple work day after day, but I had to appreciate it for saving my life. I was a better portraitist than was Syamsyulin, so I didn't need any help from him, but I imagined that he also had the job of keeping an eye on me so I wouldn't run away. Honestly, his portrait technique was not so great that he could teach anyone. In essence, he was not making portraits, but rather just drawing pictures of Stalin and Kim Ilseong. I sensed that he knew his weak points. When we started our job, he had a struggle with his own work, and his expression showed dissatisfaction with what he did. I finished my work more quickly, so had time to look out of the corner of my eye at what he was doing. He had trouble with Stalin's moustache. It looked something like Stalin, but somehow the whole ambience was wrong.

"Give it to me."

I politely held out my hand for him to give me his brush. He handed it to me like that was what he had been waiting for. I completed the mustache, where he was having difficulty, and touched up a few other places. When he saw the completed portrait, he was as happy as a child.

From that time on, he did 90% of his work, and I completed the final 10%. Whenever a portrait was finished, he was as proud as if he had done the whole thing himself. Syamsyulin was a simple person, not egotistic; if the end result was good, that was all that mattered—he was easy-going in that way. He had grown quite fond of me since we had started living together. If there was one thing that marred the situation, it was that he was drinking too much.

I needed to maintain a good relationship with Syamsyulin, since he was watching me all the time, and I had to appear trustworthy so I could be alert for an opportunity to get away from there. I was always vigilant, looking for the right situation for my escape back to Seoul. I hadn't graduated from art school to paint pictures from morning to night of men I had never seen.

It wasn't easy to find that opportunity. Even though I could get out of our studio,I had to have a detailed plan to get safely across the thirty-eighth parallel.We had been painting our portraits for a long time, when, one day the high ranking officer came in with another man I had never seen.

"Comrade, you are working so hard. Because of the comrade, our project is going very well."

"Thank you."

After greeting me, his eyes moved to the stranger, who also, seemed to be someone of high status. Perhaps sensing that I was curious, he said with a smile,

"Greet each other. This is Comrade Kim Dubong, who is the president of the Kim Ilseong University. He was head of the Yeonan Group."

At that time, in North Korea, there were four big political power groups. One was against Japan with strong military power, the head of which was Kim Ilseong; another was the National Communist Party, headed by Hyeon Junho, O Giseop, and Ju Yeonghwa; another group was the National Party headed by Jo Mansik; and the fourth was the North Korean Independent Alliance, which was supported by the Chinese Communist Party, called the Yeonan Group, at the head of which were Kim Dubong, Heo Gai, and Choe Changik. Later, Kim Dubong was eliminated by Kim Ilseong, but at that time they were on the same side, and he even became the vice president of the People's Committee.

"You are a hard worker. I have heard many stories about the great contribution you are making."

He spoke gently, as he was examining the half-done portrait I was working on. I was uneasy, but also curious about why he was here.

"This is nothing," the high official said. "He is really here to paint much more special portraits."

"Special portraits?" I asked.

"That's right." Kim Dubong entered the conversation.

"At this time, we need a portrait to hang at Kim Ilseong University. Do you understand? This is different than the usual government office."

"Yes ..."

"Please paint a special portrait of Kim Ilseong with a size of fifty ho."

"Fifty ho? That is very large." I was shocked. Now I understood why he had come to see us in person. It was not like the copying of photographs, but an important project. I said, "I understand. I will do that, but it will take a long time, and require a lot of concentration."

"Of course. Do not worry about the time, just do a good job."

"All right."

He examined my paintings again, and left, seeming very satisfied. I started the fifty ho portrait right away. Syamsyulin watched me, interested in my new project. Perhaps he sensed that I was more excited than other times. As a matter of fact, whatever I worked on, I was first and foremost an artist. In addition, I was so bored with doing the same thing over and over, and planning the new project was stimulating. It wasn't important whether it was Kim Ilseong's portrait or not, I had a passion for my work as a painter.

After that, the high official came to the studio often to watch me work, but Kim Dubong didn't return, though I was sure he was receiving reports on my progress. Then one day, as I was approaching the end of the work, Kim Dubong arrived with the official. I showed him the almost completed portrait.

"Umhm.... Of course." His tone and his expression both showed his satisfaction.

"As the comrade had said, his art-skills are superior."

"Yes, sir. In my opinion, there is no one better." The official also appeared very pleased.

"But...."

Kim Dubong's sentence trailed off, and he frowned a little, and appeared to be uncomfortable.

I was concerned, and asked, "What's the matter? Is there something that you don't like?"

"No, not that." He shook his head, and continued, "If anything's wrong, it is just that this portrait is dependant upon the photograph."

"Is there a difference between the photo and his real face?"

"Not really, but if General Kim Ilseong doesn't approve of this portrait, we might all be in trouble."

That was true. In many cases, even when the photograph and the face are alike, the portrait might not be pleasing to its subject. Everyone wants to be drawn better than they actually look. I understood what he was saying, and nodded my head.

"So what would you think about my bringing General Kim Ilseong here...."

"If he wants to do that, it's fine with me. I could finish the portrait by seeing his real face." After he heard my answer, his face again took on a satisfied expression.

"I understand. I'll meet with Kim Ilseong and discuss this matter." He left, but he didn't return with General Kim Ilseong right away. About ten days later, Kim Ilseong arrived at the studio with his body guards and several other men. I had seen him often in photographs, but when I saw him in person I thought he was quite a handsome man. He had a distinguished face with harmoniously arranged features. He was a big, tall man with piercing eyes, the power of which was overwhelming.

"Comrade, you are working hard." He held out his hand in greeting. I shook his hand, and responded modestly.

"Where did you study?"

"I graduated from the Tokyo National Art School."

"Oh.... Tokyo National Art School...." He seemed mildly surprised.

"That's wonderful!"

"Thank you." He turned away, looked around the studio, and inquired about how the work was going on his portrait.

"I have almost finished. If you approve it, I will add some finishing touches, and it will be done." I showed him the painting, which was waiting for its final touch-up.

"Umhmm—" He examined his portrait intently. That was a sticky, sweaty moment for me. Then, he raised his head, looked at me, and smiled.

"Beautiful! It is like Comrade Kim Dubong told me." I was relieved. A burden had been lifted from my shoulders.

"Then, this part...."

"Yes?" He pointed to an area around the eyes in the painting.

"Over all, it is a little bit too dark. And, it would be better if it were softer around the eyes."

He wanted to be shown to the people as someone with charisma, but also with an air of kindness and geniality. As he requested, I started to correct the art work, and I developed an aura in it which had not been apparent from the photograph. He was drinking tea, and looking at all of the other portraits, including those of Syamsyulin.

"I can see that you can do portraits, but what was your specialty when you studied art?"

"In college, I learned western art, but I prefer to do oriental-style art."

"Do you mean drawing with India ink?"

"India ink, yes, but I am primarily a painter with colors." He nodded.

"If I have a chance, I would like to see more of your work. I don't know why, but I have high expectations of you." It took about two hours to complete the corrections to the portrait, and when I showed it to him he was satisfied.

"Good, good! Very good work!" He laughed uproariously, and put his hand on my shoulder, saying,

"Do you want anything?"

"No, sir."

"I'm sure you must be uncomfortable about something...." In my heart, I wanted to say, "Please send me to the South," but I could hardly tell him that. I pushed that wish aside, and told him that I was quite satisfied. He left, telling me to let him know if I needed anything. That one day was harder than all of the other painting days put together. Within two weeks, I could wash my hands of the portrait. I called Kim Dubong to pick up the painting, and it was delivered painstakingly from my hands. All of my energy and concentration had been poured into that picture, and, while I was relieved to see it go, I felt sorry at the same time. I have not seen that portrait since, into which I had put all of my strength, because there has been no crossing between North and South Korea. But, now, I miss that painting, and I would like to see it again.

Recently, a reporter from NHK in Japan, visited North Korea, and saw my painting, which hangs in Kim Ilseong University. He saw my signature, "Seolcheon." I was pleased to hear that my painting was still displayed there. In the future, I hope I can visit North Korea, to draw Gumgangsan, and to visit my painting at Kim Ilseong University.

A Season in Hell

The complicated year of 1945 had disappeared into the past, and the new year of 1946 had begun. I was beginning to settle down in Pyeongyang. There is a saying in the North Korean province of Hamgyeong-do that the wind there is enough to break a cow's skull. That means that the wind is so strong that it can blow rocks through the air with sufficient force that if one struck a cow in the head, it would be fatal for the cow. In the early part of that year we had to travel north to Hamgyeongbuk-do. The old saying was not an exaggeration. The wind was unimaginably strong, so that we could not walk outside with our eyes open. We arrived in Cheongjin, and stayed in one of the houses which had been vacated by the Japanese when they were expelled. The sound of the howling winter wind made me very depressed. We made a fire in the fireplace, but there was no way to get rid of the chill, and the windows rattled in the wind. I was depressed about the weather, and about the fact that I was even further away from Seoul than I was before. I thought about going to Manchuria, passing through China to Hong Kong, and from there to Seoul, but it was obvious that I would be frozen solid before I even got to Hong Kong. I had to postpone my plans to run away.I thought that, since I had been brought to Hamgyeongbuk-do, I might have a chance to get to the thirty-eighth parallel; I had to wait for an opportunity to do that. If that opportunity should arise, I must not waste it, because it might not come again. I had to be patient and quiet until that time.

Syamsyulin and I began the portrait drawing for the government office in Cheongjin. During the day, we could work, but the temperature would drop drastically during the night, and the strong wind continued to blow, making it much worse for us. We dressed in layer after layer of clothing, so that we could scarcely move, but still our bodies shivered like aspen tress. We could hear the wind gnashing its teeth, and we could only lie down and cover our heads with a blanket. If the house had had the Korean floor, the ondol, the fire would have warmed it, and made it bearable, but there was only Japanese tatami on the floor, and so it remained frigid. Syamsyulin handed me his bottle of liquor.

"Thank you."

I poured the booze into a glass, and drank down more than one. The Vodka was like fire going down my throat, and my stomach was burning. Syamsyulin was gulping it down directly from the bottle. The warmth from the liquor was only temporary, though, and soon I was trembling all over again. Syamsyulin also continually complained about the cold. Finally, we decided to sleep against each other under one blanket, to share our bodies' warmth. But, I hadn't considered his hairiness. It was all over him; his legs and his chest were like a forest. Maybe that was why he had such a strong smell. So, though the cold was less, I still couldn't sleep. Then something occurred which was no laughing matter. I noticed that the blanket over Syamsyulin's lower body was rising up like a little tent; he had an erection! Then he groaned and tried to find my hand to put on his penis. I was dumbfounded, and didn't know what to do, besides blush. Then, after satisfying himself, he went to sleep, snoring mightily.

After that night, Syamsyulin was kinder to me than ever. I used that circumstance as an opportunity to gain his trust even more completely. My escape plan was already developing. While we stayed in Cheongjin, we traveled around Hamgyeong-do to towns and villages where there were government offices, and drew portraits for them. As we traveled, we met Russian people everywhere. They were armed, and were supposed to be maintaining the peace, but, instead, they were lawless themselves. It was normal to see men wearing several watches on each arm. That was not a symbol of wealth, but of plunder and exploitation.They all took from Koreans. The worst was a man who was wearing ten watches. The Russians who were occupying North Korea were mostly peasants with very little education. They had never seen a watch before arriving in Korea, and thought of it as a mysterious and magical object.

After we had finished the work at Cheongjin and returned to Pyeongyang, we saw even more Russians in the streets. Sometimes, they brought dried octopus to the shoe repairman under the impression that it was leather—that is how ignorant they were. If they saw someone who was wearing a watch, it was gone; and they often raped women, even those who were young virgins or elders. One day, the high official came to see me.

"Oh, it has been a long time!"

"I'm sure you had a hard time in Cheongjin."

"It was hard because of the cold." I could see that he had something he wanted to say to me, but was having trouble getting it out.

"Do you have something to tell me? Has anything happened?"

"As a matter of fact…." He spoke in a low voice, and I immediately tensed up.

"This is my private request. Can you accept it?"

"Please tell me what it is. If I can do it…." I thought of him as the one who had saved me from Haeju prison. But for him, I could have been killed as a pro-Japanese, so I didn't want to refuse unnecessarily.

"Comrade, can you do a portrait of me? I know this would interfere with your duties …" His words trailed off.

"Don't worry. I'll gladly do one for you." His face brightened. I did his portrait because he recognized and appreciated my talent. Not only did I want to repay his kindness, I wanted to gain his trust, which might aid in my escape.

"Thank you. That's great." He was well satisfied with the portrait I made of him, and took me to a restaurant to show his appreciation. When he had loosened up and was feeling mellow, he got a secretive expression on this face, and said,

"Comrade, do you want to join the Communist Party?"

"Well...."

"I could recommend you. Once you become a member of the Communist Party, you could become the head of the artists' group. I would support you." I knew that his intentions were good, but it was difficult to say either yes or no.

"Oh, this is an unexpected offer. I need to think about it for a few days."

I didn't want to ruin the atmosphere, but I had not the smallest intention of joining the Communist Party. Also, I wasn't sure whether his intentions were entirely good, or whether he just wanted to have me and the artists' group under his control. In any case, it was clearer than ever that I had to escape as soon as possible. If I stayed, and accepted his offer to join the party because I could not refuse it, or if I did refuse it—either way I would be in big trouble. If I joined the party, I could become well known, but what would that kind of fame mean to an artist? In order to express myself freely, I needed to be in Seoul.

Spring had come, and Pyeongyang was windy in the season of flowers. I had kept postponing giving my response to the offer of membership in the communist party, but one day I had an opportunity. I received an order for an official trip to Haeju. That was the place I had been caught by security guards, and it was not far away from Sincheon. While I was in Haeju, I visited Jeonggak-sa temple. "Jeonggak" means the end of careless thinking because of attaining enlightenment into the true Buddhist practice. Jeonggak-sa was the most famous temple in Haeju. At that time, communists did not yet control the temple, and I wanted to talk to the head monk about my situation, and, perhaps, find help in escaping to the South. I told the head monk about my relationship with the Seu-nims Mangong, Tanong, and Dongsan. He asked me how I could possibly have attained a close relationship with such famous monks.

"That was karma. I had an especially good relationship with Sudeok-sa."

"Oh, speaking of Sudeok-sa, there is a female monk Kim Ilyeob who stays in Gyeonseong-am ..." I was surprised and pleased by his words, and I felt all would turn out well.

"Do you know Seu-nim Ilyeob?"

"Of course. She is such a famous poet that every Korean knows of her, and I met her a couple of times."

"As a matter of fact, that Seu-nim is my mother."

"Is that so!" The monk's eyes widened, and he looked in my face carefully, and nodded his head.

"Yes, I can see that you resemble her."

"Perhaps you might keep me in your thoughts." I didn't want to plead my case too soon, because it might make for problems. Luckily, Syamsyulin was so trustful of me that he gave me few restrictions. Moreover, when we were not working, he tried to give me some free time. Whenever we had some leisure, I went to Jeonggak-sa, and he went to a bar to drink. One day, when I visited Jeonggak-sa, I heard a story from the head monk about the owner of an orchard at the bottom of the mountain. I was told that this owner was also a painter. On the way back from Jeonggak-sa, I stopped by the orchard house.

"Well, is it Masao? What are you doing here?" I was as surprised as he was. He was Bak Seonghwan, whom I had previously met in Tokyo. He had been a student in Tokyo, majoring in western art.

"The head monk at Jeonggak-sa told me that the owner of this orchard was also a painter … It is a small world!"

"In any case, I am happy to see you. Let's go inside."

When we were in the house, I told him briefly about my situation, and he nodded in understanding.

"By the way Mr. Bak, do you have any worries that you might have your orchard confiscated for being a landlord?"

"It's all right so far, but who knows?…."

"The communist party does not allow any private property?"

"If something like that should happen, I am planning to escape to the South."

He spoke calmly, and appeared composed. I was happy that I had met an ally. I thought that maybe if I discussed the matter with him, I could find a way to escape, but I didn't say anything further. It wasn't because I didn't trust him; rather, I thought that it was not the right time to bring it up. Most importantly, I could not escape from the North before visiting my hometown.

Maybe, it was through God's help that an opportunity came to me. I was traveling with Syamsyulin, making portraits, in the province of Hwanghae-do, and I had the chance to visit Sincheon. I was both uneasy and excited as I walked to my old home. I was imprisoned as a son of a pro-Japanese, so, surely, my father could not be safe. The scenery of my hometown was the same. I saw the field where I had played, and was flooded with bitter nostalgia.When I got to my home, it looked like no one was living in the house. When I indicated my presence, Mother looked out of the kitchen.

"Who is this? Oh, it is Yeongeop!" Tears ran down her cheeks as she hurried out to embrace me.

"Mother!" My nose got red, and my eyes filled with tears, too. In one year, Mother had aged so much.

"Where is Father?"

"Your father is in prison. They regarded him as a Japanese collaborator...." Mother couldn't go on.

"Those villains took away the lands, too ..." Mother nodded, and suddenly became very tense.

"By the way, how come you are here?"

"That's not important, Mother. If you stay here, the whole family might die. I'll try to find a way to escape, so please get ready to go to the South." I spoke urgently, but Mother was stroking my hands, and said gently, "Escape is not that easy. Also, there is no way we could escape without Father. And, where could we go if we left our heritage behind!" My chest ached to bursting. I knew that if she stayed there, there was no hope, but Mother showed no willingness to consider leaving.

"You might have to exchange your property for your life."

"They would not go so far as to kill me."

"Don't be so sure. The situation is not what you think. I'll take care of you—we'll go together." Mother was gripping my hand, her eyes full of tears.

"Don't worry about me. Your future is unlimited. You must go south and live well. If we survive, I'm sure we will meet again." I cannot forget the expression in her eyes that day, as she said that we would meet again. We never did. Even now, when I think about her, I have feelings of guilt and sadness. Maybe, if I had taken my mother at that time, and escaped, my escape would have ended in failure; maybe she knew that already. After that, I didn't want to think about what might have happened to my parents in Sincheon. I continually tried to erase that picture from my mind. My land in Dura-myun had been confiscated already, and I realized now that my plan to sell my property had been very unrealistic. I could not meet with the Japanese monk, Kanegio. He had disappeared from Sincheon upon the liberation of Korea.

The Prajna-para-mita Sutra

Since I had been able to visit my hometown, I had no reason to stay longer in the North. I wanted to escape from this nightmare as soon as possible, and I needed to escape while I was still staying in Haeju. If I returned to Pyeongyang the high official would pressure me to join the communist party. It would be difficult to refuse him, but joining the party would be a blot on my honor. I visited Jeong-gak-sa feeling very uneasy. I was planning to ask for help by telling the head monk and Mr. Bak Seonghwan everything. I was afforded a ray of hope, not from either of them, but from someone unexpected. When I got to the entrance of Jeonggak-sa, someone was approaching on his way out. I stopped first, and the other man stopped as well, and recognized me. We each called the other's name simultaneously.

"Oh, aren't you Dr. Jang Jubu?"

"And, aren't you Song Yeongeop?"

He was originally from Sincheon, and his name was Jang Unsaeng. He was a well-known doctor of Chinese medicine. When I was young, he was our family doctor, and often visited our home. Of course, whenever I was sick he gave me restorative medicines; I had received a lot of help from him. We called him Jang Jubu. When I met him so unexpectedly, I could almost have cried with happiness.

"Dr. Jang, how come you are here?...."

"One of my patients stays in this temple, and I came to treat him here. I wanted to see if he was progressing, and to take his pulse and prescribe whatever he might need."

"Then you are now living in Haeju instead of Sincheon?"

"I moved here a few years ago. By the way, what is going on with you? What brings you here?"

When I hesitated in answering, the doctor took me to his home. Then I told him in detail everything that had happened to me.

"Oh, dear, it is too bad that such a thing could have befallen you." He regarded me anxiously.

"I have to get to the South. Is there any way you know of that I can do that?" He listened, and thought for a minute.

"There might be a chance. If you give me a few days, I might be able to figure something out."

"Thank you, Doctor." I was tearful with relief.

"You look very fatigued. You must recover your health first of all, then escape." He gave me restorative tonics to take home. I gave thanks to Buddha that I had run into him. If I hadn't met him, I couldn't even have dreamed that I might reach my present life. I met him at the temple, Jeonggak-sa; this was not just happenstance. Dr. Jang did not let me down. When I had almost finished the tonics he had given me, a message came from him. I went to him with high expectations, and he spoke to me in hushed tones.

"Tomorrow night, go to the harbor, Yongdangpo. When you get there, try to find a certain person, Lee, and tell him that Dr. Jang sent you to him. Then he will help you."

"Thank you. How can I ever repay you?" He said, "You're not safe yet. Now is the most critical time. You will meet a lot of circumstances upon which your life will depend, and which will determine whether you can accomplish your purpose."

"Yes." I was thinking about how I could repay him, then I thought that it was possible he might come to harm because of me.

"If I get caught by guards, I would never mention your name."

"I have lived long enough. Whatever happens to me is secondary. The future depends upon the lives of the young."

"I understand. Do you yourself have any plans to go to the South?"

"I don't have much life left, so it doesn't matter where I live. Wherever there are patients is the place where I belong. Under communism, there are still sick persons, and I have a lot to do. I have no desire to get famous or wealthy. I will just live and die where I am."

"If you change your mind later, please come to Seoul. If you come there, try to find Master Idang, Kim Eunho, in Waryong-dong, and I will be there."

"Thank you for your good words. If our Karma is good, we will meet again."

I bowed low to Dr. Jang, and he followed me to the gate, and blessed me. I never saw him again. By now, I am sure he is in a better world. It hurts that I could not again be with someone who had given me such special care, especially because only the thirty-eighth parallel was to blame. The next day, I fed vodka to Syamsyulin from the first daylight. He had no idea about my plan, and drank up. By early evening he had passed out completely. Without hesitation, I went to Yongdangpo. It was easy to find the man Dr. Jang had told me about.

"Follow me." He took me to the shore of an estuary. There, the tide was going out.

"From here to the South is about four kilometers as the crow flies. When the water has drained, you must run as fast as you can. No matter how fast you go, the tide will begin to come in before you get to the South, but if you can swim about one kilometer you will be OK."

"One kilometer?" To swim a kilometer in the ocean is a difficult thing.

"So, run as far as you can, so you can swim less. Don't worry too much. As the tide comes in, there will be a boat leaving from the South. If you float on top of the water, you will be saved." I was a bit relieved that a boat would be coming, but he could tell that I was still uneasy.

"You are not the first. Many people have successfully escaped in this way."

"I understand. Thanks for everything."

"Good luck!"

After we said goodbye, I started running across the silt left by the retreating tide. It was May, there was a full moon, and the gleaming expanse of silt looked endless. The night wind was chilly, but I didn't have time to get cold. Yongdangpo in Haeju in Hwanghae-do is the place where the ocean and the river meet, and there are south and north facing bays across from each other. At full moon, at ebb tide, the South and the North are connected. If someone was a runner of marathons, he could be in the South before the tide came in, but, even though I ran with all my might, there was no land showing. Running in silt was more difficult than running on land, and my legs were getting as heavy as lead when I met the encroaching sea water. At first, the tide came only up to my ankles, then to my knees, then to my waist, and then to my neck. It was useless to try to walk, so I just floated on top of the water. I could hear nothing but the sound of the waves, and the moonlight was cruelly brilliant. It was no longer a fight with communism, but a fight with nature. I thought, "I have come this far—I can't give up."

For the first time, I felt the fear of imminent death, and I began to paddle with the all the enthusiasm of a suckling baby. Escaping had not turned out to be easy! Perhaps it wouldn't have been so difficult for a talented swimmer, but, after swimming 500 meters or so, my strength was gone. My legs wouldn't move, and I regretted not bringing an inner tube or a piece of wood. I had already emptied my pockets so that my possessions wouldn't interfere with my running. My strength was gone, but I could see no boat coming from the South. A straight line might have been four kilometers, but if one went diagonally at times, it might be six or eight kilometers. I was at the doorstep of death. I asked Buddha to rescue me from dying. Unconsciously, I had been reciting the prajna-para-mita sutra:

"Gwan ja jae bo sal, haeng sim ban ya ba ra mil da si …" As I was finishing, I heard a squeaking sound across the quiet water. The noise was repeated over and over, at first faint, then louder and clearer. It was the sound of oars. I shouted,

"Na mu gwan se eum bo sal." The boat approached quickly. I grasped the rower's hand and was pulled into the boat. he oarsman gave me a towel and said, "You've had a hard time. Now you can relax."

"Thank you so much, thank you, thank you." I kept repeating my thanks like a crazed person. I looked like a drowned rat. Before drying off, I put my hands together and said again, "Na mu gwan se eum bo sal." Hot tears flowed down my cheeks. The rower gave me thick winter clothing.

"It is cold. Change into this." The ocean from the boat was boundless. I didn't know how I had made it, but it felt like a great accomplishment. Finally, I had succeeded in escaping from hell.

The bow of the boat turned to the South.

2

Between Two Worlds

Another Tragedy

I stayed overnight at the home of the boatman, and the next day caught the bus to Gaeseong. When I arrived, there were many people there who had escaped from the North. Generally, they had either crossed the ocean, or the Imjingang or come through the mountains. In Gaeseong were hordes of people. Everyone from the North was sprayed by the U.S. Army with DDT to kill the lice, and then given C-rations. I was given a free ticket to Seoul by the Americans, and I arrived there safely. My family, including Idang Father, were as glad to see me as if I had returned from the dead.

"You didn't listen to me, and went on your stubborn way. You got into a lot of difficulties, right?"

"I regretted often that I hadn't listened to you."

"I'm sure you learned a good lesson. Now, take care of yourself and try to forget your nightmare."

I believe that my escape was due to Buddha's blessing. Also, the strength it took to refuse the high official's offer must have come from Buddha. After I had been in Waryong-dong for fifteen days, Gwangyun, my brother from Gimcheon, arrived.

"What happened? How did you get here?"

"Oh, Big Brother, Father ..." He couldn't continue.

"Has something happened to Father?"Gwanggyun's eyes were full of tears, and I felt my heart sink. I had been to visit them a few days earlier, and Kim Bongyul had been in good health.

"The police came and took him. He has been released, but now he is very sick. He must have been tortured severely."

"Torture? What a bolt from the blue!"

"Mother asked me to bring you home." I explained the situation to Idang, and went with Gwanggyun to Gimcheon.

"Father, who did this to you?" Tears ran down Father Kim Bongyul's cheeks, but he said nothing. I couldn't tell whether he lacked the strength to speak, or didn't wish to talk about what had happened. I questioned Mother, who was sitting beside him.

"During the Japanese occupation he helped the independence movement, but he was safe. But now ... who could have done this?"

"I don't know what's going on. If I did know, perhaps I would feel better. A policeman came and took him away, and when he came back he was like this. I didn't know what to do, so I asked you to come." Mother sighed, and started to scold me.

"He is your biological father, and if you are his son, you are my son, too. I always thought of you as my son, but you seem to want to roam around all over the place." As I listened to her complaints, my heart ached. Mother believed that I was the biological son of Kim Bongyul, and she was looking daggers at me. Perhaps she was blaming herself for not treating me well enough. It might have been a good time to tell her the truth, but Father's condition caused me to postpone saying anything.

"From now on, I'll try to spend more time at home. But now, the most pressing thing is getting Father to the hospital." I pushed Mother to help me get him ready to go. I could see the marks of torture on his body.

Later, I discovered that Kim Bongyul had been treated in this way because he had been a member of the underground Labor Party; the real reason was that he was against Seongman Rhee. Father was a patriotic member of the party of Bekbeom, Kim Gu. They had actively worked together in Manchuria for the independence movement, so it was natural that he should support him in his candidacy against Seongman Rhee. An effort was being made on Seongman Rhee's behalf to get rid of all of those who were opposed to him. Whether in the past or in the present, it seemed that anything could be done to get rid of political enemies. I had to do something for my father; I had an obligation to take care of Kim Bongyul, because he had given me so much love. I had to worry right away about the cost of hospital care, as well as the living expenses of the family.

"Mother, do not worry about the money. I graduated from college, so maybe I can figure out something to do." Mother, who was holding onto my hand, said,

"Oh, when I hear you say that, I feel much easier in my mind."

"I'll go to Seoul and bring my painting materials and equipment here." When I arrived at Seoul, Idang gave me a job to do.

"You know Master Suwun? He is Choe Jewu, the founder of the Cheondo religion. I was asked to draw his portrait, but maybe you could do it instead...."

Of course, I could not refuse Idang's request, and I was delighted that the problem of hospital costs had been resolved. I took my painting materials, and went to Gimcheon to get Gwanggyun to be my assistant.

We went to Yuseong where headquarters of the religion, Donghak, was located. It was a little farther than the Yuseong Hot Springs, in a rural area. We were greeted by an aged woman, who appeared to be the head of the Suwun religion. She was an elegant person. She showed me Master Suwun's picture, and took me to a place where I could work. I had been used to speeding through the drawing of Kim Il Seong's portrait, but now I wanted to put all of my effort into a traditionally done picture. I studied the photograph, and tried to perceive the atmosphere it conveyed. I roughed out a first draft, then transferred it to a silk canvas. I tried to do my very best, and Gwanggyun helped me. I completed the portrait in about a month. When the portrait was done, the followers of Suwun had a great dedication ceremony. Those who attended put bolts of silk and wool as well as money on the altar. After the ceremony, without reckoning the value, they put everything into one big bag and gave it to me. I thought that was to be my recompense, but they then gave me another envelope containing the actual payment for the portrait. It was a truly unexpected windfall. We took the bag and the money to Gimcheon, and gave everything to Mother.

"Oh, Oh! How much is all this worth?"

"I have no idea." I'm sure there was a huge amount. We paid all of the hospital fees, as well as what was necessary for later expenses, and still there was money left. But Kim Bongyul's body did not heal; though we gave him many good herbs, still he made no progress. Mother and I took him to Dongsan Hospital, which was the biggest one in the Yeongnam area. Even there, they couldn't cure his illness. Finally, we took him to the Gimcheon home, and in two days, he passed away there. The sadness was more than I can describe. I had not been raised by my own birth father, but Kim Bongyul had made me feel the love of a real father. I had roamed around like a dead leaf blowing in the wind, and he had taken care of me.

This was murder. He was a healthy person, and now he is dead. Who would not consider this a murder. I was filled with rage. That this tragedy had happened in a liberated country made it all the worse. The death of Kim Bongyul was not just a private problem; rather it illustrated the dark side of our people's history. I often addressed him in my mind: No one could have been more loving, kind and generous to me; you have been my shelter and my support. It was true that the connection between us was thicker than blood, and bound us together with bonds of love and obligation. My sadness and my status as the first son made me the chief mourner. He was memorialized in a Buddhist ceremony which terminated in the cremation of his body. I had watched at the death bed of Kim Bongyul, but he had been unable to express any last wishes. However, I had read in his eyes, "Jeongung, please take care of our family."

I had become the first son of the family as soon as he had passed away. It was ironic that, with the death of Kim Bongyul, my life was completely changed. My sense of responsibility gave me a purpose and a way of emerging from my alienation which I had not experienced before. Someone who had not experienced the life of a wanderer like mine, might not appreciate the importance of family ties. I kept busy comforting the mourning members of the family, and trying to restore some measure of their animation. I often took my sisters, Songja and Jukja, on walks. We would sing children's songs together, like *Thinking of Brother.* Gradually, the family began to regain some measure of its old life, and started laughing and talking together again. One day, my Seongnae-dong mother spoke to me with a worried expression.

"This is the time for you to marry. I must look around for an appropriate woman. You are already twenty-five years old."

"Ah, yes ..."

"I know a good bride for you. Would you like to meet her once?" It seemed to me that Mother knew her already. We met at a tea room, and my first impression of her was that she had a very beautiful face. She was a very nice person, but I had no intentions of marrying her.

"As a painter, I am not famous, and I don't have a regular job. If you married me, you would have a very hard time. Is that what you would want?" She said clearly, "How could you be famous? You are still too young. If you work hard, someday you will be a noted painter. I can endure suffering, and you are the only person in Gimcheon who graduated from the Tokyo Art School. As a college graduate, you will always be able to make a living."

She was right. Idang Father had let me know that he could find me a college teaching position whenever I might want to take it. Even without a job, I could earn good money. I had already been asked by more people than I could satisfy, to make portraits or folding screens. I had just wanted to prepare her for the worst, and I also wanted to know what she had in her mind. I told her,

"I have a big family—a mother, two brothers and two sisters. If you married me, could you accept and treat well my mother and my sisters and brothers?"

"Oh, that is only natural," she said, very formally. In spite of that, I still had no confidence that I was prepared to marry. I had to travel very soon to Japan to get art materials.

"May I give you an answer after I return from Japan?" She spoke quickly, "I'll wait." After that, we dated a few times. Sometimes we went alone, and sometimes I took along Songja and Jukja. One day, in a half-joking manner, I said, "I am very conservative; I like a woman who is as faithful and patient as Chunhyang."

Right away, she understood that I would be staying long in Japan.

"I will wait, even though you are gone a long time. Let me know if you want to marry another woman—if I don't hear directly from you, I will wait, and not marry another man."

Doctor Seo Jepil and His Daughter

During that time, I was largely in Seongnae-dong in Gimcheon, visiting my Waryong-dong home once in a while. I visited Idang shortly before leaving for Japan, and he was angry with me.

"We have so much to do. Why are you staying only in Gimcheon?" I explained to him what was going on there.

"Is that so? Then, what can we do?"

"And, Father, I must visit Japan because I need more colors." Idang showed some uneasiness. "Before you leave for Japan, you should finish Dr. Seo Jepil's portrait." Then he gave me his colors, so I had to postpone the trip.

Dr. Seo Jepil was a gentleman accustomed to Western manners. He provided a big photograph which had been taken in America. I started sketching both from the photo and from his person. Dr. Seo visited Waryong-dong two or three times a week to model for me, even though his schedule was very busy. One day, he said, "Mr. Kim, are you busy this weekend?" He called me that, because Idang had told him that my name was Kim Seolcheon.

"No.... I don't have any special plans."

"Oh, good. You have been working so hard I would like to invite you to dinner. I will send a car and my secretary for you. Please say you will come." Dr. Seo did send his secretary with a car on Saturday. The secretary treated me very formally. The vehicle was a jeep, and it stopped in front of the American Officers' Club. The interior of the club was so luxurious and beautiful that I could scarcely believe it was in Seoul. Dr. Seo hugged me like an American. With him was a formally dressed woman of about twenty.

"This is my daughter," he said. As soon as he had introduced us, she smiled at me.

"How are you, Mr. Kim?"

She held out her hand, and I took it without realizing what I was doing. The daughter of Dr. Seo had been born and raised in America, and did not speak Korean well, so I could find little to say to her. Dr. Seo led the conversation.

For the first time I ate the food which is called "steak." Salad, soup, dessert—these all were new to me. The environment was completely foreign, as well, and made a strong impression on me. A few days later, Miss Seo came to my studio in Waryong-dong with Dr. Seo's secretary.

"Wow! This is wonderful," she exclaimed loudly when she saw her father's portrait. She was different in many ways from a typical Korean woman. She was very active, and had no trouble expressing her honest opinions. Gradually, I became attracted to her progressive and westernized kind of beauty. She said, "If you work too hard, you'll get tired. Why don't you take a break and we'll go to the Secret Garden?" I accepted her offer, and we walked to the Secret Garden, which wasn't much more than an arm's length away from home. It was a clear day, and her face was smooth and bright. She took my arm without hesitation. She was much more aggressive than I, the man. It was strange to me, but it felt very natural. Moreover, she asked me first for my opinion.

"What do you think about me, Mr. Kim?" Before I answered, I observed her carefully. She had big eyes, shining like black pearls, and strong eyebrows. Her nose was sharp, and she looked very intelligent. Her waist was willowy, and her legs were slim. The overall effect was of beauty.

"Miss Seo, you are very beautiful." She jumped up when she heard that, and said, "Really? Thank you!" She looked into my eyes, smiling. At that moment, I thought of the face of the woman I had met in Gimcheon. Suddenly, our conversation disturbed me.

"Let's go home." Still, she held my arm and continued to speak, but I couldn't remember any of what she said.

When the portrait of Dr. Seo was almost finished, Idang spoke to me seriously.

"The daughter of Dr. Seo wants to be married to you. What is your thinking about that?"

"Marriage?"

"Yes. Dr. Seo also wants to have you as his son-in-law." I had not been drawn to Dr. Seo because I knew he had political power at that time, but I was attracted to his daughter.

"I'll give it some thought and let you know."

"When opportunity knocks you should respond."

A few days after I had heard the proposal, I handed the completed portrait to Dr. Seo, and he, himself, broached the question of marriage.

"I really like it! It's wonderful—exactly like me!"

"I'm glad it meets with your approval."

"By the way, did you think about what I said a few days ago?" When I hesitated, he patted my shoulder, and said,

"After you are married to my daughter, you can go to the United States to study. You needn't worry about finances; I will support you until you have finished your studies."

As one interested in Oriental art, I didn't think I needed to study in the USA. But … Dr. Seo's idea was different. He said, "I'm not saying you need to learn Western art techniques, but once you master English in the USA, you could represent the frontier of Oriental art there." When I heard his words, I was tempted. He continued,

"You could lecture about Oriental art in art school. Oriental art should not be loved only in the East, but rather known all over the world. When I saw your work, I saw in you the qualifications to be in the forefront of that development."

I grew more and more attracted to what he was saying. It would be good to live in a third country, not Korea, and not Japan. I had always felt an unwelcome alienation in both countries. To Koreans I was Japanese, and to the Japanese I was a Korean. In the United States I would not have that nationality problem, and that sounded good.

"After I consider all this seriously, I will let you know my answer."

"Why, is there something about my daughter you don't like?"

"Oh, no, there is no problem there. I have many obligations, too many families that I have to take care of."

"Oh, that's no problem! Take the whole family!" Suddenly, my head was spinning.

"My daughter would not be lonely if you have a big family."

"I have another issue. I must visit Japan, and after that, I will let you know my decision."

"If you will give it serious consideration, I'll wait."

Dr. Seo Jepil gave me a lot of money for the portrait. I gave it all to my mother in Gimcheon, except for my traveling expenses.

"Mother, while I'm gone to Japan, use this money to live on."

"Won't you need some of this?"

"I saved out enough to buy the materials I need, so don't worry."

"If you expect to marry, we'll need a lot of money. I've already saved some so that you can have a place to live. Don't worry. Just be careful and come back soon."

"Mother, even if I marry I wouldn't need to make separate living arrangements right away."

"What are you talking about? That's nonsense!"

"Please get good clothes for my sisters and brothers, and give them pocket money, too. I don't want them to want for anything."

"Oh, thank you. When your father died I thought the sky had fallen, but you have been so much more generous than I could ever have expected." More than ever before, we experienced the love between mother and son as we said good-bye. Mother's eyes were wet. Eventually, I would have to tell her that I was not Father's biological son, but that was not the time. She relied on me completely, and I could not disappoint her. My Seongnae-dong mother was a warm and kind person, with a big heart. I had gotten a lot of love from my Sincheon and Waryong-dong families, but I was more emotionally attached to my Seongnae-dong family. I wanted with all my heart to live with this family as a real brother.

Before I left for Japan, I told that mother about the proposal from Dr. Seo. I knew that she liked the girl from Gimcheon, but she said that, after I returned, she would like to meet Miss Seo, so she could assess her character.

That night, I took Songja for a walk. She told me carefully, "I feel like maybe, if you go to Japan, you would not be able to come back soon."

"What are you talking about? I'll be back right away."

We talked about many things, and sang the song, "Thinking of Brother" together. Mostly, I clapped my hands, and Sister sang. Since that evening, that song has been my favorite. The next day, I went to Busan. Even after the liberation, there were many Japanese remaining in Korea. I was one of a group of these taking a repatriation ferry boat for Japan, but I had no doubt that I could return by ferry whenever I wanted to. That was a miscalculation. I could easily cross the Sea of Japan away from home, but I found that it would be very difficult to get back.

The Ruins of Japan

The ferry boat arrived safely in Shimonoseki. I went immediately to Kudamatsu in Yamaguchi-ken, where my uncle lived. I supposed that I could ascertain my father's fate from him. As I have mentioned, I had worried about my father ever since the liberation, and I was determined to find out what had happened to him. Kudamatsu is only an hour away from Shimonoseki, and is where my father had lived prior to becoming a university student. I had visited there once, so had no trouble finding it. Uncle greeted me with surprise.

"Where have you come from?"

"I'm coming from Korea."

"You stayed there until now? How was a Japanese like you able to leave there safely?" My aunt spoke sharply, "Oh, Masao can pretend to be a Korean!" When I heard her speak, I felt the old alienation in my blood. Aunt had shown before that she considered me to be a Korean who should be eliminated from the family. Uncle cleared his throat, and continued, "Your father came back from Korea after liberation, and now he is in Germany as ambassador."

"Then, he is safe?" Uncle nodded, and I was very relieved.

"Your father told me to take care of you, but I had already determined to do so as much as I can. How can I help you?"

"Up to now, I'm OK." Then, Uncle told me some unexpected news.

"By the way, Grandfather passed away." At that moment, I felt a vast emptiness. He had been my strongest guardian. Grandfather had accepted me as a part of the Oda family, and I was sure he had left me some inheritance, but Uncle did not mention the subject. I didn't bring it up, either, as I was not interested in inheriting from the Oda family. Uncle didn't shun me, and I felt the blood-connection with him, but Aunt was different. I could sense that she was worrying that I might be expecting to stay in their home. One day, when I returned to the house, I heard arguing between Uncle and Aunt.

"Why is Masao staying in my home?!" When I heard her furious voice, I stopped in mid-step.

"What is wrong with a nephew staying in the home of his uncle?" When I heard Uncle speak, I gave a sigh of relief. After the war, most Japanese were very poor, and had to depend on food distributions to live. But, Uncle's house was different, and they were still very well-off, so Aunt's rejection was all the more painful to me. I didn't want to get my uncle into more trouble, and that night I took a train to Tokyo. Uncle accompanied me to the station, and offered to give me money, which I refused at first.

"Ignore your aunt. Just stop by to see me. Your father and I were very close as brothers." Uncle seemed to be sincerely concerned about me, and I felt healed from the pain caused by Aunt's harsh words.

Tokyo was very different than when I had last seen it. Many buildings had collapsed under bombing, and the ruins were charred black. The restoration had barely begun, and Tokyo presented a picture of devastation.

I went to Goenji, where Mr. Araki's house was. I had lived there through middle school and college for eight years, and was very familiar with the area. But, when I got there my heart sank: there was nothing but empty space where the house had stood. The air raid damage in that area was extreme compared with other parts of the city. No one could tell me what had happened to Mr. and Mrs. Shindo. Neighbors thought they might have been killed in the bombing, but nobody had seen their bodies, either. Later, I tried to locate them through newspaper and radio ads, but could not find them. Without them, I could never have finished my college training safely. They were my Japanese guardians, and their death was hard for me to accept.

Now, I had nowhere to go. Mr. Shindo's house was destroyed, and my classmates were all dead. I stayed in a hotel, and decided to return to Korea immediately after acquiring the materials I needed. However, when I went to the art supply store, I found out that it wasn't so easy.

Many art stores had burned, and I could find only one still standing. In addition, the price of materials had gone up fifteen or twenty times over what I had paid as a student. The money which I had brought was not even close to what I would need. In those days, I could not buy the coloring supplies I needed in Korea, so I would have to earn money to get what I needed there in Japan.

But, there were many people looking for work, and very few jobs to be had. As soon as I opened my eyes each morning, I would leave the hotel and roam around looking for a way to make some money. I visited Hongo Middle School, and the National Art University. Both schools had been damaged in air raids. I felt ashamed to be the only one of my classmates still alive and roaming around. The public security in Tokyo at that time was under the auspices of the American army. Since the Japanese police no longer had any power, a Korean could walk the street with confidence.

Art Teacher at Baekdu Institute

When I no longer had any money in my pocket, I went to a Korean organization. Luckily, they had a need for a person who could speak both Korean and Japanese. I helped them, and stayed in a small shed, where I could sleep, curled up. Finally, I got a call from the Tokyo Provincial Office, asking whether I would take a job as a school teacher. I responded immediately by going to see the person who had called. He explained, "The man who is in charge of the Geonguk Middle and High Schools, as well as the Baekdu Institute, is Korean. The institute is a private school which teaches Korean students. I know you are in bad straits, but, as a graduate of the National Art School, would you be willing to work under a

Korean boss? If not, don't apply for the job." He had assumed that I was Japanese, which was natural, since he knew me as Oda Masao, the name I had gone by in school. After I found out the situation, I was more interested than ever. I went to the Baekdu Institute in Osaka.

The institute encompassed elementary, middle, and high school. I introduced myself to the principal in Korean, saying that I had been referred by the provincial office, and gave him my resume. He glanced at it, and said, "You graduated from the National Art School? How come, as a Japanese, you can speak Korean so well?"

"I am a Korean."

"Then, you changed your name to Oda Masao? Do you have a Korean name?"

"My name is Kim Seolcheon."

"The director will make the final decision, but we need someone right away, and since you are a graduate of the National Art School, there is no reason for him to reject you. You can assume that we will be able to work together. The director is not here today, but I will let you know for sure by tomorrow."

"I can't stay here for long."

"But, maybe you can stay for two or three years."

I was going to say six months, but, finally told him I would have to return to Korea after one year.

"If that is your position, I will try to get you approved for the job, even for one year only."

When I returned to the Baekdu Institute the next day, I met the director, and he hired me on that basis. So, my first job was as a teacher in the Baekdu Institute in Osaka. The director asked me to stay in the dormitory, and that was not too bad either. My sleeping and eating requirements being taken care of, I had an opportunity to introduce myself to the school staff. There were about sixty teachers in the institute. I shook hands with everyone. Among them, I shook hands with the history teacher. He had been watching me closely.

"I am Sato."

"I am Kim Seolcheon."

"I feel like I have seen you somewhere before."

Actually, I had been feeling the same way, but I could not recall where I had seen him. Finally, I remembered: he had been the soldier who brought the inspectors to snow-covered Mangwol-sa, putting us all in fear. This unexpected meeting surprised us both; clearly, we had some special karma before we were born. Teacher Sato may have been a military inspector in Korea, but as a colleague, he was a gentle and intelligent person. He had graduated from Waseda

University and now taught history at the Baekdu Institute. He was about twenty years my senior, and did not appear to care that I knew about his previous career. He was helpful to me in many ways; our reunion appeared to be a good omen.

Ferry Service No More

My first class was at the senior level. As I introduced myself to the class for the first time, I felt fifty pairs of eyes staring at me, a twenty-six year old teacher, but when I spoke, I tried to give the appearance of calmness and experience.

"If you like, you may take notes while I lecture, but it is not necessary to do so."

I wanted to create a free atmosphere before I started my lecture:

"Art is not a painting which you paint with a brush; rather it lies in the objects of our everyday life. You must utilize your sense of beauty even in selecting the dish you are to eat off of. I added that a well-lived life, even our posture when we sit, are also aspects of art. Beginning now, become aware of the beauty around you, which you have not noticed before.

"In whatever you do, it makes a difference whether you just act by habit, or whether you add your sense of beauty to all of your seeing, hearing and thinking.

Enriching your life is impossible without developing your sense of beauty. The development of this aesthetic sense is what I hope to accomplish with you."

The students appeared to be paying attention, and I told them, by way of example, the story I had written to my mother earlier, of the artist Sesshu."....

Finally Sesshu became a very famous artist in Japan. I want to impress upon you that Sesshu's accomplishments rested on his perseverance and refusal to give up. I'm sure he was talented, but it was his hard work that most accounted for his success."

The students applauded and cheered me after the lecture, and I became a popular teacher right away. Because I was young, I tried to relate to the students as a friend, and to understand and counsel them. I wrote a letter to my mother in Seongnae-dong in Gimcheon, explaining why I had to get a job at the Baekdu Institute, and told her that I would be home as soon I a got enough money for my art supplies. Gwanggyun wrote a reply: Mother had started a business with the money I had given to her. The business was doing well, and yielding enough money for the family to live on, so I did not need to worry. Until then, I had planned on returning to Korea after one year. But, I didn't go back to Korea. There were many reasons, but the major one was that the ferry service had been cut off, and even the postal service between the two countries had almost ceased to exist.

The other reason was that I had registered to study in the Department of Buddhist Art at Buddhist University at Goya-san. I had been interested in this type of art for a long time, and the Buddhist University was well known for the quality of its art department. At first, I thought in terms of one year of study, but I became so interested in what I was learning that I did not wish to stop.

There was another reason, too. In 1948 I got the Asahi award, which had been sponsored by the Asahi Newspaper. The work for which I got the award was entitled *Jihasamcheoncheok.* After that, I received a lot of attention from Japanese artists, who advised me to remain in Japan; I decided to stay.

The Asahi award was very respected in Japan. At that time, I was using the name Kim Seolcheon as an artist. Later, I learned that there were fifteen judges, all of whom agreed that my work was the best, but, who, because I was Korean, had a hard time determining to give me the prize. My Japanese master, Ito Shinsui, had emphasized that in art there are no borders, and his influence enabled me to win. If I had used the name Oda Masao I would not have run into that problem, but I had used Kim Seolcheon because I wanted to live as a Korean in Japan, and I wanted to emphasize to my students that a Korean artist could succeed there. When I received the award, my students were delighted. In my life I have had no regrets, except for one: that I didn't return to Korea at that time. Because I didn't go back, I was able to continue working in Japan, but this decision continues to cause me pain. Because of it, I became famous in Japan, but not in Korea where my heart is.

The strait of Hyeonhaetan has known my sorrow and regret. I could not explain my longing to anyone, but, as I looked at the ocean, that strait, the path to Korea, knew.... but said nothing.

3

Love and Loss

Hide and Seek

Among the teachers at the Baekdu Institute was a music teacher, Kim Cheongin. She was from Jeju-do, and had studied voice at the Osaka Music School. She was twenty-four, two years younger than I, and was the prettiest of all of the female teachers. She was tall and long legged, and had beautiful eyes. But I was planning on returning to Korea, and the daughter of Seo Jepil and the girl in Gimcheon were both waiting for me, so I tried to keep my distance from her. I tried to relate to her only as a colleague. Luckily, there was a science teacher, Kim Chango, who was very fond of her. He was two years older than I, and from Busan. There was a Korean Language teacher, Yu, who liked him. So, there were four single teachers, relating in various triangles and squares, trying to discover their inner feelings. If they liked someone inside, they tried to hide it on the outside.

For example, Kim Cheongin liked me, but pretended to like Kim Chango; Yu liked Kim Chango, but pretended to like me. We all had coffee or tea together after classes, and had a good time, but, from the outset, I was stand-offish, because I didn't want to become involved in a love affair. We were all intelligent enough not to create a situation of jealousy and intrigue. We played ping-pong, ate dinner, and sometimes went to the movies or a dance-hall after work. One day in the fall, when I didn't have a class, I set up my easel on the school grounds, and started painting. In front of a building was a flower bed full of cosmos and sunflowers which were bending down from the weight of their seeds. The chill wind awakened sadness in me. Suddenly, when I lifted my eyes from the canvas, I became aware of the sound of a piano. It was a gentle sound, very sweet to hear. I immediately recognized Beethoven's *Moonlight Sonata.* I looked toward the window from which the sound was coming, sure that it was Kim Cheongin playing.

I tried to control the pounding of my heart. I folded up my easel, and went into the music room. I opened the door quietly, so as not to disturb her, and she didn't notice me, continuing to concentrate on her playing. When she finished the piece, I clapped my hands. She looked at me and began to blush. I went up to her.

"Please pardon me for entering rudely, without your permission."

"It's OK."

When I stood near the piano, I could look out of the window and see the spot where I had been sketching. Perhaps she had intentionally played the piano so I would hear.

"It was a very moving performance."

"Oh, thank you. But, compared to a professional musician, I am nothing."

"You are too humble! As a matter of fact, I have been wanting to learn to play piano. Could you teach me when you have time?"

"On one condition."

"What?"

"I am interested in painting, too. Can you teach me sketching and dessin?"

"That wouldn't be difficult."

So, on Sundays we would meet at the school, and she taught me the basics of piano. Then we would go to a suburb of Osaka, where I taught her sketching. By meeting with her every week, I discovered her many good points, but I didn't think that was love. Kim Cheongin's parents had returned to their home province of Jeju after the liberation, and her brother had moved from Osaka to Tokyo so she was staying with an aunt.

I was tired of staying in the dormitory, and thought about renting a room where I could cook my own food. I told Kim Chango about this, and he suggested that we move out together. We found a suitable place in Tokuyama in Sumiyoshi-ku.

On Sundays, Kim Cheongin and Yu visited us. The two women brought side dishes, and we made the rice for our meals. Kim Cheongin came to see me, and Yu came to see Kim Chango, but Kim Chango still liked Kim Cheongin and not Yu. Kim Cheongin and I would meet for piano and drawing lessons, and we would all meet once a month for our dinner. I was attracted to her, but my planned return to Korea caused me to keep my distance.

After I had been on the job at the Baekdu Institute for two years, a new Gumgang Institute was established in Osaka. It was also a private school. That new institute needed many experienced teachers, and they offered me a job there. After I received the offer, I worried about what to do. I felt an obligation to the Baekdu Institute, but the new school desperately needed me. I talked it over with Kim Cheongin.

"In my opinion, you should make the move to the Gumgang Institute."

"Why do you think so?"

"You don't know yet?"

"What are you talking about?"

"There are rumors among the students that we are lovers, so it would be better for you to go." After I heard what Kim Cheongin had to say, I was worried that I might have to marry her. I hadn't realized that others perceived us as more than colleagues. If I changed positions, I could consider our relationship from a distance, and, in addition, Gumgang was in need of more hands. So I moved to the Gumgang Institute, and Kim Chango followed me there.

The director at Gumgang was Mr. Hong, and the principal was Kim Yongdae.

I became an academic dean. Because of the newness of the school, there were many things to do. There were plenty of students and buildings, but they had not yet received formal permission to operate from the government. My first job was to secure that permission from the government at Osaka, but it was not easy, and I had to resort to using my Oda family name.

The Gumgang Institute was a little bit smaller than Baekdu, but the system was the same, covering from nursery school to high school. I spent a lot of time roaming around the school buildings and the different classes. One day, as I was passing the nursery school classroom, I spotted an organ in the room, and went in. No one was in the classroom, so I sat down in front of the organ without hesitation. Suddenly, I thought about Mr. Shindo. I had learned to play the organ from Mrs. Shindo at home, and I had learned piano from Kim Cheongin, so I had no trouble playing. I opened the cover, and, since there was no music, I played "Thinking of Brother" nicely. Before I came to Japan, I had often sung with my sister, Songja. My heart ached for my Seongnae-dong mother, and my sisters and brothers, who were waiting for me.

Suddenly, I was overwhelmed by the wish to go back to Gimcheon. I wanted to give up my teaching job and my Buddhist art studies. But, if I saw the family in Gimcheon, perhaps I would have to tell them that I was not the biological son of Kim Bongyul. I shook my head; no matter how much I loved them, I didn't want to cause them pain. That was probably why I kept postponing my return to Korea. I shook my head once more, and Mr. Shindo's face came back to me. My eyes filled with tears. The Shindos were the parents of my nursery days, and the parents of my middle school and college years. They loved me more than if I had been their own biological child. I could not repay everyone, but perhaps I could have repaid them. I railed at God for allowing this to happen, and I realized at last how much I owed them. I played the organ and felt sad and regretful. As I began to recognize the need to change my mournful thinking, I began playing fast. After a while, a female teacher came into the classroom. I was embarrassed, and dropped my head.

"I'm sorry I took over this room without permission."

"It's OK. This not my room, but belongs to the Gumgang Institute. Any staff member is free to come in."

"Thank you for your understanding. I am Kim Seolcheon, and I teach art here."

"I know, I know. I am Teacher Hong."

"You know me already, but I don't remember seeing you before, Miss Hong."

The staff of the nursery and elementary schools used different offices than the staff of the middle and high schools, so it was not surprising that I didn't know her. But, how did she happen to know me? I didn't ask her about it; she could have heard about me, or seen me from a distance.

"I knew you were a good painter, but you play the organ well, too."

"You are over-praising. Really, I'm not that good at either thing."

"You are very humble. I wish that I could play the organ that well."

"You don't play organ?"

"I didn't have a chance to learn, so another teacher helps me teach music to the children." She blushed as she spoke.

"Then, begin to learn now. You can learn in a month enough to teach nursery school music."

"There is no one to teach me."

"I am willing to teach you the basics."

"If you would do that, I would never forget your kindness."

"Oh, let's start right away."

I felt sorry that a nursery school teacher didn't know enough about the organ to teach her students nursery songs, and I was pleased that, though she was embarrassed, she was able to ask me to help her.

After that, I taught Miss Hong organ two or three times a week. That was purely being helpful to a colleague. She learned so fast that I was sure she was practicing hard between our lessons. After a month, she could indeed teach the children by herself.

"I have taught you all that I know, Miss Hong."

"Because of you I can do my job better. How can ever I repay you?"

"You don't have to do anything."

"Perhaps I could serve you a good meal."

"I appreciate the offer, but no thanks. I'll just go on home."

Miss Hong was biting her lips. I felt sorry for turning her down, but, having a meal might lead to other meetings, and just cause problems, and I thought it best to refuse. Then, I forgot about her.

Confusion

The director of the Gumgang Institute had been looking for me, and when I entered his room cherry blossoms were blooming outside his window. It was one Saturday in May.

"Please come in, Mr. Kim."

"Were you looking for me?"

"Do you have plans for dinner tonight?"

Kim Cheongin might stop by to see me at Tokuyama, but we had not made definite plans.

"I don't have anything scheduled. Why?"

"Good. Why don't you come to my house for dinner. This is a formal invitation."

"Is today a special day?"

"Not really, but you have been working so hard that I would like to show my appreciation. And, since you are single, I am sure you have not been eating properly.

I'll tell my wife to prepare a good meal to show off her cooking skills, so, please say yes."

"Thank you for your concern. I'm happy to accept."

The director's house looked big and luxurious from the outside, clearly an upper class home. I hadn't been able to find a proper gift, so I brought a bunch of roses; I was sure that housewives love flowers. I transferred the bouquet to my left arm, and rang the doorbell. To my surprise, the door was opened by Miss Hong, the nursery school teacher. She must have been invited, too. She smiled radiantly.

"Welcome, Mr. Kim. Please come in. I'm happy to have you in my house."

Then, I realized that the director and the nursery school teacher shared the same last name: Hong. She saw my bouquet, and said, "Wow—is that for me?"

I had to give it to her, and she jumped for joy. A little later, the director and his wife appeared. Director Hong introduced me to his wife, and we all went into the living room. Miss Hong served coffee. She was dressed up, and her face was tremulous and full of smiles, and she couldn't take her eyes off of me. The food was unbelievably good. Meat, fish and other dishes looked delicious, but, because of Miss Hong I couldn't fully enjoy the meal. When I stood up to go home, Mr. Hong said to his daughter:

"Why you don't walk with him to the station?"

"Of course."

"It's late already. I'd better just go by myself."

"No, I'll be glad to walk with you."

I tried to refuse, but was not able to convince her, and we went out together. It was a pleasant evening, with a fresh spring breeze blowing through Miss Hong's hair. She was twenty-three or twenty-four, a very lively young lady. She was as pretty as a greenhouse flower.

"I didn't imagine that you were the daughter of Director Hong."

"For the first time, I realize that you didn't approach me just because of my father's wealth. I had thought that you realized who I was, and just pretended not to know me."

"Of course not."

"I apologize for my misunderstanding."

Except for us, the street was deserted and silent. I didn't want it, but I began to feel some attraction to her, and she was looking at me with dreamy eyes. She said, "You are so different from everyone else I have met."

"What do you mean?"

"I have never been drawn to other men, but when you taught me the organ, my heart skipped and I couldn't breathe. If you want, I would give you everything, even my life."

"It is too sudden; we do not even know one another."

"It is not necessary for me to know you well to know that you…."

"Before jumping into anything, we have to think about lots of things. Sometimes, one can like someone, but finds that there are situations which they cannot accept. So, acting too quickly can cause trouble when you really get to know the person. To avoid regret, you must be absolutely sure that you have found the right man."

"I don't think that I will meet many people I could love—maybe only one or two in my life. When I do meet someone, I would not want to let pride get in the way." She was telling me directly that she could love me. We parted uneasily. When I got to the house in Tokuyama it was almost eleven o'clock. Out of the darkness, I saw a woman waiting for me; it was Kim Cheongin.

Oh, dear! …

"I have been waiting for you."

"Why didn't you wait for me inside?"

"Kim Chango is there. You know how he feels about me."

"He's a pretty good guy."

"Does that mean you are asking me to go out with him?"

"I didn't mean that."

"Then why did you say what you did?"

"He's a good person, so we can all be friends."

"But he keeps looking at me. How could I act natural around him?"

"Please forgive me if I said something wrong."

"Can I ask you why you are so late?"

"I was invited to the director's home for dinner."

"Then, is it true that you are in a relationship with Miss Hong of the nursery school?" "Where did you get that idea?"

"I know someone who tells me what goes on at the Gumgang Institute."

"I don't know what you heard, but tonight was the first time I found out that Miss Hong was the daughter of the director."

"Then why did you give her organ lessons? I heard, even at my school, that you and Miss Hong had something going on."

When I heard Kim Cheongin's words, I realized that rumors truly have legs, and, without my knowing it, the story about me and Miss Hong had spread throughout Osaka.

"I don't know what you could have heard, but there is nothing between me and Miss Hong."

"You keep saying that, but my friend and others think differently. That is the problem."

"By the way, why do I have to undergo this interrogation from you?"

"Does that mean that I am not entitled to ask that kind of question? For more than two years now, we have been going to movies, sketching trips, weekends and Sundays—and all of those memories were just between colleagues? Is it the story that it was only I who felt strongly about those experiences?"

As she said, we had spent a lot of time together, beginning at the Baekdu Institute.

It was during that time that we found out how much we liked each other.

Surely, the daughter of Dr. Seo Jepil would not have waited this long for me. But, the girl in Gimcheon might have done so. If I didn't return to her, I wanted to marry with Kim Cheongin. Because of that girl, I had not even held Kim Cheongin's hand in all of that time. Now, Kim Cheongin was reminding me that our relationship was important, even if I had not held her hand.

"It is too late tonight. Why don't you go back home, and tomorrow we can have a serious talk about all this."

The next day was Sunday. When I met her, I suggested going to Nara, an old city about an hour and a half away from Osaka. Now it is the capital of Nara-ken, but, at that time, it was a place of historical interest and ancient ruins. Nara was famous for its India ink and narasuke. We did a lot of shopping while we toured the place.

When we returned to Osaka, we went to a tea room.

"If our meeting is only for our marriage, I cannot see you any more."

"Are you thinking of marriage to another woman?"

"I don't mean that. It's just that I cannot marry anyone in the near future."

"But, you will marry sometime."

"I won't marry before I graduate from the Buddhist Institute. I couldn't ask you to wait forever."

"If you don't have someone special in your mind, I will wait."

"As a matter of fact, there is a woman who is waiting for me in Korea. After I graduate, I must return to Korea and marry her."

"Then, do you communicate with her by letter?"

"No."

"Then, do you think she is still waiting for you?"

"If she has married, then I could marry someone else."

"That is a pretty ambiguous answer."

"All I can tell you is that I am not going to marry soon, and I can't ask you to wait for me."

"I'll wait. You finish school, visit Korea and come back. If she has not waited, please marry with me."

"If I disappoint you, what will you do?"

"That is fate. I like you too much to look for someone else to marry."

Kim Cheongin had expressed her feelings clearly, and her liking for me was stronger than mine for her. I thought about visiting Korea. If I could not go under the current rules, I would have to find a way to go secretly. If both the daughter of Dr. Seo and the girl from Gimcheon had married, I would marry Kim Cheongin.

After I visited her home, Miss Hong became more aggressive. She sent me a letter saying that, though she had tried to change her feelings, I was still the only one she could love. She said that she would never regret loving me, even if the outcome were sad. She even stated that, should she not win my love, she would just have to die. I thought that the best way to change her mind was to let her know that I already had a girl friend. Though it seemed a bit cruel, I believed that it would be better to do it as soon as possible.

Kim Cheongin understood well what I was going through, and acted accordingly. She came to Gumgang from Baekdu as soon as her Saturday classes were over. As soon as she got to my school, I walked with her out of the gate, to show others our relationship. After this had gone on several times, Miss Hong sent me a note asking to meet with me after class for a talk. We met at a tearoom. Her appearance had changed, and she seemed like a person who had been ill. My heart sank. While I waited for her to speak, I lit a cigarette, but the taste of it was bitter.

"Is the person who visits you often your girl friend?"

I simply said, "Yes."

She bit her lip. "When did you start dating her?"

"I knew her at the Baekdu Institute."

"Then, is she a teacher there?"

"She is a music teacher."

"If you married, you would be an artist-couple."

"…"

"I feel resentful that God does not help me. Why do I have to love a man who already has a lover?"

"There are a lot of better men than I; you are very pretty, and I'm not rejecting you. But, I have known her longer, and I don't want to betray her."

Suddenly, I felt irritated, not only with Miss Hong who was in front of me, but with women in general. Did I really have to marry? I'd rather be alone. I always seemed to have to pay attention to women. I had wanted to be a monk, after all—maybe I was just a man who was not interested in women.

"Can't you separate from her?" "…"

"I know it's nonsense, and I shouldn't say it. But how about me? Do you want me to die?"

"It is not something to take so seriously."

"My heart is breaking. I can't eat or sleep. Even though I don't commit suicide, I don't think I can live much longer." Her eyes continually bored into my face. Even when I dropped my gaze I could feel her looking greedily at me.

"Please understand me even if I do crazy things. I can't just step out of the picture."

I sensed how difficult it would be to resolve the situation. A few days after the conversation in the tearoom, I saw Kim Cheongin, and she was livid with anger.

"The director at my school called me in and told me that I should not go to Gumgang anymore. He had been called by Mr. Hong, who told him that it was not good for the children to see us together. I'm sure that it was Miss Hong's doing."

I recalled Miss Hong's words about nonsensical actions. I was sure she had used her father to get Kim Cheongin barred from the Gumgang Institute.

"It's true that we are educators. Maybe it would be better if we did not meet a school."

The next thing Miss Hong did was to ask her father to request her marriage to me. Director Hong spoke to me privately.

"Mr. Kim, my daughter is a girl impossible to find fault with; she is a good girl,"

"I think, too, that she is a very good person."

"She is very introverted, and once she gets something in her mind, she can't think of anything else. She is good and pretty. Are you willing to marry my daughter?"

"I already have a girl friend."

"I have heard about that. But, I'm sorry to say, my daughter is not paying any attention to my advice. If you marry my daughter, I will transfer the Gumgang Institute into your name, because I have seen your ability to take charge."

"Thank you for your confidence in me. But, you shouldn't tie that kind of important matter to the marriage."

"I know that, but please understand that she is my daughter, and she is going through something serious."

"I'm sorry, and grateful. But if I chose Miss Hong because of your offer, what about the other girl? She would be devastated, too. I deeply regret that, because of me, others are so worried and upset. I'll just act like your offer was never made."

Shortly after I rejected the director's offer, I heard that Miss Hong had made a suicide attempt. Luckily, her parents had found her in time, and she survived. She had left a note to her parents asking forgiveness, and one to me saying that she would get to Heaven first, and wait for me, so that no one else could have me. After I saw the suicide note, I was at a loss. I could hardly help visiting her, because she had acted because of me. I comforted her, and told her that her recovery was the most important thing for me, and that we would talk more about the future when she was feeling better.

Endless Love and Hate

After Miss Hong got well, Kim Cheongin became more aggressive with me than she had been before. She visited me often at my Tokuyama home, and publicly showed her affection for me. The change in her behavior distressed Kim Chango, because he was still very fond of her. In contrast, Miss Yu approved enthusiastically, because she still liked Kim Chango. Kim Chango became gloomy, and tried to avoid me. He told me one day, "Mr. Kim, I should leave here and return home." His mother lived in Sakai City, not far from Osaka. His only reason for living here was to see Kim Cheongin more often, and now that was painful for him. Moreover, it was probably uncomfortable to be around me because of the situation.

"If that's the way you feel, don't worry about me—just go on back home."

If Kim Chango left, I could not continue to live in that place, either. It was too expensive to live alone, and, if I was alone, my relationship Kim Cheongin might get out of hand. I didn't want to get into something I couldn't be responsible for. About that time, I ran into Mr. Sato, who taught at Baekdu Institute. I asked him to find a rooming house for me.

"If you like, you could move into my upstairs room. No one lives there."

"Your home?"

"I'd let you live there rent-free, so you could save money toward your marriage."

"I wouldn't want to do it for nothing. That would place me under too much of an obligation."

"Anyhow, the room is empty, and I don't think you would eat too much."

"Please talk it over with your wife. But, I won't do it unless you let me pay rent."

Mr. Sato soon called me to let me know that his wife was in favor of the plan.

"My daughter is a college student. She would like to learn painting from you. Let's exchange the rent for the tutoring fee. Let me be a father who can provide his daughter with a private teacher. Please visit us, and if you like the place, we can make a decision."

"I understand."

Mr. Sato knew that I was a member of the Oda family, even though I acted like a Korean, and he knew about my father, but I didn't get the feeling that he was doing me this favor because of my background.

Mr. Sato's home was big. He lived in the upscale residential area of Kishiwada, in Osaka, and I liked it there because it was so quiet. He had a wife, two sons and one daughter. The first son had graduated from college and was working, and the daughter attended Hagamoro University. The whole family lived in the first floor rooms.

"Nobody uses the upstairs, so there is nothing to worry about. Just move in."

I accepted Mr. Sato's offer. I enjoyed the quiet and roominess. I set up my studio first, as well as my bedroom. Because they wouldn't accept rent, I taught painting to the daughter, and thought about giving the family a gift of some of my art work. Hagamoro University, where Miss Sato went, was one of the most famous women's colleges in Osaka. I learned that the president and financial officer of that school was the younger brother of Mr. Sato. Mr. Sato had three brothers. An older brother who lived in Hashimoto City was the wealthiest, and, indeed, was the richest man in the city.

One day the older brother came to visit in Osaka. He was an old gentleman of about sixty years. We greeted each other with a handshake, and Mr. Sato said, "Mr. Kim is a very skillful painter who graduated from the National School of Art. He already won the Asahi award, sponsored by the Asahi Newspaper. In addition, he attends the Buddhist University at Goya-san twice a week to study Buddhist art. He is a very dedicated person." His brother nodded, "To get to Goya-san, you must pass by Hashimoto City."

"Yes, that's right."

Hashimoto is located between Osaka and Goya Mountain. To get to Goya-san, I had to transfer at Hashimoto City.

"When you go there, if you have time, please stop by my house."

"I would like to do that."

On Tuesdays and Thursdays I finished my classes in the morning, and in the afternoon would go to Goya Mountain to study Buddhist art. This was only possible because Gumgang Institute cooperated with my plans. After Miss Hong's suicide attempt, I often went to Goya Mountain on Saturday afternoons as well.

If I stayed in Osaka for the whole weekend, I would have to see Kim Cheongin, and, since a woman had already attempted suicide, I was much more comfortable avoiding the situation.

The campus of the Buddhist University covered the whole side of Goya Mountain; it was the largest Buddhist community in Japan. Every mountain valley held a temple of historical interest. A visitor there would be overwhelmed by the solemn grandeur of the place. There is an ancient legend of the place: A rich man from Kyushu once brought his wife and young son, Ishidomaru, to picnic there, and to view the cherry blossoms. A gust of wind blew a cherry blossom into his wine cup. This incident made him think how quickly a human, too, can perish. Humans, in all their pride and opulence, will vanish, too, like the blossom. He thought about the randomness and brevity of life. Upon returning home, he told his wife, "I'm considering becoming a monk. I realize now that life is meaningless and short, and before it gets too late for me, I want to be awakened to eternal life. I will give you all of my wealth; please do not stop me."

To his wife, these words were like a clap of thunder, and she tearfully asked him, "How can I live alone with this young child?"

"That is hard, but it is momentary. Just recognize it as Karma, and do not try to hold me."

The rich man broke away from his wife, and went to Goya Mountain to become a monk. Later, his wife became ill, and was unable to care for her son. She took the son to Goya Mountain, but, since women were prohibited, she was unable to get in, and stayed at a hotel at the bottom of the hill. She instructed her son to climb the mountain, and to bring back his father. On the path upwards, Ishidomaru met a monk. He told the monk that he wanted to see his father from Kyushu, and gave him his father's name. After the monk heard Isidomaru's story, he said, "Alas! He passed away just a few days ago."

After Ishidomaru learned that his father was dead, he was distraught, and returned to the hotel where his mother was waiting. When he got there, he found out that his mother had died just before his arrival—he had become an orphan. He climbed the mountain again, and found the monk he had spoken to before. He told him that his mother had died also, and since he had no place to go, he begged to be allowed to stay there as his apprentice. That monk was his father. To sever the ties of blood, he had lied to his son, but another kind of bond developed, that of teacher and pupil. Ishidomaru became an important monk by studying hard with his father/teacher.

Whenever I hear this legend, I think of my mother who was at Gyeonseong-am in Deokseung Mountain. This legend helped me understand my mother's coldness. The person whose vocation lies in ascetic practice must be strong enough to reject his own flesh and blood. For that reason, I had a special attachment to Goya-san. Each time I came and went from Goya-san, I reflected on Mother, and on the futility and vanity of life, and the meaninglessness of either love or hate. I usually went to Goya-san on Saturday afternoon and returned on Sunday afternoon. One Sunday, I decided to return in the morning, in order to visit the old gentleman in Hashimoto City on the way.

His house was huge, and one could see that he was the richest man in town. Usually, Japanese houses have no gate, but just an entrance door; one had to pass through three gates to get to that house. When I rang, the door was opened by a beautiful girl about twenty-three or twenty-four years old. She was dressed in cheerful garb, and held a pair of electric pruning shears; I took her to be a helper in the garden. She looked at me searchingly, and asked, "Who are you and where did you come from?"

"I am Kim Seolcheon, and I come from Osaka. Is Mr. Sato at home?"

"Oh, you are here to see my father."

"Is he home?"

"Yes. Please come in."

She stepped aside and lowered her eyes. Then she looked at me again. My eyes met hers, and both pairs of eyes sparkled. At that moment, my heart lurched in my chest. She was tall for a Japanese woman, and her skin was as white and beautiful as a pearl. Her eyes were deep as a lake, and the pupils were like moonlight on the water. I viewed her with a feeling of rapture, and I asked myself whether it was indeed possible for such a beautiful woman to exist in this world. I had never seen such a beautiful a woman in Japan. There are many kinds of beauty in the world, but the woman whose beauty is as fresh as a flower blooming after the rain is fascinating. While I was tempted to clip that rose and keep it for myself alone, I knew I could control that kind of desire. Still, I was not made of wood or stone, and I could not ignore that beauty.

The rich man in Hashimoto spent his leisure time at home on Sunday afternoon, and he greeted me happily. He introduced me to his family. I greeted his wife, who had probably been as beautiful as their daughter when she was young, and the daughter whom I had met at the door. She told me her name with a smile.

"I am Gaiko.

"I am happy to meet you. I am Kim Seolcheon." We shook hands. Then Mr. Sato said, "I have the good fortune to be wealthy, but I haven't had the luck to have many children. I don't have a son, I have only that one." He looked fondly at his daughter.

"She just graduated this year from Hagamoro Women's College, where her uncle is president." The daughter of my friend, Mr. Sato, also attended that school. That meant that two cousins had graduated from their uncle's college. As we talked, I looked out the window. The garden was huge, with many decorative trees, and grass as smooth as a carpet. I also saw many servants, who prepared good food under the direction of Mrs. Sato, and even though I had just dropped in, I was provided with a delicious meal. After eating, while we were drinking tea, Mr. Sato asked me, "I understand that you won the Asahi award."

"Yes."

"What sort of work got you that award?"

"The title is *Jiha samchunchuk.* As you can tell from the title, I drew coal miners working in the pit."

"I heard that you major in Oriental Art?"

"Yes. I use the materials of oriental art, but I experiment with unique and special techniques in my work."

"Do you think one of your pieces would look right in my house?"

"Well.... if you want, I will make you one as a gift."

"I don't want a gift. I am asking because I want to buy one from you."

I returned to Osaka very pleased at having gotten a commission for a piece of artwork, and I again visited the Hashimoto house after I completed the painting. I went, not on my way home, but on the way to Goya Mountain. This time, too, Gaiko met me at the door. She had graduated from college, and now she was learning how to run a household. Gaiko was very glad to see me. My Korean name, Seolcheon, is Yukimura in Japanese.

"I felt something good would happen today, and here you are!"

"Thank you for your good words."

We conversed while she ushered me into the house.

"It is strange, even though I have seen you only once before, Mr. Yukimura, I feel as though I know you well. Perhaps me met in a previous life?"

"Who knows?...."

Mr. Sato was at home, and greeted me warmly. The whole family was entranced when they saw my painting. Mr. Sato nodded and said, "No wonder you earned the Asahi award. You really are an excellent painter."

"Thank you." Gaiko asked her father, "I would like to learn the principles of oriental art from Mr. Yukimura. Would that be all right with you?"

"You have to ask Mr. Yukimura first, not me." As soon as her father had spoken, Gaiko turned to me.

"Please, teach me. I'll visit you so you can give me a lesson. If you don't want to, I'll just visit with my cousin. Is that OK?" Her father said,

"Hey, if you want to be a student you don't know how to ask. That girl just doesn't know how to behave!"

Gaiko had been raised as a spoiled only child, and tended to tease to get what she wanted, but, to me, that appeared as an attractive winsomeness. I was already tutoring Mr. Sato's daughter on the days I didn't go to Goya Mountain, so I thought it would be a good arrangement to teach the two cousins together.

"Miss Gaiko, if you really want to learn, come to Osaka on Monday, Wednesday and Friday evenings."

"Wow! Wonderful!" She jumped up. Mr. Sato gave me a lot of money for the painting, and for lessons for Miss Gaiko. I had intended to make a gift of the painting, but he insisted that I take the money.

Miss Gaiko came to her uncle's home every Monday, Wednesday and Friday to learn painting from me. I did my best to teach her and her cousin. For the first subject to paint, I used the orchid. Then, Mr. Sato's daughter started coming home late one evening a week, and missing her lesson. I thought that she was doing it on purpose to give Miss Gaiko and me time alone together. Usually, Miss Gaiko came early, cleaned my studio and put flowers in a vase before I got home from school, and I started feeling an unwelcome obligation to her. Of course, that doesn't mean I didn't like her. She was truly beautiful. She seemed to be of higher status than everyone else, while actually she was very understanding, as well as being beautiful and witty. But, I had determined that I was going to marry a Korean woman. As soon as I finished the Buddhist art program, I planned to travel to Korea by any means that I could locate. If either Dr. Seo's daughter or the girl in Gimcheon hadn't married, I would marry her. If both of them were gone, my next choice was Kim Cheongin. That was my plan, so it was natural to feel somewhat burdened by Gaiko. On the days that Mr. Sato's daughter didn't come, Gaiko's outfits were especially gorgeous. I tried to approach the matter rationally, but I could not overcome my youth. Her curvy bosom made me dizzy whenever I looked at her, and her legs below her short skirts shone like ivory. I couldn't catch my breath. When we were alone together, even her voice touched me.

"Oh, let's have tea before we start." I tried to avoid Gaiko's eyes, and said,

"Hurry up with that." Gaiko held my teacup out to me, and when I reached for it and our hands touched, I felt an electric charge throughout my body. Gaiko was at a loss for words, and lowered her head, but I could see that she was blushing. When Gaiko was in my studio, Mr. Sato and his wife never dropped in. The whole family was conspiring to bring Gaiko and me together. Occasionally, Gaiko did not return home after our lesson, but stayed late in the studio and slept in her cousin's room. While she never put it into words, her eyes, her expression, her body, all showed her love for me. I was overwhelmed by the presence of such a beautiful and loving woman. My reason struggled with my growing desire to become involved with her. If I chose Gaiko, it would be against my vow not to marry a Japanese woman. It would represent, as well, a betrayal of the Korean woman and of Kim Cheongin, who were waiting for me. My reason told me constantly not to do it, but my emotion overcame my reason. This was the first time that my desire for love could not be controlled by my will.

Suicide of Gaiko

I went to Goya-san from Saturday afternoon to Sunday afternoon, and, except for three or four hours of sleep, I spent all of that time reflecting on the five human desires, and the seven human passions. I recited the Sutra of Banyasimgyung, thinking that meeting Gaiko was Buddha's testing of my faith. When I saw her, I could not find any fault in her. If I betrayed the promise between human beings, and followed my desire, surely I would be headed for Hell. I was not afraid of that fate so much, as of causing a lifetime of sorrow for others, that I could never make right. I had always tried to live as though my life were an examination, and I wanted to submit a perfect answer sheet. But, since I met Gaiko, my rational purpose was often threatened. I greatly desired to make a mistake then atone for it, but I still struggled to reach a solution. To calm myself, I had gone to Goya Mountain, and recited the Sutra again and again and again. After a time, I reached a certain moment of freedom from worldly thoughts, and I felt my fever gradually draining away.

After Goya Mountain, I felt a change in my body. When Gaiko, in my studio, gazed at me, or even touched me, there was not the electricity I had experienced before. I was conscious of this change even though I did not make a purposeful effort to distance myself from her. I felt that Buddha's power was with me, and that I had finally emerged from the prison of my own desires. The perception of my new serenity seemed to cause Gaiko to become even more passionate. One evening, after the lesson, she said, "Mr. Yukimura, can you walk with me to the bus stop?" For a moment I considered refusing, but then thought came that she might not be safe alone in the night, so we went out together. Until then, she had been accompanied to the bus stop by her cousin, or else she had gone home earlier. There was no one on the street. As soon as we reached the sidewalk, she took my arm, and she stopped in a dark spot far from a street light. We didn't say anything. She stepped in front of me, openly indicating that she wanted me to hold her. I stepped back until I was up against a wall. She came close, and collapsed against me. I was going to push her away, but then I held her gently, as if I was holding my sister.

"Gaiko!"

"Do not say anything now."

She came even closer, and I could feel that she was trembling. She held up her face for me to kiss. I turned my head, and gently pushed her away. Maybe Gaiko, like Miss Hong, realized that she could not catch me by herself, and she told her father that she wanted to marry me. Mr. Sato came to see me.

"My daughter loves you, Mr. Yukimura, and wants to marry you. I don't have any objection to that, but, as you know, I am the richest person in Hashimoto, and I do not have an heir, except for my daughter. Could you be the kind of son-in-law to me that would be like a son and live with me?"

I looked down. If I inherited his wealth, I would not have to worry about money for the rest of my life, and could concentrate on my painting; but, would I not have lost my integrity?

"Thank you for your offer. But I am the only son to my parents, and could not be the son-in-law you wish for."

Mr. Sato clearly understood my position, but he requested, before he left, that I think it over. When he got home, he advised Gaiko to forget about me, as he was determined to have the kind of a son-in-law he had described, and he stopped her painting lessons. It seemed to me that he simply couldn't stand to see his daughter suffer.

Two weeks later, Gaiko came to see me. I realized that I now had to make my position clear to her.

"Miss Gaiko, your father wants me to be a son-in-law in your family, but I can't do that."

"If you didn't have to join our family, but, rather, I came to you, would it be OK then?"

"Miss Gaiko, you cannot go against the will of your parents."

"It would be nice if I could please my parents, but, even if it is against my father's wishes, I want to be your wife."

"Oh, that would be impossible."

"Why? You don't like me?"

"It's not that I don't like you, but I cannot accept you."

"May I ask you the reason?"

"I already have a girlfriend."

She kept gazing at me with her sad eyes. At that moment, I experienced a sharp pain under my ribs. Her eyes glistened with tears, and, the next moment the tears began flowing as though a dam had broken. She sobbed sorrowfully for a long time, and then she left. It seemed as though she had given up, but she left me feeling very uncomfortable. I felt that I had lost something very precious, and all night I could see her sad face before me. I felt as though I was mired in a swamp.

Fortunately, about that time, I received a letter from my Japanese teacher, Ito Shinsui, from Tokyo. He sternly asked, "Did you graduate from the National Art School in order to become a school teacher?" He offered to help me with my living expenses if I would come to Tokyo, and threatened to disown me if I failed to do so. I felt a surge of affection for my teacher. I re-read the letter, and thought that it would perhaps be better for Gaiko, too, if I left Osaka. It was vacation time, so I was able to go to Tokyo to see my teacher.

"Thank you for your letter."

"So, have you resigned from school?"

"No. It was vacation so I came to see you."

"If you stay in Osaka, you will be isolated from the art world. If you come here, I can find you a position in a college in Tokyo, so please come."

"If I left Osaka, I would have to give up my studies at the Buddhist college at Goya Mountain. I want to come back to Tokyo, but after I finish my course there."

"You have studied enough, you stubborn boy!"

I stayed at Ito Shinsui's home for my whole vacation, and then returned to Osaka. When I opened the door of Mr. Sato's home, his wife met me, and, as soon as she saw me, she started to weep.

"What has happened?"

"Gaiko…." I was struck by an dark premonition, and Mrs. Sato spoke the words which were like a blow to me:

"She is dead."

"Oh, no! What happened?"

"After you had been gone a week, she hanged herself. I was going to let you know, but it was such bad news that I didn't."

Gaiko had not merely made a suicidal gesture like that of Miss Hong. I felt a strong guilt that a beautiful life had ended because of me. I was flooded with sorrow, but tried to maintain my composure, and went to my room, where I threw myself down and wept silently for a long time.

The next day I visited Mr. Sato in Hashimoto. It had been more than two weeks since Gaiko died, but her parents were still in a state of utter devastation. I told them how guilty I felt, and asked their forgiveness.

"Gaiko died because of me."

"It was not you, Yukimura. If I had not insisted on having my way about the issue of the son-in-law, and just allowed her to marry, she would still be alive…."

He couldn't finish, and began to sob. Mr. Sato thought that her death was because of him. He didn't know that I had told her that I already had a girlfriend. Well, it wouldn't bring her back to life to argue with him about whose fault it was. I stood in front of the memorial shrine they had arranged for her, and burned incense. Her face in the picture was flickering in front of me. Life is vain, indeed.I could not imagine that such a beautiful person would abandon her life that readily. But, if that was her fate, what can we do? I murmured *Na mu gwan se eum bo sal,* and I confessed my sins to myself. If she had met some other man, how happy she could have been.... *Na mu gwan se eum bo sal.* I touched my aching chest, and prayed for her heavenly bliss. I left the Sato house, and went directly to Goya-san. I prayed for Gaiko's soul over and over every day until the beginning of school.

The Korean War

On June 25, 1950, war broke out in Korea. The news came to Osaka right away. I worried that I might lose my mother and siblings in Gimcheon. I wanted to go to Korea immediately, but there was neither an airplane nor a ship that could take me there. There was not even an illegal passage to be found. The only thing I could do was to pay attention to the news. When I learned the war was over, I was determined to go to Korea by any means. Even then, it was not easy to find a way. After exploring many possibilities with no success, I obtained a position as a special reporter for a newspaper. By this means, I hoped to get to Korea. There were no diplomatic relations between the two countries, and neither civilians nor government officers were allowed to come and go from one place to the other. Visiting as a reporter was not legal, either, but I obtained permission from the Korean side, and so was able to go to Seoul.

For the first time, on this trip, I took an eighteen passenger jet plane into the airport. The plane flew into Yeouido Airport. After I cleared customs, I found one person waiting for me in the waiting room. He was from the Korean Intelligence Office, and he provided a car for my transportation. He assumed that I was Japanese, and asked me in Japanese where I was going. I answered in Korean,

"I am going to Waryong-dong."

"How is it that you speak Korean so well?"

"I learned."

"As you know, you are visiting illegally here, so you can't be out of Seoul. While you are here, one of our men will be keeping an eye on you. Don't feel bad—just help us."

"I understand. But, one thing, I have to get to Gimcheon. Please help me with this."

"I'll think about it."

I had finally gotten to Korea, where I had longed to be for so many years, and I was being treated like a foreigner. I couldn't roam around freely, as I wished to do, but was bound by many limitations. When the car arrived at the center of

Seoul, I could see a great deal of war damage. Seoul was in far worse shape than Tokyo had been at the end of WWII. The buildings were burned, and the Pagoda Park entrance to Waryong-dong was a mess. Idang Father was surprised and happy at my unexpected arrival.

"How is it possible that you are here?"

"Are you doing OK?"

"Our family took refuge in a shelter, and I heard that Ilyeop at Gyeongseong-am is also OK."

"Well, that is one good thing among all of the bad." I imparted to him all that had happened to me.

"Dr. Seo Jepil went back to America. He waited for you until the last minute, then he and his daughter both went back. You missed out on a good opportunity." When I heard that Miss Seo had returned to America, I felt a bit of regret, but also some relief. The intelligence agents who were supervising me gave me only one chance to visit outside of Seoul. I had heard from Idang Father that my mother in Gyeonseong-am was safe, so I decided to go to Gimcheon. When I got to Gimcheon, I was very devastated: the home in Seongnae-dong was completely gone. It reminded me of Mr. Araki's home following the war. I looked for members of the family, but there was no way to find them. The house of the girl who may have been waiting for me had also disappeared. I assumed that no one had survived. I was deeply grieved at my failure to return sooner. Probably, Mother and my brother and sisters didn't make it to a refugee shelter; if I had been there, I might have been able to do something. I recalled what Songja had said:

"Brother, if you go to Japan, I feel that I will never see you again."

Hot tears ran down my cheeks. Seu-nim Tanong, of Jikji-sa, had also passed away, and I saw no Seu-nims there whom I knew. I could stay in Korea fourteen days. As my departure day approached, Idang said,

"If you go back, it might be ten or twenty years before we see you again."

"It won't be that long. I am sure that there will soon be diplomatic relations between Korea and Japan."

"You are my son. Once I had said that you are my son, it meant that you are my son until we die. Whenever you want to come back, come back. I know you have the ability to become the best artist in Korea, and I will give you my support; don't worry about that."

I left the house only reluctantly. At the end of the sidewalk I looked back and saw Father and Mother watching me and waving goodbye. I ended the Korea trip which I had wanted so much, and returned to Osaka, but my mind held heavy thoughts that made me sad. Suddenly, I wanted to see my mother in Gyeonseong-am, as well as my father in Germany. I was saddened at the loss of my family in Gimcheon.

To calm my mind, I decided to take a trip, and, in March, 1953, I traveled to the western area of Japan. I took a bus from Osaka to Okayama, and from there a boat to Tokushima in Sikoku. Sikoku is a huge island, and is Japan's holy land, containing many temples. The high priest, Gobo, in the Kuga Era, made Goya Mountain a holy place, and his disciples developed Sikoku as a sacred land. They built eighty-eight temples. Tour groups were divided into those who had the time to visit all eighty eight, and those who toured only forty-eight. Japanese visitors who wished to pray for the dead, ensure their attainment of paradise, and those who were praying for the granting of a wish, would also be successful. Most of those making the pilgrimage were those who had lost a loved one, or who were starting a new business, or old people who prayed for their own entry into paradise.

Between Okayama and Sikoku was a group of small islands called Sedonaikai, strewn across the ocean like a handful of beans. It reminded me of island groupings in the ocean south of Korea.

When I arrived at Tokushima, I decided to make the forty-eight temple pilgrimage. All of the pilgrims were required to don white attire and carry long staffs. As we completed the tour of each temple, the white garment was stamped with a red stamp, and by the end of the pilgrimage it was almost completely covered with the colorful markings. In each temple, I blessed my dead ones, and sketched, as well as observing the architecture and Buddhist paintings. Every temple was the size of the famous temples of Korea, so you can imagine what a huge complex was the whole. The temples lined every hill and valley, and important points of the area. The disciples of Seu-nim Gobo built the temples to glorify Buddhism, but nowadays it represents a popular tourist attraction. The area was filled with an ocean of people, and I heard that it was that way every day of the year. One of Japan's three famous parks was in Sikoku, called Dakamas Ritsurin. The lake there looked like a pool of blue paint, and was surrounded by pine trees hundreds of years old. It seemed to me to be paradise on earth. It was warm there all year long, like Hawaii, and was a natural tourist spot.

After my pilgrimage, I was finally able to find some peace within myself, and I returned to Osaka by way of Kyushu in June, after an absence of three months.

Marriage

As soon as I arrived in Osaka, I met with Kim Cheongin. She asked me,

"Is your mind more settled now?"

"Sort of...."

"Good!"

"We.... let's get married." I saw tears in her eyes.

"No more postponing?"

"Of course not."

But, our wedding plans did not go smoothly. When Miss Hong heard the news, she attempted suicide again, but this time she did not wake up. I was stupefied by my responsibility for two women's deaths. Even now, I cannot forget that. One of the reasons I became a monk was in order to lead their spirits into Heaven.

I had no family with whom to discuss the marriage, and Cheongin's family had returned to Korea, so it was a matter for just the two of us to decide.

"Just come with yourself alone. We will start with empty hands and go from there."

We married on July 1, 1953, in a temple in Kishiwada, officiated by a temple officer. The guests were Mr. And Mrs. Sato and their daughter, my student. I wanted to invite Kim Chango and Miss Yu, but then all of the teachers knew about it anyway. I wanted to have a quiet wedding because of the suicides. A big wedding doesn't guarantee happiness. We went on a honeymoon trip to Tomogashima, in Wakayama-ken. It resembled Jeju Island in Korea, both in size and in being the site of a volcano. From Osaka Harbor to Tomokashima took seven hours by boat. We got a bungalow there, where we spent our first night. The ocean was clean, and the waves were crested with white foam. We held hands and walked on the beach, where she collected shells. For a few days it was like a dream.

When we returned to Osaka, Mrs. Sato had rented a room for us, as I had asked her to do. She gave us pots and pans, and food enough for a few days. Mr. and Mrs. Sato were like parents who launched us on our family life. As a couple, we went to the market and bought two soup bowls, two rice bowls, two spoons and two sets of chopsticks. We were like children playing house.

My wife was so frugal that she bought one green onion and half a radish, but she made delicious soup, and served wine at the table. She had lived so long in Japan that she had learned the thriftiness of Japanese housewives, and, being from Jeju, she had the legendary energy of the women from there. She came to me with only one suitcase, but she made me happier and more comfortable that one who brought a huge dowry.

After we had been married for two months, Master Shinsui increased the pressure on me to come to Tokyo. In Osaka we only went to ball games and movies, and drew and painted, so we packed all of our belongings up, and moved to Tokyo. Leaving Osaka, where I had spent the golden period of my youth, caused me some regrets. There was love and loss, great happiness and severe pain, so maybe these memories would not fade.

We heard the news in Tokyo that Kim Chango and Miss Yu married. That fall, diplomatic relations were established between Japan and Korea, and they moved back to Busan, which was Kim Chango's home. After that, we had no more contact with them.

4

The Light and Shadow of Tokyo

Asaoka Yumegi

Master Ito Shinsui had prepared for my coming by finding a home for us in Toshima-ku Otsuka; that room was small, having only three tatami floor mats. In addition, he found me a job at Rikkyo College at Ikebukuro in Toshima-ku. I went to Rikkyo College three times a week to teach oriental painting. The other days I went to Mr. Ito's house at Yamanouchi in Gamakura City to draw and paint. Ito Shinsui was considered the best in Japan at portraying beautiful women, just as Idang Kim Eunho was considered best in Korea at that specialty. I had met Mr. Ito during my junior year at the University, and had become his student. He seldom asked students to mix his colors, only the ones who were especially skillful at color combination. The student he asked to do that chore must be his favorite, and that student was me. He taught only me how to make the colors look antique. This is not a technique found in Western painting, and requires a special feeling for color. These colors look ancient, and, in addition, they do not fade. I was indebted to Mr. Ito for that knowledge. I used that technique in my best known works, *Bangasayusang, and Budongmyungwang.*

Mr. Ito Shinsui had a pretty seventeen-year-old daughter, Asaoka Yumegi. She called me "brother," and was cheerful and open-hearted because she received so much love from her father. The problem was that she was too brash. Yumegi often smoked in front of her father. That was allowed in Japan, but, because I was accustomed to the Korean ways, I had a hard time accepting her behavior. Also, her clothes were too grown-up for a girl her age.

One day, I asked her to think about whether smoking in front of adults and dressing as she did were really proper, but, my words went in one ear and out the other. I was irritated, but I didn't push it, and just returned home. The next time I went to my teacher's home, she had on an outfit that showed her whole leg. I couldn't help frowning, but was determined not to say anything. Then, she took a cigarette from her case, and, holding it in her long-nailed fingers, put it between her lips, and lit it. I couldn't stand it, and went directly to her, and slapped her face hard. I took her cigarette from her and put it in the ashtray. Yumegi began shouting, "Why did you hit me?"

"I told you not to smoke in front of adults, and you did."

"You say that because you are nothing but a Korean, and that's the way you are thinking!"

"You think I slapped you because of a Korean custom, but that's not it. In Japan, children are expected to obey their elders, and I clearly told you not to smoke in front of adults, and to wear appropriate clothing."

Yumegi started to cry big tears, and left the studio after giving me a dirty look. Mr. Ito, who was in the room, looked on, mouth agape. All at once I realized that I had actually hit his beloved daughter.

"I'm sorry for creating a scene." Mr. Ito slowly shook his head.

"No. You did well. I knew she was spoiled, but I couldn't scold her because I love her too much. If you can fix her bad habits, I would be much relieved." I was relieved, too. My teacher didn't see me as having done something bad, but rather as setting a good example. From then on, he seemed to trust me more.

"Is it really true that children don't smoke in front of their parents in Korea?"

"Yes. Not only parents, but in front of all adults, even their older siblings."

"Well, that shows training in good manners in Korea that we could learn from."

In Japan, it was common for children to smoke in front of their elders; even a daughter-in-law might light up in front of her husband's parents. Maybe they accepted Western culture faster than did Korea.

My slapping Yumegi was an important incident in the family, and even the other students gossiped about it. They speculated that she was trying to get me into trouble so that, perhaps, I eventually wouldn't be able to come to that home, but, they were mistaken. Within a few days, Yumegi came to me privately, and said,

"Brother, I was wrong. I'll try not to do it any more."

"Are you holding a grudge against me?"

"No. I know you were trying to help me."

"Thank you for your understanding. I just hope for you to grow up as a well mannered girl. If you act rudely, people will point their finger at you, and not only you, at your parents, too." Yumegi's attitude was completely different after that. She didn't smoke in the studio anymore, and her clothing was more appropriate for a young girl. And, instead of shunning me, she was friendlier, and listened to what I had to say. She treated me like a real big brother, and discussed her future with me at times.

After her graduation from high school, Yumegi went to the Takarazuka Drama School. After graduating, she joined the Shogiku Movie Company, and worked as an actress. Her beauty and talent led to great success. In Japan, everyone knows the name of Asaoka Yumegi. She acts in movies and in traditional musical dramas. When she has a recital, she often sends a ticket to me. Her name appears in newspaper entertainment columns with regularity. One day I visited her backstage, and she greeted me with a smile.

"Brother, is this costume too revealing?"

"It's proper for the actress, just not for the high school student...."

"You were the first one ever to slap me, and no one has done so since. So—you are the only one, and I'll never forget it."

As she said, no one would dare to hit that famous actress! Whenever I think about my Tokyo life, she comes first to my mind. Maybe I still feel a little guilty for that slap. In any case, I didn't hesitate to endanger my relationship with my teacher in order to do the right thing, and that thought, too, is a part of my Tokyo memories.

Japan/Korea Friendship

In the late fall of 1953, a Korean man called me. He had a letter of introduction given to him by Idang. His name was Kim Uhyeon, and he was a pastor working for the YMCA. At that time, while diplomatic relations between Japan and Korea were not yet on a normal basis, there was a Korean consulate in Tokyo, and there was a special correspondent there from a Korean newspaper. Reverend Kim Uhyeon and I, along with the first consul-general, Kim Yongju, the first trade representative, Jin Hakmun, and the special correspondent, Kim Ulhwan, started a friendship group made up of Koreans living in Japan.

Before liberation, the Japanese Prime Minister was Suzuki Gandaro, and his son, Suzuki Hazimae, was a friend of mine. Suzuki Hazimae worked for the Judiciary Department, and his job was to control the entry of foreigners into Japan. He helped many Korean students, and Koreans who had entered the country illegally, to attain legal status, and he was known as a friend of Koreans. He was also private secretary to the emperor, Showa. I told him about our friendship group, and he suggested that we include in the organization Japanese citizens who were interested in reconciliation. Representatives of both countries agreed to the idea,and Suzuki Hazimae became the group's first president. Our meeting was observed by such individuals as Tanaka, who later became Prime Minister, and such politicians as Hukuda, Miki, and Gishi. Representatives of the Jimin political party frequently attended. They were pursuing the normalization of diplomatic relations, and supporters of extending highways, subway systems, and technologies in Korea were all involved in these meetings. The organization was not simply focused on the issue of friendship, but was also interested in attaining political goals in both countries.

There were also artists and other cultural figures in the group, because we thought that the sharing of cultural activities was the quickest path to understanding between peoples.

I represented painting, and the writers, Yuasa Gachie, and Miss Kamada were also in the group. We published a periodical called *Friendship,* of which Miss Kamada was the head, and Yuasa and I were editors. My job was to design the covers and provide illustrations.

Members of the Korean lobby and Japanese politicians provided a good foundation for the development of friendship and cooperation. There was networking with various groups and with Japanese political figures. One group was Shimiyoshi kumi; others were Yamaguchi kumi, and Kato kumi, the head of which was a Korean, who was rumored to be an associate of President Park. That Korean leader had the nickname "Tiger of Ginza," and there was a story about how he got that name. Once, while Japan was under the American Army of Occupation, a GI tried to force himself on a Japanese woman in broad daylight. This was observed by this man, Jeongmachi, who intervened and killed the GI. He was arrested by the American army, but released by General MacArthur, who said that he acted justly in defense of the woman. After that, he became a hero and the "Tiger of Ginza." His father was the wealthy head of a steel company, and was also a member of the friendship organization.

I attended the meetings a few times, and tried to figure out the best way for me to contribute to the group. I was close to both Japan and Korea, and could be a good mediator. I was especially close to Mr. Fukuda because he happened to be an alumnus of my father's school, and was my mentor. While the group provided fellowship, because there were so many politicians involved, it also had the ability to guide the direction of Japanese politics. The members were often aware of secrets before they appeared in the newspaper.

The Japanese members and observers, though concerned about Korea, had as a primary interest the furthering the welfare of Japan. Whenever there was a conflict between the interests of the two countries, I tried to help them appreciate the Korean point of view. My efforts may not have completely affected their policy, but I am sure I contributed to their understanding of the Korean nation and people.

As a painter, my primary interest was in art, but, because I had the blood of both parents, I also wished for the two nations to attain the status of good neighbors. I had the idea of arranging an art exhibition to showcase the work of artists from both countries as a way of promoting understanding and friendship.

Three Works of Art

The complicated year of 1953 was past, and we faced the year 1954. I was busy completing an art work commissioned by the Nichigetsu Group, an organization composed of artists with which Ito Shinsui was involved, along with artists Gomada Gibo, Teragima Shimei, Machayashi Geigetsu and Yano Gyoson. My painting, which was to be submitted to a competition, was titled *Nostalgia.* The title reflects the painting's subject, which was homesickness. My body might have been in Japan, but, when I closed my eyes, I saw the mountains of Korea: Mother in Gyeonseong-am in Deokseung-san, Jikji-sa, embraced by the Hwangak-san, and the pine-wind sound around Dasol-sa—these, and the thirty-eighth parallel were always in my brain. From Gaeseong past the thirty-eighth parallel, and into North Korea—I remembered Sincheon, and wondered if my parents there, and my brothers and sisters, had perished because they had been landlords, and so regarded as wicked persons. The thirty-eighth parallel was now a symbol to me of Korea itself, and was as real a barrier as the Hyeonhetan Strait that divided Korea from Japan. My feeling about that imaginary barrier was expressed in *Nostalgia,* and was appreciated by the judges of the competition; I was the winner of that contest. I did another painting, a very large one, entitled *The Double Headed Drum,* for which I used as a model the dancer, Mrs. Jo Taegwon. I tried to express the beauty of a Korean woman playing the drum. I gave this work to Mr. Jin Hakmun, and he later donated it to the Korean University.

My work emphasized Korean scenery, emotion and beauty, and I believed that these Korean elements were also universal in the world. I wanted to show my own homesickness, and to impart to the Japanese the nature of true Korean beauty. The judges and my painter friends recognized my work as being, not Japanese, but as something novel. Some praised my work, but some were critical of it because it was not Japanese enough. I was the object of admiration, but also of avoidance, and I was somewhat isolated, but, I was still determined to be true to my roots. At that time, Kim Wonguk, who majored in political science at Waseda University, came to me to learn painting. He was a tall and multi-talented young man. He was dating the niece of Mr. Baecheol, who worked for the

Tiger of Ginza. When he came to me, he often complained of being physically attacked by members of the opposition parties. After Kim Wonguk graduated from Waseda, he went to America to earn a doctorate, and became a citizen there. I met him again much later, when I had an exhibition in the USA, and he was supportive of me in many ways.

The next year, 1955, I entered the Lippu competition. On that occasion, my subject was Buddhist dancers. The painting showed two dancers performing a traditional Buddhist dance. The judges admired the composition and the lively movement, as well as the clear colors, and, again, I won the highest award.

While I worked on that painting, I tried to maintain the mindset of Buddhist meditation. The subject was, at the same time, Korean and Buddhist in spirit, and I put into it all the passion of my desire to attain enlightenment, which is also a universal quality.

The Lippu was a very influential competition, and I used my name, Kim Tae-Shin, which I continued to use from then on. The judges thought they had discovered a hidden genius, and I was endeavoring to be judged as a new person.

I had received the Asahi award, and the Lippu award, so I was now recognized as an important artist in Japan. The Lippuu award came in April, and in February I had welcomed my first son, Yongil, so in two months I had received two important blessings.

In June, my uncle in Yamaguchi-ken transferred to my name about 40 acres of land to congratulate me on my son. I first refused the gift, as I wanted no part of the Oda inheritance, but he insisted, and, thinking about my newborn son, I finally accepted.

Nostalgia, Double Headed Drum and *Buddhist Dancers* not only made me famous, but they were also demonstrations of my artistic technique. I tried to make fully apparent my Korean influences, and then to elevate the work to a universal level. I put a lot of effort into deciding upon a subject, then executed the work employing experimental techniques, a method of working I have continued to utilize.

Gift from Mother

I must talk a bit more about Jin Hakmun, the journalist, who became the first head of the Trade Commission, providing a bridge between Korea and Japan in regard to imports and exports. He was married to the second daughter of Soma, the president of the Shinjuku Nakamuraya Cake Company. Soma's first daughter was married to Jangarubuz, who at that time was a political exile in Japan, and who later became Prime Minister of India. So, the first daughter became a prime minister's wife, and the second daughter met Jin Hakmun when he rented a room from the Somas.

Soma helped many Koreans who were affiliated with the opposition activist Kim Okgyun. He gave some of them jobs with his company, and so can be viewed as strongly pro-Korean. Jin Hakmun was a brilliant man, and, after he became Mr. Soma's son-in-law, traveled frequently between Korea and Japan, contributing greatly to the development of international friendship. He was acquainted with my mother in Gyeonseong-am, and when he returned to Japan from Korea in 1955, he brought to me from my mother a gift of Korean ginseng and dried seaweed.

"Your mother smiled with pride when I told her that you were a famous artist in Japan."

"Is she well?"

"She's OK, but she said that she was going to have cataract surgery."

"Is it serious?"

"You don't have to worry. Cataract surgery is not a problem even in Korea."

Jin Hakmun told me not to worry, but my heart lurched in my chest. In those days, it was not easy to obtain permission to travel between Korea and Japan. I thought about going to Korea by illegal means, or even going there to live permanently, but decided to work a while longer in Japan. It had been ten years since I last saw my mother. I had visited with her briefly after my escape from North Korea, but hadn't seen her since. Mother had always been uncomfortable seeing me, and I had matured enough not to want to cause her that distress, but I regretted now that I hadn't made the trip to visit her when I had last been in Korea, right after the war. I didn't eat the ginseng and seaweed, and when I looked at it I saw my mother's face. One day I heard the news that Mr. Dokudomi Soho had been hospitalized. He was an old friend of my grandfather, Oda Hosaku, and was a writer, and the first publisher of the Gyeongseong daily newspaper. In addition, he was a friend and an advisor to the Showa Emperor. I didn't know his exact age, but believed him to be close to one hundred years old. He knew my mother, Seu-nim Ilyeop, so when I visited him in the hospital I brought the Korean ginseng and seaweed my mother had sent to me.

Mr. Dokudomi was in bed, but recognized me, and was glad to see me. We talked about my grandfather's passing.

"Your grandfather died without suffering, and the day of the funeral was clear and beautiful. I hope I die like him. Oda Hosaku.... he was a nice man, but he made a mistake. His mistake was not allowing the marriage of your father and mother. Ilyeop was a genius who could have been his daughter-in-law, and he could not recognize that. What does it matter if we are Japanese or Korean? All human beings are the same. Nationalism, the worship of the emperor—that is only wasted emotion."

"..."

"Your grandfather was filled with regret about that matter at the end of his life. Before he closed his eyes, I know he left a lot of his wealth to you...." I had assumed, when my first son, Yongil, was born, that my uncle had given me forty acres as a gift.

"Yes, I received it."

"And, your grandfather had asked me many times to help you, but I haven't done anything for you. Even though I'm in bed, if I say something in Japan people pay attention. So—please tell me what I could do for you."

"I don't need any help. Please don't worry about me. Just get well and get out of the hospital."

"You are the son of a prominent family. I know you can stand alone, and also that you can easily get help from others. Your family is full of pride; that was always the problem."

He turned his head, seeming to be unhappy that I had refused his offer. As a matter of fact, I had lived up to that time in a single rented room, but I needed nothing more. I earned enough money to live by lecturing in college, and the demand for my paintings was increasing, so the price was going up. I had saved enough money to lease a whole house, but my wife was thrifty and never complained, and I could use the studio facilities at the college as well as Ito Shinsui's big studio, so one room was sufficient. My position in the art community was getting stronger.

In the spring of 1956, I received an offer to become a member of the Creative Arts Association, and to become a judge of art competitions. There were three categories represented in the Creative Arts Association: Western Art, Dyeing, and Oriental Art. There was no Japanese art category, but they were trying to develop one, with a judge, to promote the growth of painting in Japan, and they selected me. However, because I was a Korean, there was a good deal of dissension about my appointment. When I formally accepted, I emphasized that there were no national boundaries in art:

"One of our goals is to express beauty with our brush, and when one becomes a painter his dream is to be recognized at an international level. By the expression of universal emotions, transcending the limitations of national cultural pride, one best fulfills the artistic responsibility. Through art, the human family is united in sympathy and understanding. In these times, that is our obligation and our goal.

"Western artists can utilize the techniques of Japanese art, and Japanese artists can work in the Western style, or that of Korea. It is a mistake to consider the worth of a painting by taking into account the nationality of the artist. There should be no borders, no restrictions on the artistic spirit. If Japan continues to consider only its own artistic style worthwhile, Japanese art will soon become isolated in the world."

The members applauded enthusiastically. From then until 1961, I was a judge of Japanese painting for the Creative Arts Association. Remarkable artists were identified through the process of artistic competition and judging. I was proud, as a Korean, to serve as a judge of Japanese painting. After that, and until the present time, I have been the guest artist and judge for competitions sponsored by three organizations, New Art Association, Asahi Newspaper, and Mainichi Newspaper. In addition, I am a judge/committee member for the Tokyo-Ueno Province Art International Exhibition and Exchange Program.

In the fall of 1956, a monthly magazine, *Baekyeop,* was founded by a Korean artist living in Japan. The editor-in-chief was Choe Seon, and artistic matters were handled by myself, representing Oriental Art, and Gwak Insik and Lee Uhwan specializing in Western art. Out of this grew, in 1959, an organization of Korean painters living in Japan, of which I was a board member. Lee Uhwan was the director, and Gwak Insik served as an advisor. There was already a group made up of Korean artists, Jochongryon, which was strongly pro-North Korean. Our purpose was to promote friendship among all of the Korean artists, while, at the same time, working against the Jochongryon political agenda. The dancer, Jo Taegwon, who had returned to Korea, supported the work of our group. Through the organizations, we endeavored to further the cause of reunification of the North and South, and presented art exhibitions showing paintings from both groups of artists. We were on the frontier of efforts at reconciliation.

Living in one room had become difficult, so in the fall of 1956 we leased a whole house, in the same area in which we had been living, Toshima-ku Otsuka. The owner of the house was Mr. Matsura, the head of the conglomerate of Kyushu, and he used the house as his Tokyo vacation home. The house was big, there was a huge garden for my child to play in, and I was happy to have my own studio at last. Mrs. Matsuura ran the Wakakusa nursery school, and Yongil became a student there.

Troubled Times

Everything went well. Sometimes I wondered about my mother and father, and had some guilt about my Gimcheon and Seongnae-dong families, but, other than that, I was content. Our financial condition steadily improved, and my family life was happy. In 1957, right after Christmas, I woke up late, feeling as usual. I opened the window and noticed that the garden was full of fog; I thought that odd at that time of year. I said to my wife, "I have heard that London is foggy this time of year; maybe Tokyo is like London."

She laughed and said, "This is a sunny day—what fog are you talking about?"

"Really? I can see only fog."

She didn't believe me. If what she said was true, I had a serious problem. To a painter, vision is life itself. I became so gloomy that my wife began to take seriously what I said.

"We should not wait. Let's go to the hospital right away."

Up to that moment, I hadn't appreciated the seriousness of my situation, since I had no pain, but just the foggy vision. We went to the Otsuka Province Hospital, where there was a world-famous ophthalmologist, Yamamoto Osamu. After he examined me, he asked me, "Did you drink liquor yesterday?"

I tried to recall what I had done the day before. I had lectured at Rikkyo College, and then had dinner with Mr. Fukuda. He had not been feeling well and didn't want to drink, so I had no alcohol either. When I got home, I had a cup of warmed rice wine. Dr. Yamamoto said, "The rice wine was the problem. Methyl alcohol was found in your blood. If you drink much of it, it will rupture blood vessels in your brain, and you will die. Luckily, you took only a little, so we don't have to worry about dying, but it has paralyzed your optic nerve."

My wife squeezed my hand, and said, "The wine you drank last night…."

She was trembling and couldn't continue, and I felt chilled as well. When I got home the previous night, my wife had handed me a package that had come in the mail, and I opened it in front of her. She said, "Oh, it is rice wine. Why is there no indication of who sent it?"

"Well, it's the holiday season, and it must be from a friend or a student. I'm thirsty. Why don't you bring me a cup?"

So, she had brought me one cup of hot wine. How lucky that I had drunk only the one cup, or I might have died. Who could have tried to kill me? We were at a loss.

"We must perform surgery immediately," the doctor said.

My wife asked, "Are you sure it is the fault of that wine?"

"Yes, the methyl alcohol proves it. Do you know the brand name of the wine? You had better make a report."

My wife explained what had happened the previous day.

"Then, did you keep the packaging?"

"I threw it in the garbage this morning, and I am sure that the trash collectors have picked it up."

The doctor told us that was the only evidence, so my wife called our neighbor, only to find out that indeed it was gone.

"Even if we had the package, it could have been stamped in any post office. But, this is a criminal matter, and we must report it to the police prior to your surgery."

I was baffled about why someone would try to kill me. I believed that I had done nothing for which someone would hold a grudge against me. But, the evidence was clear that someone was trying to kill me. I looked back at my life. I had tried my best not to shirk the responsibility to survive with integrity. I had never harmed others for my own benefit. I was hesitant to make the police report, but, if I didn't, I wasn't sure what would happen to me. If there was a search for one criminal my innocent associates, who were all busy in their own lives, would be disrupted, and I might be the one to get the blame, so I shook my head.

"I would prefer to be the only victim, so let's just let it go. But, Dr. Yamamoto had a different opinion.

"Well, he didn't succeed this time, but you don't know when he might try again."

"I'll be very careful from now on."

"Who could want to do away with this nice person? Clearly, we should try to root out the evil."

"I'll try to find the culprit on my own. Is there a chance for me to recover my sight through the surgery?"

"It is a serious operation, but, if all goes well you will recover. You need to be aware that it is also possible for you to lose your vision."

A bolt from the blue! To eliminate the methyl alcohol from the optic nerve, the eyeballs had to be removed. It was a very delicate surgery. My wife was prepared for it, and, since it was a very expensive operation, Mr. Shinsui deposited a security fund. I was worried about my wife because she was pregnant, and had not only to take care of me, but of Yongil, our son. I sent an express mail to my cousin, who lived in Yamaguchi. My wife and I talked things over.

"Maybe I won't be able to see you after the operation, so I must look at your face very carefully to remember it in detail. I can see in your face that you have gone through some hard times since you met me."

"Why are you talking like that? You have to be optimistic about what is going to happen. I could go to work, if necessary—we can always get along. I'll pray to Buddha."

The surgery was done by Dr. Yamamoto. Since it was done under anesthesia, I felt no pain, but afterward my eyes were covered with Vaseline and bandages, and my head was immobilized. Everyday I was given a milk injection which was so painful that my body was covered with sweat.

Experiencing the inability to see made me realize the importance of eyesight, and I was fearful and despairing that I might be permanently blind. My younger cousin from Yamaguchi came to visit. I couldn't see, but I sensed that he was the only one in the room with me.

"Older brother, older brother!...."

He was holding my hand, and I could tell from his voice and his breathing that he was very upset.

"Calm down! What's the matter with you?"

"I know it! I know who sent the poisoned wine!" I was horrified.

"How did you come to know about that?"

I held tightly to his hand, so he couldn't pull it away.

"I have struggled with myself, but I know I must tell you...."

"Then who did it?"

"It is to the shame of our family, but it would be unfair for you not to know; so, I'm telling you, but please don't make it a criminal case."

"I understand. But, tell me quick! Who did it?"

I almost fainted in surprise when I heard the name, one that should not ever have been connected to this situation. Perhaps my wife heard what was going on, and she came in.

"I beg you, please forget it," she pleaded. "Think of it as only a bad dream."

She was telling me those things, but she was very angry.

"Even though they are greedy for their inheritance, how could they have wanted to murder an innocent person? But still, we must put it behind us." I wanted to confront that person immediately, but I was immobilized and my face was covered with bandages. Tears welled up in my unseeing eyes. When the surgeon removed my bandages, he remarked in a shocked voice that it appeared that I had cried a lot.

"I fear your operation has failed. We must perform another surgery."

The second surgery did no good, either. Cataracts were covering my pupils. I was more fearful than ever that I would become a blind man. Three months later, I had a third surgery. While I was in the hospital, many people came to see and comfort me. Every member of the Japan/Korea fellowship group visited, and my painter colleagues came to comfort me, especially Mr. Ito Shinsui, who worried as much as if he were my father.

On the day the bandages were to be removed, my fear was indescribable. In a darkened room, when the eye covering was removed, I could perceive a faint light, then, gradually, foggy objects appeared, and slowly, things became clearer.

"I can see!" I wanted to shout it out.

"Yes, your surgery has been a success. Your methyl alcohol syndrome is almost cured, so the crisis is over. I don't know how many years it will take, but you will have to have more surgeries in order to recover completely."

After the first three surgeries, I had two more. I stayed in the hospital for six months, and was in outpatient treatment for a year before I could use my eyes normally again. My wife went through her pregnancy without complaint, and took care of me very well.

My second son, Seonryang, was born on September 15, 1958, during the most difficult period of my life. When I heard the crying of the newborn baby, I shed tears of joy; not only had I recovered my eyesight, I had another son. Dr. Yamamoto advised me not to drink, and to limit my intake of meat. He told me that if I followed his advice he could guarantee me thirty years of vision, but, if not, I could have trouble again in three years. I followed his counsel, and I spent thirty years without a problem. After thirty years, I did experience trouble with my vision, and required another surgery. I still take medication, but I can draw, and I give thanks to Buddha.

Happy Days

Some time after my hospitalization, I experienced another turning point in my life. I was still under outpatient care, when, one day, I visited Master Shinsui.

"You have really had a bad time, but don't get discouraged. Just study hard."

He sat quietly for a while, then looked at me and said, "Teragima Shimei told me that he would like for you to become his adopted son."

"Adopted son?"

"Yes. He has never had a good disciple, and, he has told me how much he envies me every time he sees you. So, if it is OK with you, I have been considering sending you to him."

These two masters had studied under Gaburagi Kiyokida. Ito Shinsui was five years older than Teragima Shimei, and was like an elder brother to him. Teragima Shimei was a great artist who was active in the western area of Japan, living in the Nishinomiya district of Osaka. To send me to him as an adopted son meant that, since the two men were like brothers, the older brother was sending his disciple to the younger. I would be his student within the circle of painters. One may study with first one master then another, so what difference would it make to be like an adopted son? In Japan, there was a genealogical record within painting circles that had great bearing upon how easily one might be accepted in that world.

I heard that Korean artists often picked the teacher they needed at the time, then, after they learned all they could, criticized him behind his back. That is not the ideal way to proceed. In Japan, the acolytes were more loyal to their masters. The masters, too, cared deeply for their students, and took responsibility for helping them to succeed.

I was the adopted son of Idang, and also the disciple who inherited his painting style, but I did not know who had been Idang's master, or the one before that. In Korea, there was nothing like a genealogical record, but many are working hard to establish something of that kind.

I accepted Master Shinsui's suggestion, and the next day I went to Osaka, a familiar place where I had spent much of my youth. Master Teragima Shimei welcomed me with a big smile, and I bowed to express my status in the relationship.

"Whenever I saw you, I envied my brother. I am so glad that now you are going to be with me. Master Teragima Shimei had lost his wife when he was young, and had not remarried. He loved me like his own son, and asked me whether I wanted to be legally made a member of his family. I had already changed my name into Korean form, Kim Tae-Shin, and lived as a Korean. I did not wish to become adopted into a Japanese family.

"I'm sorry. But, even though I am not formally registered as a member of the family, I will serve you as a real son."

Teragima Shimei was always disappointed that I had not taken this action, and Ito Shinsui, even though he had sent me away, continued to be concerned about me. I had two masters who loved and supported me, my eyesight continued to improve, and I could overcome my past difficulties and concentrate on my art work.

My first solo exhibition was a few months after the birth of my second son. It was held in the Hibiya Art Gallery. It was attended by the members of the Korea/

Japan friendship group and my artist colleagues, and other friends came to offer congratulations. During the exhibition, I met two people who were unforgettable.

One was Mr. Meiya, who was an officer in the Dutch consulate in Japan. He had been on his way to the Japanese Department of Justice, and stopped in the art gallery. He was fluent in both Chinese and Japanese, and was knowledgeable about oriental art.

Mr. Meiya's Japanese home was close to the house of Mr. Shinsui in Gamakura.

Whenever painters came from the Netherlands, Mr. Meiya would introduce them to me, and I would take them to Japan's museums and art galleries. He offered me the opportunity to have an exhibition in the Netherlands, but I was so busy I couldn't do it. In 1965, he transferred to Washington in the USA. He invited me to visit him there, but I was unable to take advantage of his invitation.

The second memorable person was the first president of the Tokyo branch of the Korean foreign exchange bank, Kim Bongeun. I had a close friend in Tokyo, Jang Sejun, who was from Sincheon in Hwanghae-do. I had known him since I was a youngster, and met him again unexpectedly in Tokyo. He introduced me to Kim Bongeun, who was also from Sincheon. Kim Bongeun was older than I, and I called him Older Brother. Often, when we got together in Tokyo, we would talk about our home town, and console one another. He liked my painting and purchased one of my works. He was always supportive, and attended each of my exhibitions. Whenever I exhibited in Korea, he took care of me like a big brother would.

As I mentioned before, in 1959 we had a joint exhibit of the work of members of the Japan/Korean friendship group, and of the Jochongryon group, which was considered to be pro-North Korea. At that time, the newspapers made a big thing of the fact that artists from North and South Korea were exhibiting together. The journalists were divided in their opinions of this project: one group was extremely supportive, the other thought it was entirely too early to begin any sort of reconciliation. For my part, though I hated Communism, I recognized how unfortunate it was for one country to be divided into two. If it were only possible to exclude politics, the artists from both halves of the country could work together to narrow the gap between them. In that sense, our exhibition was very meaningful.

In 1960, I had an exhibit in the Seibu department store gallery, which was sponsored by the Japanese/Korean fellowship group as well as the Asahi and Kirin Beer Companies, and I sold sixty paintings, all I had for sale.

The same year, in October, my third and last son was born. His name was Jungbaek. Now I had three sons, and I regret to say that my wife was the one to raise them all. I was busy, not only with painting, but with meetings of various kinds. In addition, I was often away exhibiting my work in other places, so I had no time to play with my sons. My children grew up very healthy, and normal in their academic development. They are grown up now, and have their own lives.

My first son is a journalist, the second teaches western art in an art school, and the youngest works for a publishing company.

In 1961, I was invited to become of member of the New Art Association in Japan. I had been a member of the Creative Arts Association, which was active in the eastern part of Japan, while the New Art group covered the whole country.

There were about 200 members, and they were especially active in experimental techniques in art. That was an area in which I was interested, and I resigned from the Creative Arts group, accepted the invitation to join the New Art Association, and became a member of the judging committee.

That same year, I had an exhibition in the gallery of the Marue department store in Nagoya. It was sponsored by *Eastern Economics* newspaper, the Japan/Korea friendship group, and a wealthy man from Nagoya, Mr. Oyama Yogi. I sold thirty five paintings.

During the exhibition, the novelist, Yuasa Gatsue, was in Tokyo with me. At that time, I was doing the illustrations for his novel, *Gannani,* which was being serialized in the newspaper. It was about a Japanese boy, born in Seoul, who fell in love with the Korean girl, Gannani, and recounted the story of their love. That love increased over time, even though both families were against the relationship. The novel seemed to be only a love story, but was actually the strong representation of an important social issue. There had been an incident where the Japanese had nailed shut the doors of a church in which a Korean congregation was having services, and had massacred them all. This incident is described in detail in the novel. As I was drawing the illustrations, I was deeply touched by the story: it was not only I, a Korean in Japan, but also a Japanese living in Korea before liberation—both of us spent our lives in the middle of a whirlwind. I worked illustrating novels for ten years, beginning in my late thirties. In illustrating newspaper serializations, an artist was required who understood literature and could express the meaning of the story well. I got many offers from Japanese newspapers, and from Korean newspapers published in Japan as well.

Illustration is helpful for the painter as a source of steady income, but it takes up too much time.

I was well acquainted with Yuasa Gatsue, and also provided illustrations for his novel *Bul Kkot ui Gi Rok,* which means "Record of Flame," as well as for other works by him. I also illustrated novels by Jung Biseok, *The Modern Woman,* and *An Unqualified Person,* which appeared in the Dong-A newspaper. In addition, I provided illustrations for the newspaper which served Koreans residing in Japan, including for Hun's work, *Yuk Gyo,* and that of Bak Seokju, *No Bang Cho.*

In all, I did more illustrations than even I can count, but I finally stopped doing this kind of work because it required me to travel so much outside of the country.

My solo exhibition in Nagoya was very successful, and from then on I had a good relationship with Mr. Oyama Yogi, and he bought many of my paintings over the years. After that exhibition, I went with Mr. Yuasa Gacheue to a hot springs to relax.

In the garden of my house in Toshima-ku Otsuka, the lilacs had bloomed and faded and the red roses were beginning to flower. One day in June I received a very welcome telephone call from Bak Naehyeon, whose pen name was Uhyang.

She was a student of Idang, and the wife of Unbo, Kim Gichang. They were in Tokyo, having received special permission to stop over in Japan on their way home from Taiwan.

When I arrived to visit with them, there was a group of several people there, all members of the Baekyang Hoe organization, including Kim Gichang, the son of Haegang Cheonggang (Kim Yeonggi), Hyeoncho (Lee Yutae), and Sosong (Kim Jeonghyeon).

I was so happy to see them! I was especially glad to see Unbo and Uhyang, who had lived in the same house with me. These were the first Korean artists to visit Tokyo after liberation.

Idang had told them that the stars of Korean art would light up the Tokyo sky. In his stutter, Unbo told me, "How … how … long it has been … Glad …" He took my hand in his own rough one, and would not let it go. Uhyang said excitedly, "We want to exhibit in Tokyo, and you must help us!"

"I'll do anything I can."

Their exhibition was held the next January in the Hibiya Gallery in the Hibiya park in Tokyo. The Japan/Korea friendship group sponsored the art show, and the Korean artists living in Japan gave their active support.

Since this was the first showing of Korean artists in Japan, it was widely reported by Japanese journalists, and there was great interest shown by various Japanese artists and collectors.

After the Tokyo exhibition, the works went to Osaka to a gallery in the Gindetsu department store. This exhibit included, not only the Korean artists, but works by me, and by my teacher, Teragima Shimei, as well as by Yano Gyoson. It was truly a Korean/Japanese exhibition.

There was a panel discussion sponsored by the Dong-A newspaper, in the Sikdowon restaurant. The Master of Ceremonies was Kim Jingeum, the editor in chief. It was not only a discussion, but also a welcoming party. This was the first exhibition in Japan after the liberation, and held a great deal of meaning in the promotion of good will and friendship between the two countries. The Japanese artists spoke about how much they had learned about Korean art. The full discussion was published in the Dong-A paper. The people who read about it in the newspaper came to see the show, making it very successful.

Uhyang passed away suddenly in Los Angeles at the peak of her artistic success. I was saddened at the loss of such an accomplished artist, and I thought about God giving such a talent, then taking it away so soon. I mourned her loss, and I was sorry for Unbo, who had lost his loving wife. His own artistic output was most stable during her lifetime. I prayed for her. If I go to Heaven, I will laugh with them about the fight they had in Osaka.

When the Baekyang Hoe members left for home, they told me that they would offer strong support if I wanted to exhibit in Korea. I was feeling much nostalgia for Korea, and longed to go there.

Later, the president of the Yeongnam daily newspaper, Kim Namjung, asked me to arrange an exhibition of the works of his wife, Cheon Gyeongja, in Tokyo. I introduced him to Master Ito Shinsui, and we organized the exhibition. It was very successful, and Cheon Gyeongja became widely known as an artist.

Perhaps I would have to postpone a permanent move to Korea, but I was very eager to mount an exhibition there. While I was enthusiastically preparing for it, Ryu Shinnosuke doused the idea with cold water. He was a Korean immigrant who had become a citizen of Japan, and was a famous movie director working for the Doei Movie Company. He was a member of the Japan/Korea Fellowship Group, and of Baekyeop. He went to Seoul to attend an Asian movie competition, and met with me upon his return to Japan.

"So, has Korea changed a lot?"

"In a sense. It has progressed, but it is not a good place to live."

When he got to Korea, he was held by the Korean secret service, and subjected to severe questioning: Why did you marry a Japanese woman? Why did you become a Japanese citizen? Why did you participate with Jochongryon against Korea?

"They really gave me a hard time. They could not imprison me, because I was a Japanese citizen, but when I think about the harassment, I have to grit my teeth. Mr. Kim, never go back to Korea!"

"Why do you say that?"

"They asked me about you in some detail. They think you are a communist who helps the Jochongryon."

Had the combined North/South art exhibition which had included the Jochongryon caused the problem? When I thought about communism my jaw would clench; and they actually considered me a communist? Something was very, very wrong. I could not believe what Ryu Shinnosuke was telling me, but then I received a letter from Idang Father saying, "It is known that you belong to the Jochongryon, so I was questioned by intelligence officers. They think that I am related to you, so it would be better if you did not plan to come to Korea for a while." Finally, I realized the problem was not a minor one. Ryu Shinnosuke thought that someone had covertly informed the secret service that I was a member of the Jochongryon. It must have been someone who was overly critical of the North/South cooperative exhibit. Why had they treated me in that way? I could never return to Korea, and my heart would always ache.

My thirties had been filled with hard work and much success, but they ended with tears.

5

Ommani Banmeheum

The Ashes of Flaming Youth

In 1962, Mr. Jin Hakmun brought me a book from Korea. The title was *Ashes of Flaming Youth,* and the author was Kim Ilyeop. My mother's picture was on the back of the book, and when I saw it I was elated. I hugged the book to my chest as though it were my mother herself.

"Oh, Mother has published a book!"

"I thought you would like a copy. It has become so popular that it is a best seller."

"Is it a well-written book?"

"Not only is the style excellent, but the content is very interesting. Recently, the wife of the famous novelist Lee Gwangsu, Heo Yeongsuk, sued the publisher on the grounds that the book ruined her reputation."

In order to sell more copies, the publisher had advertised that the book was a memoir by Kim Ilyeop, the former lover of Lee Gwangsu. Later, I learned the real story from Seu-nim Beobseong, who was next in position to my mother at Seon-graam. After we had become acquainted, I referred to Seu-nim Beobseong as my sister. It was believed that Mother had written *Ashes of Flaming Youth* in Seongra-am in Seongbuk-dong, but she had actually written it in Sudeok-sa.

When the publisher had promoted the book by saying that Ilyeop was Lee Gwangsu's lover, his wife came immediately to Seongra-am. "How could you do such a thing!" Mother answered with a smile,

"We both know it is not true. Why are you so upset?"

"Because they are putting out false information which defames me, and I am very angry."

"The publisher wants to make some money. Just let it be. What does it matter now whether I was his lover or not? If you want me to clarify the situation, I can do that."

"I am not a spiritual person. If someone harms me for their own advantage, I can't just let it go."

When Seu-nim Beobseong told me this story I realized what a generous spirit my mother had. The problem of materiality, I thought, is that we make errors of the physical body by being inexperienced or too influenced by others. The more important thing is not the physical but the spiritual sphere, and Mother knew that, and was proclaiming it.

After I read the book, I was sure that Mother had no intimate relationship with Lee Gwangsu. In that memoir, there was no mention of my father, and I wondered why. Was it because he was a Japanese? In addition, there was no mention of me, her only child. By reading the book over and over, I tried to figure out why that should be.

According to the book, and also from the memory of others, before she met my father, my mother had once become deeply involved with a man in Tokyo, whom she referred to as "R." He was a married man, but Mother didn't know that, and they became very close. When they realized they could not be together, they attempted suicide, but it was not successful. After that, she returned to Korea, and there met "B." He had lost his parents and had been raised by his aunt. He was a participant in the Independence Movement of 1919. After that, he went to study in a foreign country, receiving a doctorate, then returned to Korea. One day, he abruptly broke off the relationship with my mother, and left. I could read her disappointment in her writing:

"We make our own world. If it is very quiet, that is because of our own stillness; if there is movement, it is through our own activity. I hear your footsteps, but you are not coming; I found you, and my heart jumped, but it was someone else—you were not there. My heart was mistaken, and my tears were angry."

I discovered that the "B" who was so missed by my mother later became a high priest, and I wondered whether it was through his influence that Mother eventually became a monk. From her writing, I tended to think so: "God soothed me with love, and taught me serenity. I became a real human being, and, thus, I came to Buddhism."

It seemed to me that Mother had an affair with one of the teachers in Boseong High School, who was a monk, and I could guess the anguish which she had endured. I'm sure that she was trying to overcome the guilt she suffered over abandoning her child by throwing herself into that situation. Recently, I found a writing which she had published in 1927, when she was thirty-one, which proved the truth of my suppositions. The title was "The Child Who Comes Only in

Dreams." In that essay, Mother described a child who appeared every night to disturb her:

"Each dream has a different setting for a pathetic story. I do not know if it is a boy or a girl, nor can I even picture the face clearly, but in every dream the lovely child is three or four years old, and walks and comprehends extremely well. In every dream, the child arouses in me such feelings of love that I am overwhelmed. What could be the relationship of that child to me?"

As a woman, she had been very unlucky, learning from failure, and from trial and error. At that point in her life she could have fallen into moral ruin, or become suicidal, but instead she chose a path of spiritual emancipation.

In that cultural era many women, in search of equality and liberation, became attracted to the idea of free love, and complicated their lives beyond repair. Examples of well educated women to whom this happened were Yun Simdeok and Na Hyeseok, and Kim Myeongsun. These women remained trapped in that circumstance, but my mother was able to escape into the world of ascetic spiritualism.

Mother shaved her head with heroic determination, and was forced to look upon me as a "Rahula." I had been very angry with my mother earlier, but, as an adult, I could perceive the process by which she had been forced to abandon her own small ego in order to find her bigger self. She had caused me much pain, but she had passed on to me her artistic talents.

Mother remembered the moment in which she was called to Buddhism: "Perhaps, Buddha experienced joy upon rejecting the life of the palace for that of meditation, and I felt some of that joy, myself, when I discovered the path to Buddhism. I had recognized that I could never render important service in this world, and that I was a being totally alone, insignificant within the masses of humanity. It would be scarcely noticed if I were to vanish from the crowd. At that moment, there appeared a wonderful boy who declared his love for me, but I could not allow myself to be moved. This was so because I felt that I had found my own place in the world, into which no one else could enter. When I arrived at the mountain, I felt myself welcomed by the mountain and the trees."

That mountain of which she wrote had been Deokseung-san, where Sudeoksa was located. Seu-nim Mangong was there. She told him that she was desperately looking for the right way to live, and begged him to allow her to learn the Buddhist path to enlightenment.

Seu-nim Mangong told her, "I heard that you are a fine poet, but that your poems are like the singing of a bird. When one becomes a human being, the poems become those of a human being. I understand how difficult it is to make changes. Could you bear to forsake writing and reading in order to learn? If a bowl is filled to the brim with something, it is impossible to add anything new."

Mother told him that she had come with an empty mind. For eighteen years after that, Mother did not read or write, but simply endeavored, from two in the morning to eleven at night, to attain the Buddhist way of understanding.

She asked, "Who are you and who is Buddha? We are all the same. Why should it not be me who finds enlightenment?" That unyielding spirit spurred her to hard work over many, many years, and she learned that attaining enlightenment is far from easy.

It is ironic, but, to become a virgin, to become human, to attain awakening, is a long, long process. I understood now that Mother did not abandon me for a man, but rather to begin that difficult journey.

Remembering Seu-nim Mangong

The great Seu-nim Mangong had been my mother's teacher, and was to me a kind, loving and benevolent grandfather. I had visited him in Deokseung-san on my way to join the army. Through my mother's book, I learned that he passed away in October of the year of liberation. He had prepared for his death beginning in the spring of that year, saying that, "This world no longer needs my Buddhist knowledge, and I must step back…."

One day, Mangong had brought to Gyeonseong-am a Korean man's ragged coat. He asked that it be mended and altered to fit his body. "The monk, who takes a vow of poverty, should dress for his memorial service in a ragged coat….

By October, the harvest will be finished, and people will have more time, and not be so inconvenienced by a mourning period. That would make me feel better."

One clear and quiet October morning he inhaled deeply, then took off his body like he was changing clothes. That was as my mother witnessed it.

Like changing clothes, his spirit emerged from his body and ascended to the sky. That kind of death was only possible for Seu-nim Mangong:

"Before I die, I have to open the way for Buddha's followers and believers to go…. If you keep seeking and seeking, you will find the path…. If I could show the way by pulling and digging…. But our communion is stained by its contact with the world, and I couldn't do it, even with your help; all that is left is to cry together.

"How sad it is! We live almost 100 years, and still our happiness or unhappiness remains a problem, so how could we ever come understand the reality of eternal life?"

In Korea, Buddhism had gone to sleep, and Mangong had endeavored to shake it up and return it to the honored traditions, and, in that way, was the father of modern Buddhism.

Whenever I think of him, I remember that winter, when I had become a human icicle, and Mangong warmed me inside his clothes, like a baby kangaroo. It was very uncomfortable, but very warm. Always, when I visited Deokseung-san, he would slip me an envelope of money. He was more a grandfather to me than the great, gray monk. When I visit Korea, I go to Deokseung-san and pray silently in front of his memorial stone.

My Masterpiece

I was good friends with Suzuki Senbatsu, a candidate for congress from the Japanese Liberal Democratic Party.

"Can you help me with my election campaign?"

"How could I help you?"

"Draw a few portraits of me, about the size of a door."

So I drew some huge portraits of him. He displayed the portraits at the department store he owned, and in the party office, and he won the election. After his election, he gave me a piece of mountain land. That mountain was about an hour's distance from Ikebukuro, and there was an American army base in the area. It was a very quiet place.

I went there with my wife. I wanted to build a country home there, with my own art studio, but my wife didn't like it because of the isolation, so we returned the property to Mr. Suzuki. He gave me cash for the portraits instead of a mountain. Not long afterwards, that mountain became a housing development for the wealthy, and was worth millions; I lost my chance to become a rich man. Not everybody is blessed with a talent for wealth.

In 1964, I was invited to exhibit my work at the cultural center of the Korean embassy. This time, too, I received the support of the members of the Korea/Japan friendship group. In 1965, I was invited to prepare a picture of a beautiful woman to submit to a nationwide competition for portraits of beauty. I was one of only twelve artists invited to take part, and I chose to paint a Gungnyo, a lady in-waiting to Korean royalty. The lady was holding an incense burner, and represented a court figure from the Joseon period. The critics admired the typically Korean artistic effects, and the picture was purchased by the leader of the Japan/Korea fellowship group, Mr. Sujuki Hajime. The twelve competing artists were the finest in Japan, and I was honored to be a member of their group, with my teachers Ito Shinsui and Teragima Shimei. When the painting received good reviews and sold quickly, I did another Gungnyo, of bigger size.

In that same year, Unjeong, Kim Jongpil, came to Tokyo to attend an anti-communist organization meeting. The director of the Korean Cultural Center in Japan, Mr. Jo, called me. "Mr. Kim, may I buy a painting from you that typifies Korean art?"

"Where do you want to use it?"

"Mr. Kim Jongpil wants to donate it to UNESCO."

"I have one. I don't know if you would like it or not, but I have one."

"Then, could you bring that painting to the Cultural Center?"

I went to the Cultural Center with the Gungnyo. The director introduced me to Mr. Kim Jongpil, and he nodded his head when he saw my painting. He decided to donate the painting to UNESCO in Japan, in the city of Hakone. After the transaction was completed, we had a meal together, and conversed mostly about paintings. Before we parted, I told him my situation: "I am not a communist, and I have no relationship with Jochongryon, and I can't understand who could have sent an anonymous letter to the Korean government accusing me of being a member of that group."

"Are you saying that they have labeled you as a member of Jochongryon?"

"Yes. I have always tried to work for Korea, and have never become a naturalized citizen of Japan. I have continued to use my Korean name. But still they do not trust me, and that is driving me crazy."

"There must be some misunderstanding."

"I wanted to hold an exhibit in Korea, but I was warned that going there would cause me serious trouble."

"Well, I'll be your personal reference."

Kim Jongpil told me that, if I wanted to hold an exhibition in Korea, to let him know in advance. Since he gave me hope that I might be able to go to Korea, I was able to produce many paintings.

In 1966, I had a solo exhibition in the Gindetsu department store gallery in Osaka. My colleagues from the Baekdu Institute, the Gumgang school, the parents of students, and my now grown-up students all came, making it very crowded. All thirty paintings which were in the show were sold, indicating how popular it was. Mr. Oyama Yogi from Nagoya bought five pieces. After that, every year until 1973, I had solo exhibitions, alternating between Tokyo and Osaka.

I built my house in 1967. I bought land at Nishioizumi in Nerima-ku, and deigned and built a two-story home. On the first floor were a kitchen, master bedroom, living room, home bar and bathroom. The second floor consisted of my art studio and bedroom, and two bedrooms for the children. When my three sons were at home, I thought the place was too small, but now, when two of them are married and gone, it seems a little too big. The cost was six million yen, but now it may be worth a thousand times more. Real estate prices in Japan have sky-rocketed since the house was built.

Between the exhibits in Tokyo and Osaka, and many meetings, I kept very busy throughout the 1960s. In 1969, I promoted the Organization for the Five Basic Principles of Art, and that changed my life.

The five principles were Earth, Water, Fire, Wind and Space. My wish was to contribute to a peaceful universe. Our purpose was, by re-orienting Japanese art, to let a fresh breeze blow through the art world.

The founding members of the group were Ito Dane, Akaba Toshiko, Ida Ichiho, and me. At the start, there were fifteen members, but, by combining the group with the New Arts Organization, the membership soon increased to sixty. Our project of holding competitions to discover gifted beginners was financed through public subscription. Winners of the competitions were sponsored by the group as they studied to become professional artists.

The first competition took place in October, 1969, and was held in the cultural center of the Korean embassy. Being the first, the competition was covered with interest by all of the news organizations. In March, 1970, we held the second competition in the Ueno Art Gallery, and in April the works were displayed in a gallery in Ginza, and after that, at Gohu, Osaka, Nagoya, and the cultural center in Tokyo. We had the competition and five exhibitions in the same year. We soon had the reputation of being the most active of all art organizations.

How I was an Undutiful Son

Nineteen-seventy was a very busy year, and 1971 was equally so. Besides the competition and displays, I had many other activities I felt required to participate in, so the green summer slipped by in a haze, and I was surprised to find fall had come. One day in late autumn, I received a call from Jin Hakmun, who had just returned from Korea.

When I reached the place we were to meet, I found him sitting in a corner chair.

"It has been a long time. Will you join me in a drink?"

"I stopped drinking after my eye surgery, but I can have a glass or two with you. Jin Hakmun and I went together to a bar, and I could sense something had happened to him, since his expression was so dark, but I never dreamed that it had anything to do with me. After a drink or two, he said, "Have you heard anything from Korea?"

"No, not at all."

"Don't you think this would be a good time to visit there?"

I explained to him about my problem with the anonymous letter connecting me with Jochongryon, and about Mr. Kim Jonpil, and how I had wanted to go to Seoul, but was deterred by the letter from Idang, telling me it was too soon to do so.

"You should have come sooner…."

"Why?"

"Don't be shocked…. Seu-nim Ilyeob has passed away."

I felt dizzy, as though I had been struck a blow to the back of the head. My mother had passed away! Somehow, I had never considered her dying. I shook with the impact of that shocking news. Though I had only had one drink, the bar had become very fuzzy.

"I'm sure it is a shock to you, but we all have to go. She lived to be seventy-six, so she had a long life."

"When did it happen?"

"Last January 28, the second day of the lunar new year, so her memorial day will be New Year's day."

Mother had not wanted to be a bother to others, and, when she knew it was time for her to go, like Seu-nim Mangong, she had chosen the day. Since her memorial day is New Year's, no extra feast foods would ever have to be prepared.

"On February 1, the funeral service for Buddhist monks was held, supported by the Buddhist organization, and at one o'clock on that day her cremation took place." That story was already half a year old, and I was only now hearing about it. Of course, there was no one who could have contacted me from the temple, but Idang Father could surely have written me a letter, and I felt resentful about that. As a son, I had no opportunity to be good to my parents, but I could at least have been with my mother at the last. How could I ever make up for that?

"I thought of letting you know, but, even if you had come to the funeral, you could not have participated in the religious ceremony anyway, so I did not contact you."

"Even so, I could have watched, and I wouldn't have such a burden to carry."

"I know your heart is aching, but what can we do? We must endure it."

I felt like getting drunk, crying and beating my breast, but I controlled the impulse. The next day I went to a temple near Tokyo. I bowed down in front of a figure of Buddha, and I cried and prayed about my mother's death. I should have gone to see her while she was still alive!

Mother, even though you didn't wish to acknowledge me, I was still your son, and I failed in my responsibility to warm you in your old age! My heart ached. I burned incense before Buddha many, many times, but I couldn't console myself.

When I got home, my wife brought my dinner table, but I couldn't even pick up a spoon, and asked her to take it away. I couldn't swallow food, but my mouth was so dry I drank a bowl of water. My wife was concerned about my change of mood.

"Honey, did something happen? Are you sick?"

"Nothing. I don't want to talk right now. Please leave me alone."

I ignored my wife, and went alone to my studio. I didn't want to ask for comfort from my wife by telling her about my mother's death. I couldn't shake my feelings of guilt. Even though the room was getting dark, I didn't want to turn on the light. The first time I went to see my mother, when I was a middle school student, in my high school uniform, and finally as a college student—these scenes passed through my mind like a movie or a magic lantern show. I called to my mother in a low voice:

"Mother, how could you leave me without seeing me one more time? Did you think so little of me? How could you close your eyes?" Hot tears flowed down my cheeks. My worried wife came into the room.

"What's wrong, my dear? I feel bad that you cannot share the reason for your unhappiness with me."

"My mother in Korea.... she passed away."

My wife closed her eyes, then approached me quietly, and embraced me. I fell into her arms and sobbed.

"I wanted to see her one more time."

"Who was the person who reported that you were a member of the Jochongryon?"

My wife had always wanted to visit my mother while she was alive. If I had not had the problem about the Jochongryon, I would not ever have been too busy to visit Korea. My hatred for whoever it might have been who had informed on me flooded my mind.

"Even though it's too late for your mother, why don't you make a visit to Korea?"

"That's what I'm thinking, too."

"Although I didn't know my mother-in-law, she was the grandmother of our children. Let us go to the temple tomorrow to worship, and to honor her."

The next day, I went to the temple with my wife and children. We brought flowers, burned incense, and prayed for my mother's speedy entry into paradise.

Far, Far Away to Home

If I hadn't been able to go to Korea, I don't think I could have accomplished anything, I bought a ticket, but it was not a simple thing because there was no guarantee that I would be allowed to return. I visited Mr. Jo, the head of the Korean Cultural Center in Japan, and asked him straightforwardly, "Mr. Jo, do you believe that I am a member of the Jochongryon?"

"What are you talking about?"

"In Korea, I have heard, they look at me as being anti-Korean."

"Who could be a better patriot than you? You have always made an effort to do what was good for Korea."

"I don't think I have done very much as a patriot, but at least I have never been a spy or secret agent against Korea. By the way, I have to make a trip to Korea. Would you provide a reference for me?"

"What can I do to help you?"

"When Mr. Kim Jongpil came to Japan, he told me that he would help me when I decided to make the trip. Could you contact him for me so that I can get back home safely?"

I had several exhibits in the cultural center gallery, and knew Mr. Jo well, and he knew I was not a member of the Jochongryon. He contacted Korea, and, after a wait of two months, we were informed that I had received permission to make the trip.

"Mr. Kim Jongpil promised me that he would be your reference, and that the matter had been cleared up, so that you will not be followed by a secret service agent when you visit Korea."

I expressed my appreciation that Mr. Kim Jongpil had kept his promise. In January, 1972, I was finally able to board an airplane to Korea. After about a two hour flight, the plane landed at Gimpo Airport; it hadn't taken long at all to cross the Sea of Japan. My last visit had been in 1952, right after the end of the war, exactly twenty years earlier. When I stepped onto Korean soil, tears ran down my cheeks. I don't know where the tears came from, perhaps from my growing excitement.

When I pushed open the gate, Idang Father came out of the house in great surprise.

"How could you have come here so suddenly?"

"I came to visit."

Because Idang had been approached so many times by secret agents seeking information about me, he could hardly believe that I was really there. After we had greeted one another, he expressed the fear that I might not be safe staying there at home, and asked me to follow him.

We went to the nearby Undang Hotel which was run by the Korean musician Park Gwihwi. Idang spoke to him discreetly, and he guided us to a very private room. Idang Father asked to see my passport. Even though he saw the stamps authorizing me to enter Korea, he couldn't believe it, and asked me, "Is it true that you are a member of Jochongryon? You must tell me the truth, so that I'll know what to do."

I could scarcely believe that he was asking me such a thing, and I realized how one misunderstanding leads to another, and finally to distrust.

"Father, as you know, I almost died because of the communists. How could I possibly work for them?"

"Communist shot their own parents and sisters and brothers. They are not human beings. I didn't believe that you could belong to that group, but I was interrogated about you so many times...."

"You don't have to worry. That was a false accusation by someone who was trying to get me killed. But now the truth is known, and that made it possible for me to come to Korea."

I reassured Idang carefully that Mr. Kim Jongpil had provided a reference for me, and that I was not guilty of doing anything against the interests of Korea. Then Idang felt comfortable, and asked me to return home with him. There was much I had to do, including visiting Sudeok-sa, and I felt that might be difficult if I was staying at his house, so I insisted on remaining at the hotel.

"Then, sleep there, and come home for meals."

Then Idang father called in Mr. Park. "This is my son. While he is here, please take care of him well."

Mr. Park looked puzzled. "Why do you want to make your son stay in a hotel?"

"He has lived in Japan for a long time, and thinks that a hotel would be more comfortable for him."

Since then, whenever I have visited Seoul, I have stayed in the Undang Hotel. Mr. Park has always treated me like family. Idang always paid the hotel bills because, he said, if he didn't, he would feel like a bad parent abandoning his son. The next day, I went to Waryong-dong, and the family talked for a long time, sharing our stories. Mother was getting old. Father introduced me to his secretary, Lee Sanggyu, and told me, while I was visiting in Seoul, to get any help I needed from him.

At Mother's Gravestone

After three days, I went to the Seoul station and took the train to Sapgyo. I sat beside the window of that diesel train and thought nostalgically about the slow old steam engines. There was now a bus to Sudeok-sa from the Sapgyo station, but I took a taxi anyhow. The road was unpaved, and the taxi bumped along, but I arrived at the gate in style. I walked past the Buddha rock, and went up the rocky path to Gyeonseong-am. It had been twenty years, but little had changed. Three steps along, the twenty-five foot tall stone statue of Buddha looked at me with a kindly smile. I climbed steadily, and got to the tower memorializing Mangong, which, I realized, had been erected to his memory by his disciples after his death. I bowed by head in prayer in front of it, and recalled his benevolent, grandfatherly face. I increased my pace to Gyeonseong-am, but was stopped in my tracks. There was nothing there now but a vegetable garden. I remembered the time I had knocked at the door, covered with snow and pacing back and forth waiting for my mother. I walked back down the path to Jeonghye-sa. There I met a Seu-nim in the garden.

"What happened to Gyeonseong-am?"

"Gyeonseong-am was moved nearer to Sudeok-sa."

"Is that so? So, did Seu-nim Ilyeop pass away at the new Gyeonseong-am?"

"No, she spent her last year at Hwanhi-dae. The new Gyeonseong-am is not like the old one. Now it is a modern two-story building, called Deokseung Chongrim, and all female monks go there for their training."

"Thank you. I understand now. Do you know whether an old monk, Byeokcho, is still here?"

"Yes, but he is away at this time."

"Then, how about Seu-nim Wondam....?"

"Seu-nim Wondam is the head monk of that big temple. Why don't you go there?"

I bowed, then walked past the stone tower, and out of the Jonghye-sa grounds.

As I walked down, I felt as though Mother was calling me, but it was only the sound of the wind blowing through bare branches. It was the same wind that had fooled me when I was in middle school. When I visited as a youngster, and had not wanted to leave, I would be tantalized by what I thought was her voice, but when I looked back no one would be there; I was still tantalized. Mother had been cold as ice to me. How could she have been so severe? There was a point where my love for her blended into hatred. I was walking down the path, past the places where years before I had run with tears streaming down my cheeks. Maybe, despite her coldness and reserve, she had held some love for me. She had been a sincere person, so, maybe the reason she had distanced herself from me wasn't because she considered me bothersome. Maybe she was wanting to make me strong and mentally independent. Maybe she had wanted me to be the kind of heroic man who could live successfully in the world, even without a mother.

As the wind sounds met my ears, I released the resentment toward my mother which had lived within my heart for so long. It was as though a dam had burst, and the yearning for my mother, now unmixed with hatred, overwhelmed me. This was the road on which my mother so often had walked while she was alive. I felt that there were places there which had been touched by my mother, and I couldn't hurry by. I finally arrived at the big temple, but there was no Seu-nim Wondam, and no Seu-nim Suyeob there, and I knew no one else.

I went to Hwanhi-dae, where my mother had stayed. I was sure that there was a place there where her portrait was displayed as a memorial, but I did not wish go there and divulge that I was Ilyeop's son, so I had to direct my thoughts and prayers to that place from afar:

"Mother, your son Tae-Shin, has come. Now, I am not Song Yeongeop, I am not Oda Masao, I am not Kim Seolcheon. Now, I am Kim Tae-Shin, who is an important artist in Japan. I didn't visit you while you were alive, so my heart is aching. Please listen to my sad, repentant cry. You pushed me away harshly, and concentrated on your own enlightenment, and I thought you would live a hundred years. How could you not call me even once before you died?

"I married a woman who was lonely like me, and I have three sons. My wife is generous and good-natured, and my children are doing well. I believe this is because you have prayed for us. Now, I am over forty, and, as your son, I want to reflect credit on your name, so I will do my best in my work.

"Mother, you have passed away, but I am sure that you have attained eternal life. If time allows, I will come back again; and, if you have something you wanted to do but were unable to accomplish, I will do it for you. Stay well, and I will return."

I stepped backward, unable to make myself turn away from Hwanhi-dae. My mother had left me with disappointment and sadness because she had died without seeing me. I believed that Na Hyeseok would be glad to see me and greet me warmly, so I went to the Sudeok Hotel, but she was not there either. She had remained permanently in my mind as a good aunt, but in reality she had passed away even before liberation.

I had memories of my mother, of Mangong and of Na Hyeseok, and, before I left, I looked around Deokseung-san mountain where they all had lived. Winter days are very short, and the sun was already setting behind the mountain peak.

Seokbong and Sanjeong

While I was staying at the Undang Hotel, I saw many people, including Brother Unbo. I met with the people from the Baekyang organization, and with An Dongsuk, who later became the dean of the art school at Ehwa University. I met Yun Songdang, president of the Jeonbuk Daily News, Bak Seonghwan, and others as well. I had met Mr. Bak Seonghwan in Haeju, while I was being forced to do art work in North Korea after the liberation. He had risked his life to get to South Korea.

One person I met at this time was Go Bongju, whose pen name was Seokbong.

He was a calligrapher, who was a close friend of Idang. He was also a respected expert in wood cuts and lithography. He was very tall and graceful, with a long beard, and was very famous in Korea, and almost equally so in Japan.

Master Go Seokbong was born in Chungnam in 1906, and went to study in Japan 1924, at his own expense. He had been a participant in the independence movement, so a Japanese policeman always followed him. However, he was protected by his Japanese friend from Shimane, Mihara, who had introduced him to the well-known calligrapher, Master Hidai Denrai. Master Denrai recognized his genius, and provided references for him. Master Denrai was a good friend of Emperor Showa.

After his sixtieth birthday, Master Denrai refused to use any signature stamp except one carved by Seokbong. The seal belonging to the Empress Showa was also carved by Seokbong. After liberation, Seokbong returned to his hometown, Yesan, in Chungnam. Twenty years later, an exhibition of his work was held in Japan, and was completely sold out. At that time, Prime Minister Ohira requested that he carve a signature stamp for him.

Seokbong, who spoke with a provincial accent, said, "I worked day and night carving signature stamps good enough to surpass anything found in Japan, and I discovered, after a while, that Japanese people are not so bad after all, and that I could like, and learn things from them."

In Japan, there were two famous calligraphers, Guwabarana, a student of Denrai, and Yoshino, a disciple of Go Seokbong. Both of them held him in the highest regard, and both had sent gifts and letters with me to deliver in Korea when I visited there. Master Go acted as a judge of the National Exhibition for a long time, and also established an international art exchange organization. He was a board member with me of the International Line and Surface Organization.

Master Go's home in Yesan was not far from Sudeok-sa, and I later learned that Master Go and Seu-nim Mangong had been close friends. Since then, when I visit Sudeok-sa, I visit Yesan as well, and vice versa.

While I was still at the Undang Hotel, I went to the Center for the Promotion of the Cultural Arts with Lee Sanggyu, Idang's secretary. I was looking for a place in Korea where I could hold an exhibition, and wanted to get permission to hold it in their gallery the following January.

After I had been there for a while, I informed my Waryong-dong mother that I was planning to return to Japan. She gave me an elegant Korean outfit for my wife, and Korean clothes for my youngest son. My wife was delighted and grateful, and treated her gown like a precious gift. She wore it whenever we went to a meeting together.

As had been planned, I returned to Korea in January, 1973, and had my first solo exhibition there, in the cultural arts center. There were thirty-five works in the exhibit, and, as they were sold, many incidents occurred.

One day, a representative of the congressional office came to buy a landscape of Seolak-san, which was 10-ho in size. He asked me the cost, and I gave him the price per ho, as I would have done in Japan, and he didn't understand. In Korea, there was no concept of ho, at that time. At that moment, Mr. Seo Seok, whose pen name was Sanjeong, came into the exhibition hall.

He said, "We don't sell art in Korea by ho; we just say a quarter, or a half, or a whole, and sell it that way."

I explained to Mr. Seo about the size of the ho in art.

"In the Western world art is sold by size, and, since we are a part of the international art scene, we should do the same."

Two days later, the congressional representative returned, and did pay by the ho. This was the first time that art was sold in Korea using this system. After that, everyone did it, but that was not a perfect system either. In oriental art, colored painting, in the northern style, is good for selling by the ho, but works in the southern style, which includes the use of much space, and calligraphy, are better sold in the traditional way. That is my opinion.

All of the paintings were sold, and I deposited the income from the sales in a Korean bank, to use in organizing an Owon exhibition to be held the following year. Once I had a relationship with Seo Seok, he helped me whenever I came to Korea, and I would do the same for him when he came to Tokyo.

Right after the Chinese "Cultural Revolution," a Japanese art dealer went to China and bought cheaply many works of art which were slated to be burned. At that time, Seo Seok came to Tokyo, and we visited various art dealers. He was fortunate enough to find a great art work which had been done by a master in Korea. That work was worthy of being a national treasure. It had been lost for a long time, but had been treated well, and now, because Mr. Seo Seok bought it, could at last be returned to Korea. It was very lucky that Mr. Seo Seok had the knowledge to recognize the value of that work, which had traveled to China, to Japan, and now back to Korea.

Blood Will Tell

In 1974 I went to Korea for a Korea/Japan art exhibition and stayed at the Undang Hotel. Somehow, my relationship to my mother had been discovered, and a newspaper reporter came to interview me. At first, I cut him off, adamantly denying that I was the son of Ilyeop. Reporters, however, evidently sensed a good story, and they obstinately investigated my background. I concluded that I should be open about the situation, since their speculation might result in worse misunderstanding, and I decided to tell them the truth. However, I thought it would be better to consult with the Sudeok-sa monks prior to acting on my own. I went Sudeok-sa for that reason, but also with the thought of being able, perhaps, to see and pray before the portrait of my mother, which I was sure was there. I went to the big temple, first to the sanctuary, then to Wondam's office. I looked around the office, and the secretary guided me to him. We talked about old times, and exchanged our innermost thoughts. I invited Wondam to come to the exhibition in Seoul. When he arrived there, I took him to the Undang Hotel.

"As a matter of fact, I have something to discuss with you...."

"You can speak freely. Tell me what is on your mind."

"As a matter of fact, Seu-nim Ilyeob was my birth mother."

Wondam's eyes opened wide, and he said, "Brother, what was that you said?"

"I said that Seu-nim Ilyeob was my mother."

"Is that so?" His expression was skeptical, but he had seen me coming to Sudeok-sa often when I was young. "If that is true, it answers a lot of questions for me. You came to Sudeok-sa every school vacation, and one of the worshipers in the temple told me that you might be a spy for Japan. After I heard that I could never relax around you."

"So, you really thought that I might be spying for Japan?"

"Yes."

Now I understood why he had shown me so much hostility when we were young.

"I had no idea that I had aroused so much misunderstanding."

"Well, I never would have dreamed that you were the son of a Seu-nim. That's why you came to Sudeok-sa for every vacation—to see your mother."

"Only two people knew the truth. One was Mangong and the other was Seu-nim Byeokcho. Seu-nim Byeokcho could bear witness, but I don't know if he would say anything. Reporters have been bothering me, and I do not know how they could have found out about the situation."

"I think it would be better not to say anything at this time. It might be advisable first to meet with the people who were taking care of Seu-nim Ilyeob at the time of her death."

A few days later, Wondam brought two female monks to the Undang Hotel. They were Wolseong and Geongjin, who were disciples of Gyeonghi, the monk who had cared for my mother on her death bed. Wolseong had never heard that Ilyeob had a son. A short while later I went to Sudeok-sa and met with Seu-nim Gyeonghi. After we had greeted one another, she looked intensely into my face, then nodded her head.

"The blood cannot be cheated! You clearly resemble her."

We went to Jeonghye-sa to see Seu-nim Byeokcho. He recognized me, and we greeted each other, but he refused to confirm that I was the son of Seu-nim Ilyeob. He was probably trying to keep the promise to Mangong that whatever happened that secret must be kept, but neither did he say that I was *not* the son of Ilyeob. He wouldn't break his promise, but he also refused to distort the truth. Those who were there didn't hear from his lips that I was the son of the Seu-nim, but they sensed that it was the truth.

I thanked Seu-nim Gyeonghi for her service to my mother prior to her death. She had done what I should have been there to do. I called her Seu-nim Sister. Sister Gyeonghi showed me pictures of my mother's ceremonial funeral and cremation, which I could not see because my eyes were full of tears. I stayed overnight in my mother's old room.

The fountain of my tears of yearning for my mother never seemed to run dry. When I was young and went to Gyeonseong-am, my thirst for her was intense. As I grew older, the feeling ebbed, but, since her death, it seemed to have bubbled up, stronger than ever. I lay awake all night keeping watch, in hopes that her spirit might make a visit to me. From then on, I called Gyeonghi Older Sister, and Wolseong and Geongjin called me Uncle. Before I left Hwanhi-dae, I decided that I would consider myself their biological relative, and I decided as well to build a memorial tower for Ilyeob.

Before I left, Gyeonghi told me that Ilyeob had been in the hospital before she died, and that, during that time, a Japanese gentleman came to see her. Around that time, my father had visited Japan from Germany, and I met with him briefly. He had planned to go back by way of Korea. The Japanese gentleman who visited my mother before she died must have been my father.

"Father!" As I spoke that word, I felt electricity through my body; I started to cry, and had to wipe my eyes. When I thought about my father, I realized that, in truth, his fate was more pitiful than mine.

My father had lived his life for one woman only. Because of his love, he abandoned his family and his country. He went to Korea, and did many other things for her. Of course, he had guided my life, which I only found out about after the fact. When I went to Idang Father's home, that was my father's doing. I had received evidence of his love while I was growing up, but, not only did I not repay him, I never even spoke to him about it; I had been very disloyal to my father.

Seu-nim Wolseong later came to the Buddhist University in Kyoto to study. While she was there, whenever she had the chance to come to Tokyo she would call me. I treated her as my niece because she had cared for my mother, but I'm not sure she really thought of me as an uncle.

Wondam's visit to Japan

Wondam and I had known each other since boyhood, and, once we became reacquainted, we became very close. He wanted to see Japan, so I took him there after one of my trips to Korea. I took him to visit temples everywhere in Japan. While we were walking around Rikugien Garden, I asked him, "What do you think of Japan?

"Everywhere I look, the land is well conserved and taken care of. We need to develop that long vision in our country, too."

While he was in Tokyo, Wolseong and Geongjin came from Kyoto to see us. At that time, the movie star, Kim Jimi, came to Tokyo on the way back from America, and stayed in the Akasaka Hotel. She was a very sincere Buddhist believer. She invited Wondam and me to dinner at the hotel, and we spent some time together. Afterwards, Wondam said, "Brother, can you make a donation?"

"What for?...."

"There is so much to do in regard to temples."

"Oh, so you must need a lot of money. Maybe I can make it possible for you to make money, and that would be better than just a donation."

"Monks can't do business. How could I earn money?"

Wondam had gone to the temple when he was very young, and by study and hard work had become a head monk. He had a special talent at calligraphy, and I could tell that he had fully mastered that art.

"Give me a sample of your art work."

"Are you planning to sell it to make money?"

"Well, I have an idea."

I obtained one of his drawings of Buddha, and entered it into a national competition in Japan. My expectation was right. He got high marks from the judges, and an award from the cultural center which had sponsored the international competition. The next year, he received another big award, from a calligraphy competition sponsored by the Sankei Newspaper. His talent at calligraphy was that good.

Wondam was the head monk at Sudeok-sa who had asked me for a donation, but now, when I visited Sudeok-sa, he offered me pocket money.

"My work has turned into money, all because of you, Brother."

"Not because of me. You had talent, and you worked hard to polish it. That is the reason you are making money."

Temple Fund-raising Exhibition

The first article published about me as the son of Ilyeop was in the *Weekly Central Newspaper*, written by the reporter Lee Ilgu. It was an intriguing article which received a lot of attention, to the extent that the edition was sold out and a reprinting was done. After that there were many articles, including in the women's magazines, *Ju Bu Saeng Hwal*, and *Yeo Won.* Some of what was printed was what I had divulged because of being pressured by the reporters, but part was made up only of rumors. Many names, dates and locations were wrong, and my mother was described as an irresponsible, overly-liberal woman. I refused to give interviews because I didn't want to seem to be courting fame under my mother's name, but the articles continued to go on and on. In 1975, Mr. Bak Euntae, the brother-in-law of the artist Kim Okjin, was my agent in Korea, and helped me in many ways. He told me that the head monk of Seongraam, who had helped my mother while she was writing her famous book, "*The Ashes of flaming Youth*" wanted to see me, and, as it happened, I had also wanted to meet her. She was Seu-nim Beobseong. I went with Mr. Bak Euntae to Seongra-am in Seongbuk-dong. The Seu-nim greeted me warmly, and remarked about my resemblance to my mother. Seu-nim Beobseong had my mother's portrait in the registry of the temple, and had arranged a small altar for her, where I burned incense, and greeted my mother.

"While she was alive, the old Seu-nim had always wanted a place where wandering monks could lay down their knapsacks and rest. If it would it be possible for us to turn Seongra-am into that place, it would be a good memorial to the Seu-nim."

Beobseong told me that she was working to establish a training institute, and I let her know that if I could be of help I would be glad to do so. She invited me to stay at Seongra-am instead of the Undang Hotel whenever I visited Seoul. At that time, I was making plans to build a Kim Ilyeop commemoration building beside Hwanhi-dae in Sudeok-sa. I had already obtained a blueprint from the architect, Professor Jo, whom I had met through Seo Seok, but the plan for that building fell through because of the opposition of Seu-nim Byeokcho. He felt resentful that there might be a Kim Ilyeop building when there was no such building to commemorate Seu-nim Mangong.

A few years later, Seu-nim Beobseong started to raise funds to build the Seongra Monks' Institute, and I staged an exhibition to help her. I consulted with masters like Unbo, Sanjeong, Cheonggang, Cheongdang, and Okju, and they donated art works for the exhibit. The fund-raising exhibition was held in 1982 at the Korean Packaging Design Center. Other artists of unsurpassed quality also exhibited, such as Namnong, Unwon, Cheongcho and Hwadang. The next year, we had another fund-raising exhibition for the renovation of Hwanhi-dae Temple. At that time, 33 artists donated their work, and the exhibition was called "Thirtythree Oriental Artists." It was sponsored and supported by Hwanhi-dae and by the *Yeo Won* magazine. It was held at the art gallery in the Lotte Shopping Mall. The opening ceremony was arranged by Brother Unbo, Mr. Seo Seok and the actress Kim Jimi. Whenever I had a project, I was always grateful to Unbo and Sanjeong, because they were unfailingly there to help me.

Some of the exhibitors were: Gangeom, Namdong, Hwyeonso, Cheonggang, Hwadang, Hwyechon, Torim, Oksan, Baekcho, Cheongwon, Kubong, Ueun, Namgang, Soam, Sogang, Unwon, Sukdang, Simgye, Chisan, Chuli, Hwyeongjeong, Udang, Changseong, Munje, Socheon, Ilgwan, Gakpo, Ijeong, and Dongcho.

During preparation of the exhibition, I and Wolsong and Jeongjin went to Mokpo to see Namnong. When we explained the fund-raiser to him, he promised to give a work of art. Other people besides artists helped in the Hwanhi-dae fund-raising. One of these was Kim Namhyeon, who had been the vice-president of Haitai, and who now was the CEO of the Jangu Corporation. He and Sin Unwon, professor in the art school in Busan, and I went to Hwanhi-dae and slept in one room. They offered me much helpful advice.

During that time, *Yeo Won* published a six-month-long series of articles about me and my life story. Another man had come forward claiming to be the son of Ileop, and *Yeo Won* was determined to prove that I was the true son. I didn't know what stories reporters had made up about me. It was an unbelievable situation. There were many stories based on rumor or imagination, without any objective evidence.

One day, Mr. Choe Jeongyeop came to Seongra-am to see me. I had met him, probably in the Spring of 1980, in a gallery in Insa-dong. We had become close friends, and he was well aware of my situation.

"Seu-nim, now is the time to prove that you are the son of Seu-nim Ilyeop."

Many people were present at that time, and one of them, Mrs. Kim Jaewon expressed her agreement with him. There were reporters there who had written about me.

"I heard that Seu-nim Byeokcho is the only one who could confirm the story, so let's ask him for the truth."

I decided to get help from Byeokcho, and went to Sudeok-sa with Kim Inbong, reporter for *Yeo Won*, and Choe Jeongyeop, who took time off from his work. We stayed over-night at Sudeok-sa. The reporter interviewed many people, and in the morning we went to Jeonghye-sa at the top of Deokseung-san. Seu-nim Byeokcho was puzzled by the arrival of so many people to see him. I introduced the reporter to him. The Seu-nim guided us to the temple, and the reporter hurriedly asked her questions, but the monk's face remained impassive, and, from beginning to end, he gave no answer. Then Mr. Choe Jeongyeop said, "The French philosopher Bergson said that truth cannot be found through analysis, but only by intuition. What do you think about that idea, Seu-nim? You are the only person who knows about this, but shouldn't you have told the truth about it by now?" Then, the Seu-nim nodded his head and sighed deeply.

"As a matter of fact.... Seu-nim Mangong told me never to open my mouth about it."

I couldn't bear to stand there, saying nothing, so I went outside. From the top of Deokseung-san I could see all the way to the ocean, and, watching the ocean, I called to Mother, and my tears flowed down my cheeks. I wiped my eyes and composed myself, then returned to the room to talk to the Seu-nim. He was saying, "The first time, I think, I was with Seu-nim Mangong, and Seu-nim Ilyeop brought the boy to us, saying that he was her own flesh and blood. Seu-nim

Mangong, without hesitation, said then that we were the only three who were to know about this, and that I should keep the secret until death." The Seu-nim took my hand.

"So many reporters have asked me whether the story was true, and I have not said a word, but today I will tell you. Yes, it is true." I had already been aware of this, but Byeokcho's words were important because they confirmed my story.

"From then on, Seu-nim Mangong loved him dearly, perhaps because he was the son of Seu-nim Ilyeop, or perhaps because he pitied him. I still remember how he put him on his lap and rubbed his own beard against his cheek."

At once I recalled clearly the rough feeling of Mangong's face against mine, and I remembered not liking that prickly feeling very much. I continued to listen to his story. "He would say, 'Boy, don't be such a wiggle-worm.'"

Seu-nim Byeokcho remembered every detail. He knew that the first time I came there was in the late spring, and recalled the time I climbed the trail and arrivedin the middle of a winter storm, which had everyone surprised and worried. A fterhis story, we took a picture, and went back down the mountain.

All during the fund-raising exhibition for Seongra-am and Hwanhi-dae I felt no impatience or anger, and I didn't seem to tire. That was because of meeting with my past and conversing with my mother.

Because of this work, I stayed almost half a year in Korea. But then, someone wrote to my wife that I was having an affair with another woman. My wife came to Korea without telling me, and investigated the situation. Upon finding that there was no truth in the rumor, she came to see me. I don't know who could have tried to injure me by spreading an untrue story, as had also happened about belonging to the Jochongryon. I could not tell who did it, but there were many people who were closely involved with me, perhaps one who felt there was a good reason to wish me harm. When my wife arrived, it was with a regretful face, for having doubted me.

"Don't you think it is time for you to stop coming to Korea and spend your time at home?"

"I cannot do that. This is my country and that of my mother. I have to atone for my neglect of my mother. Perhaps you can't understand my point of view."

When I mentioned my mother, my wife made no more argument. I whispered, "Om Ma Ni Ban Me Hum, Om Ma Ni Ban Me Hum."

"What do you mean?"

"I said, 'Om Ma Ni Ban Me Hum.' Om refers to paradise; Ma to demons; Ni means human being; Ban means beast; Me means hungry ghost, and Hum means hell. These words are the basis of precious truths about the blessings of wisdom and goodness."

The phrase Om Ma Ni Ban Me Hum refers to the six doctrines of salvation, closing the gate on the demons of hell. If we recite these six words, we can accomplish a life of merit and virtue. I murmured the words again, for my mother, my wife, and the people I knew. My wife closed her eyes, and recited only once, "Om Ma Ni Ban Me Hum."

6

Together But Alone

Conversing with the Goddess of Mercy

After I became forty years old, although my painting and drawing still remained very important, I began thinking about other ways in which I might contribute to the welfare of others, to the Korea I loved, and to humankind as a whole. There was a dream I had first experienced after I was arrested in North Korea in the year of liberation. Many years had passed, but that dream is as fresh in my mind as one I might have had last night:

The visiting of a temple, becoming a monk, the old Seu-nim who had shorn me and asked me to come back, then the meeting with the Buddhist Goddess of Mercy—all that was as clear as a video picture in my mind. In that dream, the Goddess of Mercy had asked me to find out who I was. I didn't fully understand, but the Goddess of Mercy had said that I had accomplished my aim, and should return down the mountain.

At that moment I had no idea who I was, except that I had been born between two countries and two cultures, and that my role was to promote understanding and reconciliation between them. That was the moment that the Goddess of Mercy told me that I had attained my goal. If so, I had a job to do: perhaps I was the one who could apologize for the reckless cruelty with which Japan had treated Korea during thirty-six years of occupation.

Maybe I didn't have to think in terms of mankind as a whole; maybe I could be the one to close the breach between my two nations. Now, in 1974, I felt an urgency to put my thoughts into action.

One day, I had dinner with Mr. Jo, the head of the Korea Cultural Center. He said, "Mr. Kim, even though a long time has passed, we cannot forget our oppression by Japan, and I don't think that we should forget it."

"I agree."

"However, we cannot bear the burden of so much hatred forever. We have to get rid of it. We hate each other, but if we do not help each other, we will never be able to promote peaceful progress."

"I also agree with you about that."

"We must be the leaders toward reconciliation, understanding and help."

"...."

"To attain the kind of environment we aspire to, politicians must make some efforts, but, artists like you can be the most effective facilitators. That is my thinking, and that of the government, too."

"By means of exchange art exhibitions between the two countries, we can promote understanding, which will lead naturally to the kind of environment you are speaking of. The problem is that, even though Korean artists might want to participate, the government looks at it as a waste of foreign exchange, and is reluctant to issue passports. Still, I think that if we continue to mount good exchange exhibitions, and journalists write about it approvingly, we will get good results.

"Can you be our contact representative? If you do, I will take over the administrative side of things. I have had communication from the government that indicates we could receive help."

"That was what I had hoped for. Let's do it."

I felt encouraged by Mr. Jo's suggestion. I had been looking for a way to contribute to Korea through my work, and he had appeared with the right job at the right time. I went to Seoul to begin organizing for an Owon Japan/Korea art exhibit, and contacted the artists whom I knew. Oriental-style artists Jeonggang (Kim Yeonggi), Sukdang (Bae Jeongrye), and Hwadang (Kim Jaebae) consented to participate, as did western-style artists Bak Seonghwan and Lee Chunggeun. These artists helped organize an Owon League in Korea.

In May of 1975, we held the first art exhibit sponsored by the League in Seoul, in a gallery of the Cultural Arts Promotion Center. Japanese members were able to show their work to the art lovers of Korea. In October of that year, the work of Korean artists was exhibited in the Ueno gallery in Tokyo. During these shows, journalists wrote many positive articles, indicating that the exhibitions were promoting friendship and neighborliness between the two nations. I totally agreed with their point of view.

From then until 1986, exhibitions were held almost every year in Seoul and Tokyo, and from the capitals the exhibits toured the smaller cities.

During the Korean tour of 1976, an exhibit was held in the Maekhyang Gallery in Daegu. I had previously held a solo exhibition in Seoul where I had shown my painting *Bibogwaneum*. This work was bought by Mr. Kim Taesu, from Daegu.

"I have an import/export business, but, since I am interested in art, I would like to open a gallery. Could you give me some suggestions?"

"Art galleries don't make money. You have to think about it in terms of culture rather than profit."

"I know that is so, but I would like to make the arts available in smaller cities. That is why I want to promote this idea."

He had already bought a building, which was being renovated and decorated appropriately. The Owon exhibition in Daegu marked the opening of his gallery. At the reception in the Maekhyang Gallery, I unexpectedly met two persons. One was Juknong (Seo Donggyun), who had demonstrated to me how to draw bamboo during my visit to Master Bak Gwang, before liberation. He was the one who first introduced me to "Sa Gun Ja," recognition of the importance of the four gracious plants in oriental art. He was over eighty, but he recognized me immediately, and we embraced. I remembered one winter, when I visited him, he was drawing bamboo alone in his room. He was so poor that there was no fire, but he had the honesty and uprightness of bamboo, and when I saw him I saw the personification of dignity. I had liked him so much that I stayed with him overnight. We wore many layers of clothing, and slept close together for warmth, but it was so cold that I couldn't get to sleep. I thought I had closed my eyes only for an instant, but when I opened them it was morning, and I saw Juknong already at work, the aroma of India ink permeating the atmosphere. The window was covered with frost and the contents of the chamber pot were frozen. It was morning, but Master had not thought about making breakfast, and I thought that there was nothing to prepare. I asked him to go with me to Master Bak Gwang's for breakfast, but he refused, saying that he could not be a guest so early in the morning. That was Master Juknong, and he had lived into his eighties, long enough for us to meet again. It was an emotional meeting.

The other person I met was Mokrang (Master Choe Geunbae). I had met him previously in the home of Idang, before liberation. At that time, Mr. Mokrang had been a teacher at the cultural school in Gimcheon, and a painter whose work had been accepted for the Korean National Art Exhibition. He had often been a visitor in Idang's home, and whenever I saw him he was friendly and encouraging. He also was more than eighty years old now. I felt especially close to him because he used the technique of stone-color painting.

I learned that both of these old masters had dedicated their energies to the art education of the young, and, for that reason, had been invited to attend the gallery-opening in Daegu. We conversed all night long. Soon after our meeting, both Mokrang and Juknong passed away, within a few months of each other. I felt strongly that two pillars of the Korean art world were gone.

Seven Japanese painters, as well a more than twenty Korean members of Owon, participated in the Gwangju exhibit. Various organizations in Gwangju got together to see that the participants received good meals and other manifestations of warm hospitality. The Gwangju Cultural Broadcasting Company and the Gwangju Daily News were especially helpful in promoting the show. There was a tea room next to the exhibition hall in the middle of the cultural center of Gwangju which we patronized often several times a day. The owner was a kind and helpful woman, who was not bad looking either. One day when I was resting in my room in the Gwangju Tourist Hotel, the tea-room manager came to see me. I was surprised that she came so late at night. She was smiling brightly when she came into my room.

"Teacher, do you think that it is possible to fall in love at first sight? I think that it is possible, and I'm the one who has fallen in love with you in one glance." She asked to sleep with me with no strings attached. Although she was attractive, I shook my head. At that time I was very busy with my own exhibitions, with the exchange shows, and with fund raising for Buddhist causes that I was kept in Korea more than half of each year. I felt guilty that my wife had to be alone so much, and I was determined not to betray her by having an affair.

"Thank you, but I cannot do that. If you want to stay here, I'll find another room for myself." I picked up the phone to call the front desk, but the lady hurriedly pressed the button.

"I'll leave."

I hung up the phone and looked at her. I couldn't tell whether her expression was one of hurt feelings or unconcern.

"I might respect you or love you sincerely, so I'll go now."

The next day I went with other members to the tea room, and she looked at me flirtatiously.

"I have refused many men, but this is the first time one has turned me down. But, for some reason, I don't feel bad about it at all."

"If that is so, I feel better about it."

I had often been tempted in a similar way, not only in Gwangju but also in Seoul, but I never gave in to the temptation. Artists sometimes have a reputation or being promiscuous, and I was overly cautious not to fall into that kind of trap. Perhaps because my mother had defined free love as being a part of the identity of a modern woman, and I had experienced the result, I was more conscious of the problem than others were. I wanted to live a reverent life, and I wanted to personify the value of art in my own integrity. Some thought that traumatic experiences were necessary to the production of worthwhile art, but I never believed that. We opened touring exhibitions three times in the city of Jeonju. There was an organization there, the Seventy-seven, who loved art and supported us. In that organization were the head of the Baekje Art Gallery, Mr. Kwon, Jeong Namsu, and Master Gangam (Song Seongyong). One day we were invited by that organizationto go to the Yonggung Restaurant. The owner of that restaurant was a woman who had been taught by Master Heo Baekryeon, and was a sincere art lover. When we went there, she said,

"Today is my treat."

"How can you stay in business that way?"

"You are right. I am a business woman; I can't lose money. There is a condition: Master Kim, you have to draw a picture on my skirt."

People looked at me, so I nodded my head. She was a person of taste and elegance. Ink was prepared was by a woman helper. Then two waitresses stretched the owner's skirt out tightly. I inked my brush, and thought that, since I was receiving a meal for my trouble, I would do my best. I drew a virile Dharma on her white skirt. People applauded.

The Mokpo exhibition was organized by Master Namnong and Jo Hyoseok. Master Namnong bought a painting of a jumping eel on a dish. There was a story about that dish that the Japanese members long remembered, because that kind of dish, known as unagi in Japan, was extremely expensive there, so that almost no one could afford to eat off of one. Whenever we had a traveling exhibition, we toured the local area to see the sights, and to take time for sketching. These tours were popular with the Japanese artists while in Korea, and with the Korean artists visiting Japan. After such a trip, the Japanese artists would draw a lot of Korean scenery and show the work on exhibition, as did Korean artists with Japanese subjects.

The Seolak Mountain is one of the most famous mountains in Korea. One winter we went there to sketch, and were caught in a sudden heavy snowstorm. The wind and snow obscured the path, and we went down the mountain slipping and falling along the way. We had to return to Seoul, but there was no way to get there. At that time Mr. Jeon Duhwan was a military commander in the area, and he helped us get to Seoul by employing a military vehicle. That is one of my memories.

When we had an Owon exhibition in Japan, we invited the Korean members to famous locations there to sketch. In Darube, naked men and women can often be seen enjoying the natural hot springs. When we were in Meiken, the hot springs there were also patronized by naked men and women. On one occasion, a foreign tourist there became so absorbed in watching them, he fell from the third floor balcony.

The Owon exhibits were enlivened by so many happenings that I could scarcely report them all. There were some love stories between the Japanese and the Korean members, and, during one trip a wife at home had an affair and was divorced by her husband. These meetings continued for more than ten years, so there was time for many comical occurrences and some strange ones. Except for one or two instances, everything that happened provides me with precious and beneficent memories. To the individual participants was offered an opportunity for self-development, and progress was ongoing in the relationship between our two nations.

I was a judge as well as a member of the management team for the Owon group from its inception until its dissolution. The reason for ending the group was that it had grown so large, and the members were so many, and of such a high quality of professionalism, that the assistance of such an organization was no longer necessary. In the beginning, we all met together frequently, but, by the end, there was no Japanese member who was not busy. It was the same with the Korean members. When the group started, they depended upon it for the organization of exhibits in Japan, but later they were well able to handle that job themselves. The cultural exchange between the two countries had also blossomed, and was continuing to thrive on its own.

My personal reason for considering that it was time to dissolve the organization, was that, from the outset, I had made many sacrifices to help the group succeed, but, later it was said that I had worked for that success only in order to promote myself. In reality, if I had not devoted so much time to organizing Owon exhibitions, I could have done much more in the way of mounting large shows devoted to my own work. When I heard of the murmurings of the Korean members, who had no idea of the amount of time and money I had expended, I decided it was time to disband. In any case, I got too old to carry that burden. A few years ago, there was established the International Line and Surface Organization, and the International Art and Culture Exchange Organization, so, even without Owon, its goals were being advanced. Therefore, I brought up to the board members the matter of disbanding Owon.

We Must Go On

As I mentioned earlier, the International Line and Surface Organization worked to continue the cultural exchanges between Japan and Korea. Its parent organization was the Japan Line and Surface Art Organization, and it was established in 1983 by Dori Seishu, Sekiguchi Goyo, Gudo Ganzi, Sibazaki Sadao and Gonoki Sangyo.

The first Japanese export item was said to be the fan, but, in actuality, the large fan came to Japan by way of China and Korea, and the Japanese later developed the small fan for export. For a long time, these fans were decorated with the mountain, the river, gracious plants, calligraphy and haiku. One of the original members of the group, Sibazaki Sadao, was a famous teacher of haiku. Gadogawa Haruki, who was president of the publishing company "Gadogawa," was a famous haiku poet. Gonoki Sangyo and Gudo Ganzi were fellow alumni of mine of the Tokyo National Art School. In Japan, it was traditional for the later graduates pay respect to those who went before them, and these two people came to me for advice and asked me to become a board member for the new group. I accepted their offer, and told them,

"Do not be satisfied with having only Japanese members. Rather, include Chinese and Korean artists as well, and make it a truly international organization."

Among Korean artists, there were a few who resented me, but the majority were understanding, and I was anxious to include Korean artists in the new organization. Because of this, I was one of the founding members of the International Line and Surface Organization, and I, along with Seokbong (Go Bongju), Oksan (Kim Okjin), and Cheongdang (Kim Myeongje), became members of the board of directors.

In addition to that organization, there was a very active group devoted to the cultural exchange of art, which we established and called the International Art and Cultural Exchange Organization. Seokbong, Go Bongju, and Oksan (Kim Okjin), and I were the Korean charter members. The Japanese were Kori Seishu, Sekiguchi Goyo, and Gudo Ganzi. The first exhibition held by that group was in an art gallery in Ginza Dagagen. Since then, both countries have continued with the exhibitions.

Korean members of the International Line and Surface Art Organization suggested that we establish a group devoted solely to Korean artists, and the Korean Line and Surface Art Association was established in 1989. When an exhibition was held in Japan, Korean artists were invited to participate, and when an exhibition was held in Korea, Japanese artists were so invited. At that time, the president of the Korean organization was Mun Jangho, and the advisors were Seokbong, Oksan, Cheongdang, and me.

If one is an artist, the first rule is to work very hard on the work. A great deal of solitary effort is required to become outstanding in that field, as it is in any other, but one cannot become famous by only working alone. It is possible to become a big frog in a little pond by limiting oneself to his own country, but to expand one's horizons, one must work with others in the same field. I, alone and with others, did my best to attain the expansion of the art world.

It is possible to spend too much time on public work, thus limiting one's own horizons, and being too solitary is limiting, too; it is necessary to attain a balance. I had been concentrating too much on public work from my forties to my sixties, and I determined to spend more of my energy on my own work. Now I could trust the ambitions of the younger generation, and, if they needed advice, I could give it. As a matter of fact, I could no longer handle the organizational work to which I contributed earlier. Of course, I didn't want to be a complete outsider to public work, but my age and my concentration on my own work, left me little time to participate. I didn't announce that I was cutting off my participation completely, because I had in the back of my mind that I could still help in the field of Korean art. Later, if I felt that I had no more to contribute, I could withdraw and concentrate on my own work for the rest of my life.

Finally, I want to talk about the Korean Coloring Association and Husohoe. I am an artist working in the Oriental style, doing color painting, which is a part of Northern Art. Color painting, like the Southern Art category, is a part of the origin of Oriental Art. Since the Goguryeo, Baekje and Silla eras, color painting has been connected with Buddhist art, and was a part of the legacy of the unique and beautiful Korean culture. During the Joseon period, however, Confucianism became prominent and Buddhism was downtrodden, with the result that the stone-color art was allowed to deteriorate. Scholars began drawing the noble plants as a hobby, and the technique of India-ink painting became popular. Color painting was pushed aside by the avalanche of black and white India ink art, and the technique was almost forgotten. People came to believe that only India-ink was appropriate for oriental art, and, of course, it is an important aspect of that genre. But, India-ink cannot express the full range of natural beauty and emotion which we want art to convey. Like Western art, the northern style of art depends upon color for its effect, and, I believe, that is what is necessary for an artistic genre to become international.

Until recently, in the National Exhibition, or in other competitions, there was no one who utilized the technique of color. If someone submitted a color painting, the judges considered that it had been submitted wrongly, and should have gone to a exhibition of Western rather than Oriental art. If even the judges thought that way, you can imagine how little the ordinary person knew about color painting.

Some people considered Kim Tae-Shin's painting to be Western art, and, furthermore, some even thought of me as producing only Japanese art. People who thought that way had never been in Japan, nor had they been exposed to truly Japanese art. Either they were uninformed, or they were criticizing just for the sake of criticizing. Of course, color painting was popular in Japan, but the technique had come to them from Korea. By the Joseon period color painting had almost disappeared from Korea, but it was adopted, preserved and developed in Japan, and was shown to the Western world as a Japanese genre. People had no idea that the technique had been plundered from Korea, and considered it to be traditionally Japanese, separating it from what was recognized as Korean art. I felt sorry for those people.

I had first learned stone-color painting from Idang Father, and, in my work, I stubbornly portrayed only subjects of typically Korean natural beauty, and always saw myself as a Korean artist. I have been deeply disappointed that, in Korea, the tradition and technique of stone-color painting have been almost lost. There are no teachers to teach it, and no students wishing to learn. I have felt it to be my responsibility to preserve and extend this tradition.

A few years ago, I had an exhibition in the Daegu Gallery, where I lectured about stone-color painting. The auditorium was overflowing with the more than 300 people in attendance. I realized, then, that people were interested, but there were no available teachers. I am thinking about writing a book covering stone color painting technique. It would provide guidance for those who might want to learn the method. My wish is that the tradition of stone-color painting would have a revival in my country.

In Korea, though the prospects for color painting are barren indeed, there is a little hope for the future because of the Korean Stone Color Association. Many years ago, I had an exhibition of stone-color paintings in the Lotte Gallery. Afterwards, the Dongil Art Gallery in Los Angeles invited me to hold an exhibition there. During that exhibition, Hong Sangmun, Lee Gyegil, Yu Jieun attended with their wives, and Hong Byeonghak and I attended alone.

We went to San Diego, Mexico, Las Vegas, Yosemite and the Grand Canyon, and enjoyed sketching and conversing with each other. We decided to form a group devoted to stone-color painting. I became an advisor to the group, and Jong Byeonghak was elected president, with Hong Sangmun acting as business manager. The first exhibition was held in the Lotte Gallery, and a foreign exhibition in the embassy in Osaka.

While the technique of colored painting was sadly neglected in Korean art, the Korean female painter, Cheon Gyeongja lectured on the subject at Hongik University, and Oh Taehak taught it at Jungang University, preserving a thread of influence extending over time, and leading directly to our establishment of the Korean Coloring Association. We had to promote the development of the association actively by holding competitions and exhibitions locally, nationally and internationally.

Husohoe was an art group which had been started in January, 1936, in Idang's studio, and was made up of Idang's students and former students. Idang was considered the patriarch of modern Korean art. The name Husohoe came from the word "hoesahuso." The founding members were Kim Gichang, Jang Useong, Baek Yunmun, Han Yudong, Lee Yutae, Chang Unbong, and Jo Junghyeon, all of whom were painters. I became a member when I entered the National Art School. When I returned to Seoul as a college student, Idang gave me a Husohoe badge, and asked me to become an active member of the group. After liberation, because I had to remain in Japan, I couldn't participate in Husohoe's meetings and exhibitions, but, later, when I did travel to Korea, I was able to do so.

In February, 1979, on an especially cold Friday in Tokyo, as I came into the house out of the freezing cold, the telephone was ringing. When I picked up the phone, I heard the voice of Mr. Lee Sanggyu, Idang's secretary.

".... Don't be shocked."

"What? What has happened?"

"Master Idang has passed away."

Mr. Lee Sanggyu had told me not to be shocked, but his news struck me like a blow from an iron bar. Idang Father had died. He had been the master who taught me how to draw, as well as a father who had been generous with his love. He had been more of a protector and guardian to me than had my biological father. Although I had not been present at his death bed, I was determined to be at his funeral. The next day, I went to the embassy to get my passport. At that time, we had to obtain a passport for every trip, and Koreans living in Japan had to obtain visas. It bothered me that I had to obtain a visa even though I was a Korean national and was returning to my own country. Not only that, in order to return to Japan, I had to obtain clearance from the Japanese government before taking the trip; I was considered neither Korean nor Japanese. There was no way that I could finish the red tape in one day. That day was Saturday, the next day was Sunday, and by Monday I had used all of my connections to enable me to make the trip, and I was afraid the funeral would be over. On Tuesday, I went home. As soon as my mother saw me, she burst into tears. Around the mourning table were many mourning guests.

"We decided on a seven-day funeral in hopes that you would be able to get here."

So, luckily, I was able to attend Idang Father's funeral. He had been born in 1892 in Incheon, and had died in his eighty-seventh year, 1979. In September of that year, we erected a memorial gallery in his honor.

The grand opening of that gallery featured a posthumous exhibition of his works. The art critic, Lee Gyeongseong, praised him as follows:

"Idang, Kim Eunho, was a giant in Korean art history. He continued the development of Korean art from the Chosun period to modern times. He was personally a very successful artist, and on a larger scale, he was a leader who guided Korean art into the modern age. His was a unique personality, marked, throughout his life, by a dignity and strength of character seldom found in an artist. As an artist, he left around ten thousand works of art, which embody modern Korean art history. Even more significant, he was our best art teacher, helping to produce many capable artists."

Assuredly, Idang was an example of virtuous person and in addition, he contributed many notable works to the history of art. He trained his students by the example of his own integrity and perseverance. The Husohoe represented a gathering together of the students who had absorbed his teachings, and continued the tradition of which he was a part.

The grand opening of the gallery show-cased Idang's work. The next exhibit included the works of the Husohoe members, including Unbo, Udang, Hwadang, Sogang, Torim, Iltang, Hyechon, Hyeondang, Sudang, Sukdang, Odang, Gumchu, Hyeoncho, Yunje, Udang, Gubong, another Udang, Woljeon, Ijeong, Hyeonso, Simwon, Ugang, and Gyedang. The sudden death of Idang presented me with some problems. On an earlier trip to Korea, I had received money from Mr. Kim Taesu of Maeghyang in Daegu, and Mr. Jeong Namsu of Jeonju, to purchase some of Idang's paintings, and I had given that money to Idang. I told him that, as soon as the paintings were ready, I would deliver them to the purchasers. He had nodded his head, but provided no receipts. He passed away prior to completing the paintings. I spoke to Mother about this, but she had no knowledge of the matter, and said, "Since I received no money, I don't know what's going on, but I know you are not a person who lies. But … he left no unsold art works, so what are we to do?"

Idang had left about 10,000 works of art, but at the time of his death, they were all in the hands of collectors, with almost nothing left at home. There was nothing equivalent to the money I had received. I worried about this, and finally confided in Unbo, asking him if he could provide a painting, and he gladly agreed. I took one of Unbo's paintings to Jeong Namsu, and explained the situation. He was satisfied with that solution. I gave one of my own works to Kim Taesu, and he, too, was understanding about what had happened. I want to express my appreciation to these two men, who had been so understanding.

Husohoe had been established in 1936, and so was almost a half century old. As a group dedicated to the preserving of tradition, it was important for it to continue to work to develop the younger generation of artists coming up. The decision was made to hold a competition and exhibition, and this took place in 1984. I was one of the judges of the competition. I was already a well-known competition-judge in Japan, and my firm belief was that a judge should be definite about his neutral position. In judging, I looked first for skill in drawing, the composition of the piece, the effort expended by the artist, and, finally, the overall quality of the work. Skill in brush-work alone is important, but not enough to deserve an award. I was careful not to be swayed by being acquainted with the artist or his teacher. I am convinced that a judge must go out of his way to be completely fair.

During the first Husohoe-sponsored competition, I was in disagreement with some of the other judges. The work that I thought of as a superior piece, another judge considered not even acceptable, and one that I thought was only good brush-work was considered by someone else to be a superior work. I wasn't sure whether I was not qualified to judge, or whether other judges were awarding points to their own favorites. Since I was doubtful, I decided to resign as a judge. At about the same time, I resigned from Husohoe, for other reasons. I had discovered that the person who had accused me of being a member of Jochongryon, thus preventing my returning to Korea, was a member of Husohoe. Under Idang Father, we had been closer than real brothers, and I still don't know why he had made up the story that I was a communist. The hurt I felt was the cause of my resignation from the group. Still, these were the students of Idang, and I have not lost my feelings for the members of that organization. As far as being a judge was concerned, everyone has his own opinions about the evaluation of art, and disagreements are natural, but I didn't want to be in the center of that sort of conflict. There were others who experienced the same thing, and resigned from the position of judge at the same time. These were Lee Yuseong, An Dongsuk, and Jang Useong. Even so, Husohoe was a part of Idang's legacy, and I sincerely wished for it to prosper.

Twin Temples

This matter has nothing to do with art, but I want to bring it up because so many people were involved. In the Fall of 1985, I received a phone call from Mr. Kim Jungsam at the Tokyo Cultural Center.

"Master Kim Tae-Shin, can you come to the Cultural Center tomorrow, if you are not too busy?"

"What is it all about?"

"I have something important to discuss with you. I'll tell you about it when I see you."

The next day, he was waiting for me when I arrived at the Cultural Center.

"This is a letter from a female essayist, Sakamoto Hisa."

I read the letter Mr. Kim Jungsam handed me. The writer introduced herself as a sincere Buddhist in the Asuka-dera Temple in Nara, and wrote as follows:

"Asuka-dera is in Asuka, which, as you know, has been the most influenced of any city in Japan by the Baekje era in Korea. Because of that, Asuka has a sister-city, Buyeo, the old capital of Baekje, with which we enjoy a cultural exchange.

"This inspires us to have sister-temples as well, one of which is Asuka-dera Temple, and the other is to be a traditional Korean Temple, which shows the most influence from Baekje. We want to give and receive cultural assistance, and other help as needed. Please assist us in finding the most appropriate Korean temple to fill this role." I read the letter, and said to Kim Jungsam, "That is an interesting request."

"Master Kim, what temple would you recommend?"

"Well, how about Sudeok-sa? There are many Buddhist paintings there which are very similar to the murals in the Horyu-ji temple in Asuka. I think the Baekje artist, Abiji, who had a connection in Sudeok-sa, went to Japan and painted the murals in Hory-ji. The main temple is formed like a pillar, not straight up and down, but bulging in the middle. That is a trademark of Baekje architects. I recommend having a sister-temple arrangement between Asuka-dera and Sudeok-sa."

"As a matter of fact, I had the same thought. That is why I wanted to see you. Master Kim's mother, Seu-nim Ilyeop, has lived there, and you have connections with other Seu-nims there."

"I think so."

"Then, can you make the arrangements?"

The next day, I went to Nara by way of Osaka. Asuka-dera Temple in Nara was huge and majestic. I met the head monk, Yamamoto Joro, who was more than eighty years old. I told him about Sakamoto Hisa's letter, and that I was interested in developing the connection between the two temples. He was very happy about the plan, and made me feel welcome there.

The head monk, a dignified gentleman, was enthusiastic about the plan, and had strong expectations for it. Once the relationship between the two temples was established, someone who wanted to go to Japan to study could expect to receive support from Asuka-dera, and vice versa. I met with Mrs. Sakamoto Hisa, who lived in Yokohama, and with Seu-nim Wondam in Sudeok-sa. Meanwhile, the head monk, Yamamoto Joro, passed away, and the new head monk was named Yamamoto Hojun. He came to get acquainted with Sudeok-sa, and, while he was there, we were entertained by General Jeong Jintae, who was a supporter of the temple. The meeting included Yamamoto Hojun, Seu-nim Wondam, Kim Gisang, a representative of the temple members, and myself. At that time, Dr. Kim Giyeong, president of the local hospital, served dinner to us. I thanked General Jeong especially, because of his help in so many ways, material and spiritual, and also his fund raising. The official ceremony for the connection of the two temples was held in Asuka-dera, in Japan. The head monk of Sudeok-sa, Seu-nim Seoljeon, the head monk of Gwangdeok-sa, Seu-nim Jindoui, Seu-nim Beobseong of Seongra-am, and members' representative, Kim Gisang, all were present.

On the third anniversary of the twin-temples ceremony, both temples opened their cache of holy relics for display. On the way to the ceremony in Japan, the Korean visitors stopped at a rest area for a meal, and Seu-nim Wondam left his coat there. To ease his worry, when we got to Tokyo we called back to the restaurant, and they promised to hold his coat for him. When we picked it up again, every thing was in it, including his money, and we felt ashamed for our previous concern.

Sudeok-sa was the place where my mother had stayed, and I had many memories there. I always visited there during my trips to Korea. At the foot of Sudeok mountain was the birthplace of Yun Bonggil, known as a great patriot, and a supporter of the independence movement. Many people made a pilgrimage to that area, but the road was not paved. I had hoped to be able to take care of that problem, but the expense would have been prohibitive. However, shortly after President Jeon Duhwan visited there for the first time, the road was paved. As a matter of fact, paving a road would not be a big problem if people worked together. But, in Korea I found many people who wanted to succeed by working alone. On the contrary, it is important to work cooperatively, if one wants to make a real contribution.

7

Memories of Love

A Letter

When I held a fund-raising exhibition for Hwanhi-dae, the women's magazine, *Yeowon,* printed an article about my life. When I returned to Tokyo after the exhibition, I received a letter from Korea:

"To Master Kim Tae-Shin:

"How are you? Recently, I read your biography in a magazine, and found it a very touching story. I wondered, after I read it, if you could be my brother who went to Japan shortly before the Korean war. My brother's name was Jeongung, so the name is different, but, I thought, you might have changed your name in Japan, so I am writing this letter.

"My father's name was Kim Bongyul, who stayed at Jikji-sa in Gimcheon, and who passed away right after liberation. I had two brothers, Gwanggyun and Gwanggi, but they both died during the Korean war. My mother is still living, with the help of Social Security, and is seventy-two years old. I am Jukja writing this letter; I am forty-two years old, and I have an older sister, Songja, who is forty-four. Our mother lives with me. My husband is the head of a department store, and he also has a super-market, so we are financially secure. This might be a boring introduction, but I feel as though you are my brother, so I am telling you about the family.

"My heart is pounding, and I don't really know what to write. This is me, but can you imagine how my mother is feeling! After she read about you in the magazine, it seems as though all of the feeling that she had kept hidden is coming out. She lost two sons in the war, and she prays to Buddha every day to see again the son who was like one of her own. My brother who went to Japan had a close relationship with my mother, as well as with the brothers and sisters here. Whenever I think about my brother, my eyes get wet because I miss him so much.

"I'm enclosing a picture which my brother sent from Osaka. Mother took this picture everywhere we sought refuge during the war. If you are not my brother, please return the picture, as it is precious to us.

"I will be awaiting your letter. Be well and happy, and your family, too. Goodbye. Daegu, in Korea, Jukja"

Of course, this was my lovely sister Jukja's letter. As soon as I saw her name on the envelope I couldn't catch my breath. While I was reading the letter, I had mixed feelings of pleasure, at hearing from my family again, and sorrow about the losses. It was painful to read that Gwanggyum and Gwanggi had died in the war. I remembered staying in the same room with them whenever I visited Gimcheon. As boys, they had especially liked and admired me. Luckily, I still had Mother and sisters, and that was a source of joy. Right after the Korean war, when I visited Gimcheon, I had found the house destroyed by bombing, and assumed that the whole family was gone. I hadn't returned there on my subsequent visits to Korea, and that was a big mistake.

At the time I received the letter, I was in the process of preparing an exhibition, and, though I was eager to go, I had to postpone my trip to Korea until after the show. I wrote a letter to Jukja expressing my heart, letting her know I was the brother she was seeking, and telling her when I would be coming to Korea. She wrote back immediately:

"Dear Brother! I gave thanks to Buddha. I couldn't stop crying out loud. Mother, Sister and I were abandoned on the battlefield, and, since then, I have cried so much I thought I had no tears left. We read your letter over and over, each time weeping anew. I am so glad you are alive, and that we will meet you again, and that you have become an upstanding citizen. We had never expected that we would cry with joy. I miss you, Brother! I still remember you clearly, and I can hear your kind voice, even after the passage of thirty-two years.When you left for Japan, I was still in grade school. You promised to bring me crayons and pretty shoes, and I still remember that very well. Every day I sang "Thoughts of Brother," and you cannot imagine how much I missed you.

"Your kind smile and loving eyes were our hope. Gimcheon became an ocean of fire, and we were waiting for our brothers and couldn't leave. We came close to death on many occasions. Sometimes we went through flame to avoid the bombs, and finally went into the mountains, from which we eventually reached Daegu. After Gwanggyun and Gwanggi had both gone into the army we suffered more, but we never stopped thinking about you.

"Anyway, that is past history. From now on we hope that we can live happily with you in Korea. Mother needs something to lean on, and she will be happy then. You can't imagine how happy she is! I saw your wife's picture in *Yeowon*. She is very pretty, and I'm sure she is intelligent, too. I hope that we can all meet together.

"You are coming to Korea in September, but time goes by so slowly. I'm counting the days until you get here. When you come to Korea, we will pick you up at the airport. Please take care of yourself until then." The letter was signed, Jukja, from Daegu. Right after receiving that letter, I received one from Songja. Her letter also touched me deeply:

"Brother! I waited every day, and it has been more than thirty years. When I found out that you were the one in the magazine, I almost cried my eyes out.

"Mother supported us by being a seamstress. Neighbors wanted her to remarry and to put her children into an orphanage, but she wouldn't think of doing such a thing. She didn't even have a sewing machine, and had to do all of the work by hand. We often went hungry, and moved from house to house like gypsies. When I remember those times, my heart still aches.

"Brother! I thank Buddha that we have heard from you, and I am proud of your success after having to overcome so many difficulties.

"Now we live comfortably. Best of all, Mother has a peaceful life. On April 9, 1967, I married Im Hyeongbin, from Poeun in Chungbuk Province, and I have a daughter and a son. My daughter is in high school, and my son is a middle school student. My husband works as a conscription inspector for the military affairs office.

"Jukja married in December of that same year, to Lee Muwung, from Seongju in Gyeongsang-do, and she has three children. Her youngest daughter is very talented, and won first prize in a piano competition. She got an award from the Minister of Educational Affairs. I am very proud of Jukja. When she was single, she worked as a typist for the United States Army, and she speaks English exceptionally well.

"Oh, Brother, while I write this I feel like I did years ago, like a child whining to you, rather than a grown-up. You left as a young man, and you are returning as a grandpa. We have lost so much time!

"When you couldn't see, our sister-in-law took care of you and our nephews so well for more than a year, and we are grateful to her for that. I saw the pictures of your beautiful sons, and I want to see them in person. I pray to Buddha that you have lots of love in your home. Please take care of yourself and your family until we see you." Her letter was signed, July 14, 1983, Songja in Korea.

The letters from my sisters made me want to give up everything, including my exhibition, and go immediately to see Mother, and to embrace them all and cry together. Until I could do that, the ache in my heart could not be assuaged, but the invitations for the exhibit had already been sent out, so I had to go through with it. I went to the temple to calm myself, and to concentrate on the work I had to do, but only my body was in Japan during that exhibition, while my heart was in Korea.

During the exhibition, which was in the Fuji Gallery in Ginza, I got a phone call.

"This is an international call from Korea."

The voice of the caller, which came by wire across the Sea of Japan, was that of Jukja. As soon as I said hello, she shouted,

"Brother!" Immediately, my heart sank, and I asked shakily, "Who is this?" The voice was shaky and full of tears.

"This is Jukja."

"Oh, Jukja! This is me!"

My sister couldn't continue speaking, and my eyes began to fill with tears. I tried to calm myself, and I finally asked, "Is Mother alright?"

"Yes, Brother. She is right here, and you can talk to her."

Then, I heard my mother's voice, the mother who loved me more than if I had been her biological son.

"Oh, Jeongung, it is really you…." She, like my sister, was too overcome with emotion to continue. I said through my tears, "Mother, please forgive your undutiful son."

"It doesn't matter if I forgive you or not. Just let me see your face!"

"Yes, Mother…. As soon as this exhibition closes, I will come there."

At that time, to make an international call was very complicated. They had learned my phone number from my letter, had called my home, and had been given the number of the gallery by my wife. After I heard the voices of my mother and sister, I missed them even more. I made an airline reservation for a date after the end of the exhibition.

Lost Years

I had thought about taking my wife to Korea with me, but decided to go for the first time by myself, and, later, to take her to meet my family.

"This time, I'd better go alone. We can go together later so that you can get acquainted."

"That'll be fine. You have been without your family for a long time…. Go—and have a good time."

"Thank you."

"By the way, they have always thought you were the father's biological son. Maybe this is the time to tell them the truth." My wife looked at me with a worried expression.

"Don't worry. We are closer than biological relations."

As my wife said, they thought of me as a blood relation, and missed me a lot, but, if I told them the truth, they might be very disappointed.

"I may leave that problem for later. The important thing now is just to see them again." My wife nodded, and bade me goodbye. When I arrived at Gimpo International Airport, I went to the Seoul station and took a train to Daegu. When the train passed through Gimcheon, my heart began to ache. I had walked around Gimcheon so many times, but now I went on to Daegu, and took a cab to my sister's house. Now my heart was pounding. I tried to control my breathing, and rang the doorbell. Through the intercom I could hear Jukja's voice.

"Who is there?"

"Jukja? It's me!"

"Brother!"

Just as I entered the gate, she burst out of the door. We looked at each other for a moment. She was an adult, but I could see the face of the child I had known, and Sister recognized me even more quickly. I learned later that they had looked at the picture I sent them from Osaka almost every day. I set my suitcase down and opened my arms wide.

"Jukja!" I could see that her eyes were full of tears as she ran into my embrace.

"Brother!"

"Jukja!"

How long I had waited for this moment, and how much I had missed this sister! I had been without a family, and they had offered me a family's warmth. I couldn't say anything, but just hugged my sister. I heard the sound of the entrance door, wiped the tears from my eyes, and looked at mother, who was coming out.

"Mother!" I drew her into the embrace with my sister.

"Jeongung!"

Mother and I hugged, and the happiness of the reunion as well as the thought of the many lost years brought tears to our eyes. Even the nephews who were watching us did so with wet eyes. Jukja started calling everyone in the family. Songja's family came, and an aunt, my mother's sister, came also. Family from near and far arrived and we had a big feast. Mother looked at my face again and again, and would hardly let go of my hand.

"You have been in Seoul a few times. If you had made a trip to Jikji-sa in Gimcheon, we could have been together sooner.... Oh Ingap, whom you know well, is now the head monk of that temple." Mother was sorrowful that so much time had been lost.

"I went to Jikji-sa once. I did not see Oh Ingap, and there was no Seu-nim there whom I knew. Right after the battle of June 25, I went to Gimcheon with much difficulty, but the house was burned to the ground, and I thought the whole family had perished. If I had met you then, I would never have stayed in Japan...." Mother said, "Gwanggyun died in battle, and Gwanggi stopped at home on his way from Busan to North Korea, and we never heard from him again. He is listed as a missing person, but I am sure that he died in battle too."

At that time, they were showing on television families and missing persons, in the attempt to reunite them, and that was touching to all of us. Thirty years may have passed since the war, but the wounds had not healed. When I saw those wounds of our divided country, I realized that I was far from being alone in my situation. Every day we had a feast. All of the neighbors were invited, as well as members of the temple where my mother worshiped. Mother danced with joy and often touched me, and I could see tears in her eyes.

"Well, I am getting old, but there are no regrets. From now on, let us live together."

"Yes. I want to live with you, Mother. But, I have lived in Japan for a long time, and I will have a lot of arrangements to make; that will be difficult to do right away. I will have to talk to my wife as well."

As a matter of fact, I wanted to live in Korea immediately. My mother in Gyeonseong-am had already passed away, but, I could still be a dutiful son to my mother in Gimcheon. However, I could not just do whatever I felt like. I was not alone, and all of my life and work was based in Japan. But, wherever I lived, I would be affected by the more than biological love I received in this family. I had already lost many of the people who had loved me. Idang had also died, so all I had left were the mother in Gimcheon, and Songja and Jukja. As I thought about my mother in Gyeonseong-am, I realized that she had been a very solitary person, and that is what I was, too.

In my mind, there was a far-reaching plan developing. First, I had to introduce my wife to this family. Next, I would invite Mother to Tokyo to look around, and have her live with us in Japan for a bit. After a while, I would persuade my wife and family to move with me to Korea. That was my plan. As soon as I returned to Japan, I began putting my plan into action.

"I want you to go to Korea to meet my mother and sisters."

"Were they glad to see you?"

"Of course, of course."

"It would be better if they were your blood relatives." Why was she still concerned about that point?

"Even if my biological parents were alive, I would do the same thing. But, since they are gone, I feel even closer to that family. I told you—we are more than blood relatives. Now that I have found my Gimcheon family, I will devote all of my energies to my mother."

My wife indicated that she understood my feelings. We traveled to Korea together, and went to Daegu. We greeted Mother, and I cannot describe how happy she was. My sisters treated my wife warmly, and took us on a tour of Kyeongju, the ancient capital. It was the first time my wife had seen that site. While we were in Kyeongju, we enjoyed spending time in Bulguk-sa and Seokgul-am. When we got back to Tokyo, my wife said, "Your mother is such a nice person. I almost feel like crying she was so gracious to me."

"She is like an angel. My sisters are like her, and even the children are good."

"I felt like they were a blessing I didn't deserve. Maybe it is time to tell them the truth."

It had been bothering me for a long time. I didn't want to deceive them, but I had the desire to live with them like we were a real family. I didn't want to disappoint my mother, who was relying on me, and I decided to put the matter aside for a little while. A year went by, and the time came for Father Kim Bongyul's memorial service. I had never attended his memorial over all of the years, but I was determined to attend this one, and made the trip to Korea. I attended the service at Tongcheon-sa in Daegu. I bowed, and said,

"Father, I am sorry. Please forgive me for being such an undutiful son. You asked me to take care of your family, but I didn't do it. Already Gwanggyun and Gwanggi are gone, and Mother, Jukja and Songja had a very difficult time. I feel guilty about that."

When I remembered my father, who had been so generous and loving, my eyes filled with tears, and I was determined to take care of the family well at last. After the service, Mother spoke to me shyly.

"Jeongung."

"Yes, Mother."

"As a matter of fact, I bought a house in which to live with you when you come back, but I didn't know when you were coming, so I sold the house, and gave the money to Jukja and Songja, half and half." This touched my heart. She had earned her living as a seamstress, and suffered so much, and, because she was thinking of me, she bought a house....

"It's OK, Mother."

"No. Since you have come back, I'll ask them for the money, and use it to buy a house."

I decided that this was the time to tell them the truth. I had to tell them that I was not the person who deserved a house, so that they would not feel burdened by me. I gathered the whole family together in the living room, to disclose this important secret. My mother, my two sisters, and my mother's sister from Seoul were there. Before I brought up the issue, I looked at my mother's face. She was already over seventy, her hair was gray, and her brow deeply furrowed. I could see the wounds the national turmoil had inflicted upon her. Her husband had died, two sons had been killed in the war, and she had survived only with difficulty. Her only hope was me, and I had to deliver still another blow. I could not do it; I closed my eyes, and felt resentment toward Kim Bongyul, who, by lying, had caused me this problem. Of course, he had done it only to insure my acceptance by his family. I thought that, no matter what the reaction of my mother and sisters might be, I had to go on treating them the same way as before. That would have been my father's wish. I opened my mouth and told them the truth. While I was talking, the room was completely silent. When I finished, I felt as though a weight had been lifted from my heart, but also empty and worried. Mother's eyes were wet with tears, but nobody spoke, and there was no sound in the room. I took a deep breath, and said, "Mother, I'm your son Jeongung, the same as always. From now on, I will take care of you better than ever." Mother wiped her eyes with her handkerchief.

"You may not be our blood relation, but still you have been a good son, and I am so proud of you. Father told a useless lie, and caused you this difficult problem. But, when I think about it, maybe it wasn't a useless lie. Maybe he realized our other sons would die, and he wanted to provide me with another son!"

"Mother!" My voice was choked.

"We are lonely people, and we have to rely on each other." I was sure that Mother was disappointed that she had no male descendants to carry on the name, but, even though we had no biological relationship, I had attended the memorial service, and cared for the family, and she was proud of that. I'm sure that my sisters must have been shocked, but they didn't show it. Songja told me, "Brother, as you have done so well by our father and mother, I believe that I should think of Seu-nim Ilyeop as another mother. I'll visit Sudeok-sa and see her memorial portrait." Songja was such a good person. It was vacation time, and we went to

Jikji-sa and took my nephew Junseok. I felt that my mother, Seu-nim Ilyeop, and my father, Kim Bongyul were there to greet me. Songja bowed in front of Mother's portrait in Hwanhi-dae. She said,

"Brother, you are my eternal brother, so please do nothing to change that."

"Yes, of course." I gave one of my paintings to my mother as a gift, and I returned to Japan.

After I got there, I received a letter from Jukja. At that time, my eyesight was very poor, and I was having symptoms of glaucoma. My sister knew about that, and she had gone to Tongcheon-sa, and bowed five hundred times every day to pray for my improvement. I thanked Buddha for my warm and beautiful sister. Her letter reported that Mother was healthy, which made me happy, since I had worried that she might have suffered from the aftereffects of the shock when I told the truth. I answered her letter, and she wrote back again on February 19. Even though we lived far apart, we corresponded at least weekly, to make up for the lost thirty years.

Songja's letter included some writing from my cute nephew, Junseok, which made me happy. My other nephews also sent me letters giving me encouragement and pleasure. I was preparing a solo exhibition in Tokyo at the time, and I could work well because of the happiness their letters gave me.

She's Gone

After the Tokyo exhibition, I talked to my wife.

"Well, dear, we are finished with that busy time, and I would like to invite Mother to come to stay with us for a while. What do you think?" My wife smiled, "That is a good idea. I never had the opportunity to serve my mother-in-law, and I would like to do that now. Before that, though, why don't you go to the hospital for a check of your eyes. It would not be good if your mother came, and then you had a bad spell."

Dr. Yamamoto had said that after thirty years the condition of my eyes could worsen, and I had been having some symptoms. Often my eyes were tired and my vision blurred, and sometimes I could hardly see at all. I agreed with my wife, but I worried that I might never get the chance to have my mother here. And, indeed, that worry became reality. The next day the telephone rang, and when I answered I heard Jukja's crying voice. My heart sank.

"What's the matter?"

"Mother collapsed."

"What? What happened?"

"I don't have time to tell you everything. Mother is asking for you."

"I understand. I will be there on the first flight tomorrow. Is her condition serious?" Jukja answered, weeping, "I don't think she will survive." That night I couldn't sleep. I was thinking that, let alone whether or not I got to bring Mother to Tokyo, I might not be able to be present at her death-bed.

My wife's turned pale as well. She said,

"What shall we do? If she is that bad, we should have acted sooner...." The next day I hurried to Korea by plane. I went to the hospital where Mother was, and I met Jukja, whose face was full of tears.

"What shall I do, Brother? I must not have taken care of her well enough, and this happened." I shouted at her,

"Don't say that. You have been the equal of Sim Cheong as a faithful daughter." I knew that Jukja had been the best of daughters. I was worried about my mother, and had little time to console my sister. I opened the door of her hospital room, and saw Mother, who was lying very still, with her eyes closed. She was not aware that I was there. I was heartsick with regret that I had told her the truth, and thought that the letters from my sisters about how well my mother was doing were sent just to comfort me.

Mother passed away that night. Shortly before the end, she regained consciousness for a brief period, and opened her eyes. She smiled at me and touched my hand. I was holding her fragile hand, and trying not to cry, but when her breathing stopped, I wept. My sisters were also sobbing.

Mother's funeral was a Buddhist ceremony, in accord with her lifelong beliefs, and her mortuary tablet was kept in Tongcheon-sa. Even after the funeral, Jukja continued crying and blaming herself.

"You took care of Mother until she died. Think about Songja. Think how sad she must be that she never had the opportunity to have Mother with her in her home. I, too—I wanted to take her on a tour of Japan, but I waited too long, so I have some guilt, as well. Don't blame yourself."

I was going to stay in Daegu until the forty-ninth day Buddhist mass for the dead, but my eyes were uncomfortable. Perhaps because of the stress of Mother's death and the funeral, my eyes got so bad that I had to return home. I went to the ophthalmologist at the Jonan Hospital in Tokyo.

"There is no time to wait. You must have glaucoma surgery right away."

So, as soon as I got back to Tokyo, I had to go through the procedures to enter the hospital. I was more worried than when I was young that the results of the surgery might not be good. After the surgery, while I was in the hospital, I received a letter from Songja which my wife read to me:

"Dear Brother, I miss you, and I am anxious to learn the results of your surgery. I am thankful to you and my sister-in-law that Mother was able to close her eyes peacefully, and go into another world.

"Brother, since Mother met you again, she was so pleased with herself that she had a son once more, and she acquired sweaters of various colors for you, since she thought that you were sensitive to the cold, and often shopped around at the tailor's and touched the suits. She read your letters again and again, and she told people that she felt so much better since you brought stomach medicine for her. And she bragged that she would soon be sight-seeing in Japan with you. But—she is gone now.

"Brother! I keep wondering where a person comes from and where they go. Life seems so futile. Do you think Mother went to paradise and reunited with Father?

"On the morning of your surgery-day, I prayed that your operation would go well, to Buddha, and to the mother who is in Heaven.

"Whenever we had a Buddhist mass for the dead, the head monk at Tongcheon-sa prayed sincerely for you and your family. August 20th is the forty ninth-day mass, and after that I will write again. I am curious about the results of your surgery, so please have somebody write to let us know." The letter was written August 17, 1984, and signed by Songja.

Luckily, the results of my operation were good, and I gave more credit to the prayers of my sister than I did to the advanced medical technology. After the forty ninth rite, Jukja wrote to me. This time, she enclosed a letter from my niece, Seungmin. Her letter was decorated with flowers, and her writing was neat and girlish. That letter is the only one that has kept its original color over the passage of years. While I was in the hospital, Sister Seu-nim Beobseong, from Seongra-am, came to Tokyo to see me, and President Kim Nam Hyeon of the Jangu Group helped me financially and psychologically. So, with the assistance of all of those people, I was discharged in good health, and had no trouble drawing. I rested a few days at home, then went to Korea in September. I went with my sisters to Tongcheon-sa, where Mother's mortuary tablet was located. Again, I wept because of the love which I hadn't had the opportunity to show her.

We meet many people during our lifetimes. Sometimes we meet good people, as we wish, and sometimes we meet bad people, whether we want to or not. We can become friends, lovers, even enemies. In short, continual meetings are what life is. I may say that chance meetings are a matter of karma. The meeting of Father Kim Bongyul and me represented very good karma. We were not of the same blood, but we shared good love. Now, Father and Mother have both left this world. They did many good things in their lives, and were faithful Buddhists, and I believe these two people were reunited in paradise, and achieved supreme happiness there. Meeting with Songja and Jukja was also good. We were solitary, but we built a family relationship wherein we could rely upon and help each other. I believe that to have this closeness is the fruit of God's blessing. If these sisters were still young, I would have tried to help them all I could. But they had both already built secure lives, and did not need my help.

After I became a monk, I cut off many of my worldly relationships, but my sisters are always in my thoughts as a blessing. When I go to the temple, I always touch the wooden gong and offer a prayer in their names. I can say that I have few regrets in my life, but one thing bothers me still. After liberation, I went to Japan, and didn't come back sooner to Korea. At that time, I could have returned, but I didn't do it. If I had gone back then, my life would have been very different. Also, Gwanggyun and Gwanggi.... There is still a painful sense that I didn't do enough for them. I don't understand fully, but, even though they are gone, I may be able to lead them in the way of providence. This is my responsibility, and I pray silently to the Buddhist Goddess of Mercy to save us.

8

Following Mother's Path

Discovering a New Land

In 1985 I was sixty-three years old. In Seongra-am, I met Seu-nim Doan who built Gwaneum-sa in Los Angeles. He told me that, if we built an assembly hall at Gwaneum-sa, it would be helpful in carrying out missionary work with Korean Buddhists in the United States.

"Mr. Kim, can you help us?"

"How can I help?"

"I'll pay all of your expenses if you would come to Los Angeles and put on a fund-raising exhibition for us." Sister Seu-nim Beobseong encouraged me to take that step, because she believed that missionary work was very important. I accepted the proposal, with one condition.

"I want to bring my wife to America with me. Could you pay expenses for her as well?"

"Of course."

"I'll add ten more pieces of art, which you can sell to defray our expenses."

In the studio at Seongra-am, I drew thirty works of art which I intended to donate to Gwaneum-sa, and ten more to cover our travel and other costs. I ordered the frames to be made at the Jongro Art Store. I sent the completed art pieces to America by ship, and received two round-trip airline tickets from Seu-nim Doan.

I had been apologetic to my wife that I had traveled alone so much, especially since her youngest sister lived in San Francisco, and she had been wanting to go to the USA. Seu-nim Beobseong agreed to join us. Beobseong and I went to my home in Tokyo, and told my wife of the travel plan. She was happily surprised, and said, "After all this time, you are going to take me to America?...."

"I'm your husband. If I don't take you who will?" My wife was so grateful that I felt quite guilty.

On October 10, we flew from Tokyo to Los Angeles. When I looked at my wife, I could see how excited she was. Like Robert Frost's poem, "The Road Not Taken," I was at a cross-road. In my old age, I could appreciate how well the poet expressed the feeling of regret concerning the path not followed. I felt sorry about the way I had chosen, and took hold of my wife's hand.

The newspaper *Korea Times,* KTE, and the Korean Cultural Center sponsored the exhibition. When I arrived in the USA, I was kept busy being interviewed for the *Korea Times,* and the Korean Broadcasting Company. Seu-nim Doan, who was the head monk at Gwaneum-sa, wrote about me as follows, on the invitations that were sent out for the exhibition:

"Master Kim is the founder of the Japan Owon Art Organization, and manages that group. He was a disciple of Idang Kim Unho, and studied with Unbo Kim Gichang. In Japan, he graduated with honors from the Tokyo National Art School. He has judged art competitions for the Mainichi and Asahi Newspapers. He is considered a master artist in the Japanese Art Organization."

I had become a member of the Japanese Art Organization in 1963—my membership number was 3280. This is the most important organization involving Japanese artists, and now has 7,000 members. I think my most important accomplishment was the establishment of Owon. I was honored by the opportunity to be a judge for competitions sponsored by the Mainichi and Asahi papers, and especially to be an invited exhibitor in their art shows.

Master Kim Bongtae, the head of the Southern California Korean Art Organization, said, "In Los Angeles we have had many exhibitions of the work of Korean artists, but yours is the most popular by far."

I sold all forty of the pieces I had provided for the exhibition. I am sure the publicity which had been provided had ensured that success. The Koreans in the United States liked best my color-added paintings. In Korea, most people prefer the Southern-style painting which utilizes India-ink, but westernized people seem to like the Northern-style colored works better. During the exhibition, I met Kim Dongil, who had learned color-painting from me. He had come to Los Angeles, and now operated a gallery. After the exhibition, Seu-nim Doan and Kim Dongil took me, my wife, and Sister Beobseong on a tour.

We started with the Grand Canyon in Arizona. When we passed Nevada and entered Arizona, the land was spacious, and I imagined I could hear the hoofbeats of Indian ponies. The desert seemed endless and the canyon was majestic, and I imagined the figures of Apache braves brandishing their bows and arrows. I looked down through the layers of rock making up the canyon, to the Colorado River far below, and I imagined I could see John Wayne riding by; it took my breath away. The sun shining through the cumulous clouds made fantastic silhouettes, making the canyon all the more mysterious and impressive. I know that Columbus discovered this country long ago, but now I had found it for myself at last, and I felt regretful that I had not seen it sooner.

We went to Yosemite, and, on the way back, stopped by San Francisco, where my wife's sister lived a prosperous life. My sister-in-law and her husband came to our hotel and took us to a restaurant from which we could see the Golden Gate Bridge. She asked my wife, with a smile, "Sister, what do you think of the USA?"

"This place is more huge and beautiful than I had heard. After I saw the Grand Canyon, it seemed impossible for couples to argue with each other."

"Why is that, Sister?"

"Seeing that great accomplishment of nature makes our human concerns seem trivial."

I said, "If it made you think that, it was worth the trip!" That made us all laugh.

After returning to Los Angeles, I received three phone calls. One was from Kim Wonguk in New York. He had studied painting with me while he was in Waseda University. He had come to the USA, earned a Ph.D. in Political Science, and was now a university professor. The second call, also from New York, was from Seu-nim Oh Beoban. He was the vice president of the Dongguk Buddhist University in Korea, and was doing missionary work by building Wongak-sa temple in New York. Both of these calls included invitations to go to New York, and I determined to visit there.

The third call was from Dr. Lee Tae Yeong. She was visiting in Los Angeles from Korea, and heard about my exhibition. She had her secretary call with the invitation to dine with her. Dr. Lee Tae Yeong was my aunt on my mother's side. Her husband, Jeong Ilhyeong, was the brother of my mother, Kim Ilyeop. My grandmother had died early, and my grandfather then married a widow with one son. That son was Mr. Jeong Ilhyeong. My grandfather, who had no sons of his own, had dearly loved this boy. My mother, with no other sisters and brothers, had grown up with him, and was extremely fond of him as well. Mr. Jeong Ilhyeong was a congressman in Korea, and busy with national affairs, but he had frequently visited my mother at Sudeok-sa, and I had known of him.

I was unable to accept my aunt's invitation as I had a previous appointment for an interview with a reporter the *Dong-A Daily News,* and I regretted being unable to meet with her, since she had freed up enough time for a visit. I had dinner with the reporter, who offered me the opportunity to write an illustrated article about my visit to America. I accepted the offer, and spent ten days working on the article for the newspaper.

New York, New York

Along with my wife and sister Beopseong, I went to New York, and Mr. Kim Wonguk picked us up at the airport. He took us to Manhattan, to Wongak-sa to meet Seu-nim Oh Beoban. We stayed at Wongak-sa during our visit to New York. My favorite place to go in Manhattan was the Metropolitan Museum of Art. When KimWonguk took us to the museum, I was agog at seeing works of the masters that I had known only through pictures in a book. There was no way we could see everything in one day, so we stayed two, but, even so, I felt I had still seen only one leg of the elephant. Because of our schedule, we had to move on. Not far from the museum was Central Park, and I spent a half day sketching at the lake-side there. The sun was glinting off the windows of the tall buildings surrounding the park, and everything was clear and pretty.

The East Village in New York appeared to me to be an origin of modern artistic expression. The poor artists there appeared to be followers Marcel Duchamps, in their rejection of traditional styles and values, and, to feed themselves, were always providing entertaining performances of every kind.

One day, Seu-nim Oh Beoban took us to Monroe in upstate New York. There was a big camp there with football fields, tennis courts, swimming pools, basketball and volley ball courts, etc., every imaginable kind of leisure activity. There were tens of bungalows, and at the shore of a lake was a yacht club. When we went up the hill, we saw deer grazing, who bolted when they felt our presence. Seu-nim Beoban said to me,

"This place is for sale. I am going to buy it, and move the Wongak-sa here. What do you think about that?"

"That would be a great idea. But, how could you manage it financially?"

"If I sold the Wongak-sa building in Manhattan, I could buy this place. We could remodel one of the existing buildings to use as the temple. In the future, I am going to do some fundraising to build a traditional-style temple, like Bulguk-sa in Korea."

"What a great idea!"

"I'll do the fundraising, and I would like you to be in charge of building an oriental university here."

"Oriental university?...."

"Is this not a bigger space than any of Korea's biggest university campuses? It is my dream to build a place where could be taught all aspects of oriental culture, art, music, religion, philosophy and medicine. Together, Brother, I believe we could do it."

"Let's think about it."

I, my wife, and Sister Beopseong, traveled past Los Angeles, to Hawaii. In Hawaii, there was Daewon-sa, which was exactly like a Korean temple. I was looking at it, and thinking that, if we could build one like it, only bigger, in Monroe, that alone would be a big accomplishment.

Seu-nim Beoban had said that he would take care of providing for the temple, and my part would be the development of an oriental university. But, money was the problem. If we could raise the funds, I thought that I could spend the rest of my life in this work.

In Hawaii was another temple, Buleun-sa. The head monk there was Seu-nim Jaeun. The beach at Waikiki was as beautiful as a painting, and we swam and surfed like native Hawaiians. Everywhere in the sky were colorful rainbows. While I was looking at a rainbow, I thought again about an oriental university.

I have visited Hawaii a few more times. Once I went to a nudist village, where, even to visit, one had to be nude. It seemed to me to be what Eden was like, and I envied the people who lived there like primitive beings who had refused the encroachment of civilization.

Support Group

After our American trip, upon my return to Tokyo, I heard from Seu-nim Oh Beoban that he had sold the Manhattan building, and purchased the camp at Monroe. He again suggested strongly that we begin building an oriental university there. I thought about how meaningful it would be to build such a university in the center of international culture and art, New York. It would bring to Americans knowledge of oriental art, music, medicine, philosophy and religion. The land was ours, but the problem was to raise the necessary funds to erect the buildings. This would require a lot more money than I could come up with, and I thought that contacting people influential in political and financial circles in Japan might provide a source for funds. First, I contacted Congressman Fukuda, who had been a supporter of mine. Mr. Fukuda thought it was a good idea, but warned me that working with Korean people would not be easy.

"I'm not saying this applies to everybody, but many Koreans will agree to something but then not follow through."

I emphasized again and again that Seu-nim Beoban was not that kind of person. When I finally convinced him to help me as much as possible, I felt like I had conquered an army. I met Abe Shintaro, who was also politically powerful, and he promised to lend his support. Through these two men, I was introduced to many people of wealth and influence. The president of the New York branch of a Japanese company promised to make a tax-deductible donation to the school fund. I was able to find ample support among business people, who promised to contribute, and I was confident that I had enough support to succeed. The following year, I held a fund-raising exhibition in the youth center at Wongak-sa at Monroe, New York. At that time, I asked Mr. Choe Jeongyeob to go from Korea to New York, to work on establishing the oriental university there. He considered the matter, but was concerned that he could not immediately resign from his current position. Therefore, he delegated a friend of his to go to New York to act as my agent. He told me that, after he heard a report on what progress had been made, he would consider joining in the project. I went to New York with this unanticipated advisor.

We announced, through a Korean newspaper in New York, plans for a new temple to be built in the traditional Korean style, and that an oriental university would be established. I talked to reporters from many different newspapers, especially to Jeong Sihun, from the *Korea Times* in New York, who gave me a very important cause around which to build my later life. His penname was Jeonghyeong, and he was a novelist as well as a journalist, and wrote stories which were printed in serial form in the paper. He convinced me that, to build the university there, I needed to gain support from Korean people living in New York. He was acquainted with many rich Koreans in New York, and built a support group among them for me, Kim Tae-Shin.

In Tokyo, I also had a Kim Tae-Shin support group, which had also been organized through the work of a reporter. In the early seventies, I had a solo exhibition at a Ginza gallery. As I was hanging my paintings, prior to the opening of the show, a young man knocked on the gallery door, asking to see the pictures. I let him in, and he examined each painting very carefully. Then, he stood, motionless, in front of a half-length figure of the Merciful Buddha.

"Do you like it?"

"Yes, it is unique. When I saw this painting, I was immediately drawn to it. As a matter of fact, this morning my mother told me she had dreamed about Merciful Buddha. I will buy this painting."

"You are welcome to take it after the exhibition."

"I'll come on the closing day and pick it up."

The last day of the exhibition, he came, paid for the painting and took it with him. He was a reporter for TV station Yomi Uri, and his name was Inagaki.

"This is a gift for my mother." His mother was a cancer patient, who was not expected to survive. She was able to contemplate from her bed, the painting her son had given her, and, miraculously, she began to improve, and fully regained her health. I didn't know whether it was just not her time to die, or my painting had a healing effect on her, but I gave thanks to Buddha when I heard that she had begun to recover the first day she saw the painting. She, herself, said that the painting had helped her, so, perhaps it is not too bad to believe it.

For a while, the reporter, Inagaki, told the miracle story to everyone he met, and people began coming to see me. One day, I got a phone call from the owner of a bar, which was called Edoko, and was located in Oizumi Kakuen. His name was Mr. Suzuki, and I went there to see him.

"Master, can you draw a Merciful Buddha for me? My customer, Mr. Inagaki, told me about your painting, which we all know has some mysterious power."

"Is that so?"

"As a matter of fact, my business is very bad lately. Maybe if I hung your picture on my wall, things might pick up."

"If you think so, I'll make the painting. But you must keep a proper mind, and respect the Buddha, if you want any good effects."

Again, a mysterious thing happened. As soon as he hung my painting on the wall of the Edoko bar, it became very popular, and was crowded with customers all the time. I don't know whether Mr. Suzuki approached his customers with a new determination to serve, or my if painting really had an effect. In any case, Mr. Suzuki gave the credit for his prosperity to the painting, and was most happy with it.

After that, I was asked to make a painting by the president of a large company. He was a regular customer at Edoko, and had heard from Mr. Suzuki that good things would happen to anyone who bought a painting from me.

"My business is not doing well. It seems to have too many ups and downs, and I can't figure out what to do."

I drew the god of fire, Acala. This god was called upon from ancient times to remedy misfortune, and good luck did indeed come to this business man. He said that, from the moment he bought the picture, everything improved for him.

He also believed that his success was due to the painting, so I had several word-of-mouth advocates. I earned money from the painting, but I also got a lot of free advertising from these people who believed that my work held some mysterious power. They told others that whoever keeps my paintings will receive blessings. I had so much business for a few months that I could scarcely handle it all, and my customers became enthusiastic fans. Whenever I held an exhibition they would all attend, and formed an influential support group. They asked me for discounts below the gallery prices, and in return, they brought prospective buyers, and made advertising pamphlets and posters, supporting me in that way.

As a group, we went on sketching trips, where I lectured to them about how to appreciate good painting, and taught them about oriental art. To show them my appreciation, I held two solo exhibitions to promote this group. With the funds received, they paid my way on our trips, and paid my expenses in various other travel. The president of the Kim Tae-Shin Support Group was a businessman, and Mr. Suzuki was the manager of the group. The ages of the members ranged from twenty to sixty, and there were women members as well as men. Their occupations were varied as well, and they gave me a great deal of help with my activities in Tokyo.

Now I also had a support group in New York, which would be of great help there. The president was Mr. Oh Gijeong, a businessman, and the manager was Jeong Sihun, the newspaper reporter. When I held an exhibition in the youth center at Wongak-sa, Mr. Oh bought five of my paintings, which was a big help. I donated the funds raised by this exhibition to Seu-nim Hyegwan, the business manager of Wongak-sa.

"Please deposit this money in the bank to be used when we start the building project." He agreed to my request.

To Become a Monk

After the fund-raiser, I had tea with Seu-nim Oh Beoban.

"From now on, building the oriental university will keep us very busy. In order to do this, Brother, you will need to live in New York, so why don't you apply for permanent residency? Talk it over with your wife. If she agrees to live in New York, send me your family records, and I'll apply for residency for you."

"Because of the children, I doubt that my wife would want to live in New York."

"Then, could you live separately for a while?"

"Well, we are close to our seventies, so maybe it would not be a problem to go our own ways."

"Then, Brother, why don't you shave your head and become a monk?"

When I heard those words from Seu-nim Oh Beoban, I felt my ears tingle. As a matter of fact, I had long wanted to take this step, particularly on three occasions in the past, the first time when I visited my mother in Gyeonseong-am. I had also wanted to become a monk at Dasol-sa, but wasn't able to do so. Then, in Osaka, when I became very confused by the problems of the two young women, I desired once more to shave my head.

Before Buddha became a monk, he had a son, Rahula. His concern for his son interfered with his religious meditations, and Rahula represented a connection with the world and an interference with Buddha's spiritual pursuits.

I was a Rahula to my mother, Seu-nim Ilyeop. Buddha's son followed his father, and became a monk at the age of fifteen, becoming one of the ten great disciples of Buddha. I had to follow my mother's way, and reach the highest goal, like Rahula. I had often thought about this, but had not been able to act on it because of my wife. She had waited for me until she was more than thirty years old, and I couldn't bring myself to hurt her by saying that I wanted to become a monk. Now we were close to seventy, and I was sure that, even if I told her I wanted to become a monk, it would not cause her pain.

After my return to Tokyo from the New York exhibition, I talked to my wife.

"From now on, I want to live in New York. Will you come with me?"

"At my age, you are asking me to live where I could not even communicate?"

"Then, can I go by myself?"

"Who can stop a stubborn one from Hwanghae-do? Even if I said no, you'd do it, so I might as well say yes."

"You really mean it?"

"Does this mean that you are going to be a monk?" She was smiling, but she could scarcely believe it.

"Yes. I'll provide for you all of your life, so please do not hold on to me this time."

"It's funny. Up to now, you have done everything in this world that you wanted to do, and now you want to become a monk. Can you handle it?"

"I can do it."

"Then, do it! Don't just keep talking about it."

My wife thought I was joking, but my mind was relieved. Though I knew what she was thinking, I decided to pursue my plan.

The next year, I went to Wongak-sa in New York and expressed my determination to become a monk to Seu-nim Beoban.

"Brother, if you feel that way, why don't you take instruction in Buddhist precepts from my teacher? He is Seu-nim Gwaneung, and is head monk at Jikji-sa; he is a well-known expert in Korean Buddhism."

"Do you think he will accept me right away if I go there?"

"I will write a letter of recommendation, and submit your resume to him. I'm quite sure he will accept you."

I took his letter of introduction, and went to Jikji-sa. I was accompanied by Sister Beobseong, and my acquaintances, Mr. And Mrs. Yun Seokho. Seu-nim Gwaneung was staying in Jung-am, and when I entered the campus there, I could see Geumo Mountain and Gimcheon in the distance. On top of the temple pillar I could read the following poem:

> Gold and diamonds are not the truth;
> Worldly relationships are not the truth.
> To the holy person, the path is blue and clean,
> And it is without end.
> The treasure is the reflection of the moon on the river.
> It is like seeing the clear sky behind the clouds.

Jukrim-won was the place where the great monk stayed, and carved there on a pillar was:

> Someday an enlightened one will come here.
> High mountains surround
> Where peach and apricot blossoms
> Have nothing to do except be pink,
> In tribute to Buddha's mind;
> A gnarled pine whispers Buddha's Sutra,
> And birds twitter around the truth.

The meaning of the poetry refreshed and cleansed me of worldly grime. The great Seu-nim lived freely in this serene place, and I would feel honored to be accepted by him. When I met him in person, and looked into his eyes, I experienced again a sense of being cleansed. Seu-nim Gwaneung read Seu-nim Beoban's letter.

"So, you are a painter?"

"Yes." He thought for a while before speaking.

"It was before liberation, so more than fifty years ago, I was a student at the Buddhist University in Kyoto, and when I came to Jikji-sa during vacations, I would often see a middle school student. He was young, but he had extraordinary artistic talent. He probably lives in Japan now, but just in case you might know him, his name was Seolcheon ..."

"That's me! I was Seolcheon!" I shouted without thinking, and the great monk was startled.

We looked at each other carefully. I could perceive in the Seu-nim's face the college student whom I had met in Cheonbul temple in Jikji-sa. The great Seu-nim also could see my young self, and nodded his head. It was a miraculous encounter after so many years, and I could see the student in the great monk. I hadn't recognized his Buddhist name, but his worldly name was beginning to emerge in my memory.

"Seu-nim, was your old name Jeon Jaeyeong?"

"Right!"

The others who were there were amazed. I explained to him that I had changed my name to Kim Tae-Shin, and told him what I had been doing in Japan. I also disclosed to him that I was the son of Seu-nim Kim Ilyeop, which he had not known before. After that, the great Seu-nim told me a story which he thought that no one knew: The person who had shaved the head of Seu-nim Ilyeop had been Seu-nim Tanong, and after that he had sent her to Seu-nim Mangong to receive the precepts of Buddhism. I believed that I had heard about that from Seu-nim Tanong himself, and Seu-nim Gwaneung had been a student of Seu-nim Tanong. So, as my mother had her hair cut off by Seu-nim Tanong, now I was to receive that service from Tanong's disciple.

What a coincidence! The great Seu-nim told me that, since I was going to become a monk so late in life, he could not train me. But, he told to reflect on the matter for a few months, then return to him if I had not changed my mind. We decided on a date of June 6 for the ceremony of ordination. A few days later, I returned to Tokyo. My wife teased me about not yet shaving my head.

"I came home to organize my affairs, and, if I leave again, it will be to become a monk."

"You are really going to become a monk?"

"Did you think until now that I was not being serious about what I intended to do?"

She realized that I had not been joking, and her attitude become very serious.

"Even though you were often gone for months at a time, did I ever complain? You don't have to become a monk."

"We've already talked about this. Let's not argue about it."

"I haven't finished with it yet. Please don't become a monk."

"I already have made my commitment; I can't change it."

"When we get old we need companionship. How can I live alone without you?"

"I am sorry, but we have sons and grandchildren, so you won't be lonely. Please don't stand in my way." I felt sorry for my wife, but I could not change my mind. I called all of my sons, told them of my decision, and asked them to take care of their mother. I made sure that she had medical insurance, and gave one savings account to her.

I met with Mr. Fukuda and others of my supporters, told them my plan to establish a university in New York, and asked for their assistance. In May, I returned to Seoul, and went to Jung-am in Jikji-sa, where I heard unexpected news.

"The head monk has gone to New York."

"Why?"

"Seu-nim Beoban in Wongak-sa has had a stroke, so he went to see him with Seu-nim Dojin. If Seu-nim Beoban is in bad shape they are going to bring him to Korea for treatment." I didn't know what to do. If Beoban had a stroke, it would be impossible to raise the funds for the college we had planned to build. I went to New York right away. Seu-nim Beoban could not use his legs and arms, and I thought that we could do little as long as he was in that condition. But he told me clearly,

"Brother, I am sure I can get well. Until then, please just go ahead with our plans. When I have recovered, I will join you."

When I heard his clear words, I thought that the situation was not completely tragic. I decided to continue with our plan without him. I had already gathered pledges for two and a half million dollars in support from Japan, and, depending on our progress, we could amass many times that amount. I didn't feel that I could stop at that point.

I planned to begin working right after the ordination ceremony. Originally, I had planned for the rite to be held at Jikji-sa, but since the great monk had come to New York, I thought it would be better to hold it at Wongak-sa, and the great monk agreed with me. My support group in New York planned to make a video of the entire ceremony.

The day of the ordination turned out to be a beautiful one, and many monks attended, from Wongak-sa, Manhattan and Washington. Many Buddhists from various congregations and from my support group, also came. Seu-nim Beopseong came from Korea, and reporters arrived from everywhere, making for quite a big event.

The ceremony began with my burning of incense before the statue of Buddha, and making an offering of flowers. The great monk, dressed in a formal robe, explained the doctrine. I bowed three times for my Korean nation, three times for my parents, and then donned the clothing of a monk. The ceremony proceeded with the shaving of my head, after which I was dressed in a monk's outer robe. Then, the great monk gave ten religious precepts:

> Do not kill any living thing.
> Do not steal.
> Do not commit adultery.
> Do not lie.
> Do not be a drunkard.
> Do not believe yourself to be better than others.
> Do not use makeup.
> Do not sing or dance.
> Do not adorn yourself.
> Do not eat except at meals.
> Do not have pets.

I continued the rite before Buddha. I bowed to the people who had come there, then burned incense before the great monk, and bowed three times. I thought of my parents, and bowed three more times, and the great monk blessed me. That was the end of the ceremony. My mother had used her pen name, Ilyeop, as her Buddhist name, and I used my pen name, Iltang, as mine.

The Rahula

My teacher, the great monk, told me, "Beoban's condition is improving through treatment with oriental medicine, so I am going to take him to Korea. You became a monk late in life, so you may have some trouble dealing with those who took that step at a younger age. Think of it as a bride adjusting to her in-laws, and just be patient.

"Please don't worry about me."

Seu-nim Dojin, who assisted the great monk, was also concerned. He said, "Seu-nim Iltang, you might have something come up which you would find difficult to endure. If so, discuss it with Seu-nim Jewon in Washington." Seu-nim Jewon was head monk of Washington's Beobju-sa temple, one of the disciples of Seu-nim Gwaneung, and like a spiritual brother to me. Until I heard the words from Seu-nim Dojin I had not considered that anything unpleasant might happen, but now I was more concerned. The great monk and the others decided to return to Korea on the twentieth of July. On the day before they were to leave, a special reporting team from Yomiuri TV station in Tokyo arrived at Wongak-sa. That had been arranged by Congressman Fukuda. We had previously discussed that we would announce through broadcasting the establishment of the oriental university in New York, and make possible for people who were interested in contributing funds to the project to visit there. Seu-nim Beoban, who was to leave the very next day with the great monk, requested of the reporter that they do a good job for us. They planned to stay for a week at Wongak-sa, and to make a thirty-minute film. Showing their film in Japan would be sure to attract lots of positive attention; however, they were forced to leave Wongak-sa after only two days. As soon as Beoban and his party left for Korea, the Seu-nim in charge of the temple, Hyegwan, stopped everything the team was doing, and did not cooperate with them at all. I was bewildered and embarrassed, and did not know what to do.

The reporting team did take pictures of Wongak-sa in Manhattan, and of the prospective location of the university, and included an interview with me, which I insisted on, describing the project. But it was not a comfortable environment for them, and they departed hurriedly. I asked Hyegwan what was going on, and he told me that it had been a decision of the board members. I couldn't figure out why such a decision could have been made.

A few days later, there was a board meeting. I strongly questioned them, and received an answer which came as a complete surprise.

"We don't want to see Japanese come and go in Wongak-sa, and we don't want Japanese funds used to develop this place."

"Why, why?"

"You don't know the reason? They're Japs! How can you trust them? They are the ones who ground Korea down for thirty-six years."

How could they be so mired in the past? Even though the Japanese might provide the funds, they would not be participating in any management decisions. Nor were they imposing any conditions on the use of their money. Even though they hated the Japanese, there was no reason to hate their money. Could a real patriot stand up to declare his allegiance, but, behind the scenes, be destroying all of the plans?

"This project is proceeding according to the plans and wishes of Seu-nim Beoban, and the board of directors should not interfere with it."

"Seu-nim Beoban went to Korea, and there's no guarantee that he'll ever come back in good health. Even though he might return, we have to run this temple in the meantime."

I thought that the board members were doing real violence by refusing Japanese funds, and, with none among them able to donate as much as $100,000, I just couldn't understand.

Because of the opposition of the board, I could proceed no further. By now, I recognized that Seu-nim Hyegwan was not on my side. Even though he held a spiritual position under Beoban, he stood with the board members against me.

"To survive, there is no way we can go against them. They were the ones who rolled up their sleeves and worked for Wongak-sa. Without them, we might have to close the temple."

I began to suspect that Hyegwan was the instigator of the trouble with the board. Even before this incident, he had disappointed me once. The previous year, during a fund-raising exhibition in the Wongak-sa youth center, we had given the proceeds to Hyegwan to hold. Later, when we asked him for the money to use, he gave us an unreasonable answer:

"You know, the head monk got sick, and we ran short of funds and had to use that money."

In New York, they had good insurance, and I was sure that the money had not gone for medical bills. If it had been used for the temple, I was sure there must be a record of each expenditure.

"Can you show me the bills and the receipts?"

"Yes."

He answered without hesitation, but somehow never got around to showing me the documents. I was depressed and heartsick. How could I explain the situation to the Japanese who had wanted to contribute to our project? I recalled Donjin's advice to consult with Seu-nim Jewon in Washington if a problem arose. I went to Washington with a young Seu-nim, Seonjin, who drove the car. Seu-nim Jewon greeted us happily. After he heard my story, he said, "Since you are in Washington, let's take a tour, and we'll talk about the future later." During our tour, Jewon asked me, "Do you really want to establish a school in Wongak-sa?"

"This was the dream of Seu-nim Beoban, so we started making the plans for the school there."

"But, if you cannot solve the problem you have encountered, even though you want it, you could not have a school there. If they give you a hard time in New York, perhaps you could think about locating the university in Washington. If you do, I'll do my best to help you."

"I'll think it over."

On our way back to New York, we stopped at the Wongak-sa in Philadelphia. The head monk there, Seu-nim Seonwu, greeted us. In Philadelphia, Mr. Oh

Seyeong, whom I had met through the Owon Art Organization, introduced me to Othmar Carli, who was famous in the field of wood-cut printing. He introduced me, as well, to the owner of the Miro Art Gallery in Philadelphia. I was invited to mount a solo exhibition there, and I accepted gladly. While I was in Philadelphia, Mr. Oh spoke to me seriously.

"I don't think that it is necessary to work within the temple to establish an oriental university. You have a great vision. If you wish to come to Philadelphia to establish the school, I will support you."

"Well...."

"First, we would have to get permission to establish the school, then rent a building, and start off with lectures on oriental art, gradually adding religion, music, philosophy and oriental medicine. That would mean we could have a growing school."

In order to strike while the iron was hot, we met with an attorney, a black man. He listened carefully to Mr. Oh's plan, and said,

"Maybe I could obtain the right to use a city building for this purpose."

When I returned to the New York Wongak-sa, my telephone line had been disconnected, and I approached Mr. Hyegwan about the matter.

"Well, we have almost no income, and a lot of expenses, so I had no choice but to do it. I regret having to ask you, but could you move out of your room? Someone wants to rent it, and we need the money."

"I cannot do that. I became a monk in this temple. Where could I go? As long as Seu-nim Gwaneung, who shaved my head, and the head monk, Seu-nim Beoban, are alive, I must consult them about whether to stay or go."

I had heard that new monks were often given a hard time by those ahead of them, and it seemed that Seu-nim Hyegwan wanted to see my tears. I was sure I had already missed many phone calls from Japan, so I went out into the city and called Congressman Fukuda in Japan. As I expected, he became very angry.

"Through Yomiuri, we reported the establishment of the oriental university in New York. I've been trying to contact you in regard to fund raising. What happened?"

"I'm sorry. While I was visiting in Washington, the phone was disconnected."

"If you don't even have someone to answer the phone, how can you proceed with this big project?!!"

"For a while, let me call you. Please don't try to call here."

"I don't understand. Some people who want to contribute funds want to visit there. What shall we do?"

"Please postpone everything until I get in touch with you."

Why would they delay their gifts? I had a feeling that something was wrong that would be difficult to straighten out. I was close to seventy years old, and dreaded being shamed and laughed at. I tried to keep my anger under control, and began to prepare for the exhibition at the Miro Gallery in Philadelphia. I already had enough paintings so that I didn't have to do much new work. I went to Philadelphia a week prior to the opening of the show, and stayed with Mr. Carli while I made the final arrangements. He made some woodcut prints of my work which were also to be exhibited. This was the first time that I had spent time in the household of an American family. Othmar Carli's house was large, and he and his wife lived there alone, since their children had grown up and left home. The couple did not take their meals at home; in the mornings, they would get up and go to breakfast at a hotel restaurant. I could not communicate well with them, but, when I had no words, I would draw pictures, and they understood me perfectly. Mr. And Mrs. Carli attended the opening ceremony at the Miro Gallery, and when she saw the pictures, Mrs. Carli shouted enthusiastically,

"Wonderful! Wonderful," and threw her arms around my neck and kissed me. I was very embarrassed, and wondered what her husband could be thinking.

In setting up the exhibition, I had a lot of help from Mr. and Mrs. Hong, faithful members of the Philadelphia Wongak-sa, who ran a grocery store. During this time, the black attorney, to whom I had been introduced by Mr. Oh, came to see me. He told me he had been impressed by my paintings, and, after the exhibit, he took me to see a five story building which, he said, was owned by the city. He told me that he had obtained permission to use that building for the university. Mr. Oh said,

"The attorney has gotten us the use of this building at no charge. Let us start the lectures on oriental art here."

I told them that the offer was so sudden that I had to have a little time to think it over. The attorney added that, since this project would benefit Philadelphia, he could help me to get permanent residency there.

After the exhibition, I returned to New York, and let my support group know about the offers I had received in Philadelphia, but their reaction was negative. In their opinion, the lectures must be held in New York, since we would not be able to get enough students in Philadelphia. I also believed that, before I made any plans, I should discuss the matter with Seu-nim Beoban, as long as he was still alive. I postponed going to Philadelphia, and, fifteen days after the exhibition, I traveled to Korea. I met Seu-nim Beoban in Jung-am, and found that his condition had not improved at all. Taking his health into consideration, I explained to him what had been happening. He appeared to be very uncomfortable.

"I am sorry, Brother, to have put all of this on your shoulders, and to have been unable to help you. Please don't feel you must pursue the New York matter on my account."

"Don't worry about me. If you wish me to continue with the project in New York, I will do so, but I will need a written authorization from you, giving me full responsibility over the building of the college in Wongak-sa. I will show the authorization to the supporting body, and get on with the project."

Seu-nim Beoban closed his eyes, and didn't open them until he had taken time to consider what would be the best thing to do. He did not give me the written authorization. Perhaps he thought that, even if I had his authorization, I would have a difficult time with the project, because of the board members, or, that until he recovered his health, Seu-nim Hyegwan and the board were more important to Wongak-sa than I was. I had no way of knowing what his thinking was. One thing was clear: he didn't write the authorization paper for me. I went to Seongra-am in Seoul. I had become uncomfortable in Wongak-sa, nor was I comfortable in Jung-am, so this was the only place I could go. Sister Seu-nim Beobseong was sympathetic.

"New monks have problems, like newlyweds. You were so new that the people at Wongak-sa couldn't take your plans seriously."

Perhaps she was right; maybe I still lacked the discipline and training I needed. After I became a monk, I felt like I was bogged down in a quagmire. Perhaps I had been too eager to satisfy my own ambitions.

The Love Left Behind

I had expected too much in regard to the oriental university. Seu-nim Beoban had a vision of teaching everything oriental in America, and perhaps I had become too involved with his dream. I had wanted to bring the teaching of oriental art to the West, so that its value could be known, and I decided that now was the time to act on my belief. I had dreamed that, after I had reached my spiritual goal as a Rahula, my second goal would be the teaching of oriental art.

I could have worked with Mr. Oh Seyeong to establish a university in Philadelphia, but, as my New York supporters pointed out, New York was a better location for the promotion of such a school. It was a center of international art and culture, and would provide more prospective students to enable me to reach my goal.

Until the recovery of Seu-nim Beoban, the existence of the oriental university remained uncertain. In the meantime, I had received many pledges of support for the project from Japanese people, who were disappointed that it had to be postponed. The reason I had sought financial support in Japan for this Korean project, was to make evident the true friendship of Japanese people for Korea. Oriental artists were also disappointed by the delay in our plans.

In 1989, I had an invitational solo-exhibition put on by my New York supporters. Although it was not a university, I wanted, by my own works, to cultivate an appreciation of oriental art in America. The exhibition in the middle of Manhattan was very well-attended. I was especially grateful for the efforts of the support group, its president, Oh Gijeong, and members Kim Byeongmo, Yun Yeongheon, Lee Byeongman, Kim Hongjo, Kim Seongyo, Lee Wonju, Lee Seokgyu, Gwak Ilhyeong, Oh Sangseon, and Jeong Sihun. The exhibition's success was also ensured by the work of Seu-nim Seonghae of Bulguk-sa temple in Manhattan.

From New York I went to San Diego. There was located the temple Bulgwang-sa, which was had been built by Seu-nim Seonjin, who had previously been at Wongak-sa. I asked him, "What brought you here from New York?" Seu-nim Seonjin smiled and said, "In the worldly sense, they kicked me out, but, in thinking of it spiritually, I believe it was Buddha's will." He had been forced out of Wongak-sa, but considered his decision to come to San Diego to be a good one.

"By the way, Seu-nim Hyegwan in Wongak-sa passed away a short time ago.

"I was beset by many feelings. He continued,

"We need funding here, but I am not able to raise much money."

"I'll try to help you, Seu-nim Seonjin." To keep my promise to help in funding the establishment of a temple in San Diego, I had a fund-raising exhibition in Busan in the spring of 1991. I decided to do something I long had wanted to do. When I was a middle school student, I had written to my mother that, if I became a painter, I would hold an exhibition celebrating her poetry by my art work. I had thought of that because of the popularity of a children's poem Mother had written about the death of her brother. Mother had passed away, and I had been so busy that I hadn't yet been able to pursue that plan. Now, hopes for the oriental university had vanished, and I could concentrate on promoting my mother's poetry along with my exhibition.

Seu-nim Wolsong, in Hwanhidae gathered all of my mother's published poems, and sent them to me. I did the illustrations, then the poems were added to the pictures by Park Siho, the head of the Korean Education and Cultural Center, whom I had known when he was a reporter on the Central Daily Newspaper. He worked hard at transferring the poetry into the pictures. The exhibition was held at the Lotte Art Gallery, where head of the gallery, Kim Taejeong, helped me greatly. I worried that by adding my paintings to my mother's poetry I might have degraded her work.

In 1990, a book of the poetry and paintings was published by Goryowon, with the title, *The Love Left Behind,* which was the name of one of my mother's poems. Many people visited the exhibition, but I was especially happy to see two persons. One was Seu-nim Doseong, who took care of my mother until the time of liberation. She became teary-eyed as she viewed Mother's poetry coupled with my paintings.

The other visitor was the congressman, Jeong Daecheol. He was the son of my uncle, Jeong Ilhyeong, my mother's brother. I knew how busy he must have been, and appreciated the fact that he took the time to come, along with the many other visitors; it was an opportunity to recover many memories of my mother. The introduction to the book of poetry and art was written by Seu-nim Wondam, head monk of Sudeok-sa:

"When we were children playing in a mountain stream, he was my close friend and older brother, Kim Tae-Shin, and he now is Seu-nim Iltang. He only came occasionally, but still he let me be his friend. When I think of the old days, I realize he must have had an unhappy childhood, but he always seemed to me to be a happy orphan, and I envied him. He would cross mountains and valleys in the storm, longing for one leaf from the tree of mother-love. Now the field is only melting snow, and the solitary leaf is gone, so he has no one to wish for. Now, Seu-nim Iltang gathers up his mother's love, expressing with his brush on the clear window of Buddhism, the poems of Seu-nim Ilyeop, which he wants to preserve as the birth-right of the next generation. In his art, he represents his pain, not hiding his yearning for his mother's love, so please console him."

It has been ten years since that exhibition. I have been re-reading Seu-nim Wondam's writing; he understood me well, and touches my heart. Looking back, I still have that hazy yearning in one part of my mind. What was the purpose of my existence? I see dimly the mother who shaped the direction of my life, and who is smiling now. It makes no difference whether it was as a mother or as a Seu-nim, my relationship with her is surely eternal. Maybe, before her spirit left her body, my mother wanted to say that which I am feeling now: I am a part of the everlasting confusion of mankind.

About the Author

Biography of Iltang (Kim Tae Shin), 1922–: Born of mixed Japanese/Korean parentage, his whole life marked by war, and, especially, by his mother's desertion of him as a newborn to become a Buddhist monk, Iltang became a famous artist, and, in his old age, a monk himself.

Summary: *The Lost Mother* is a memoir in which Iltang imagines the romance of his parents, an aristocratic Japanese man and a Korean poet and feminist leader, in the early 1920s, and its effect on his life Marriage would have been unheard of, and was made completely impossible by the woman's decision to follow the spiritual path of Buddhism, and retire from the world to become a monk. Iltang, reared in loving foster families, found out about her existence at the age of fourteen. His longing for a relationship with her, which she could not permit, persisted throughout his life. His father never married, and eventually died in Germany, where he was a representative of the Japanese government after World War II. That war, as well as the Korean Civil War marred the whole of Iltang's adult life. He utilized his growing fame as an artist to attempt to mediate reconciliation between his two nations through cultural exchanges, and became a Buddhist monk in his later years.

2) Author's Notes:

My mother is Kim Ilyeop, a Buddhist monk. The famous monk, Mangong, called me Rahula, after the one who had been fathered by the Buddha before he began his holy and ascetic life, and who was a cause of such concern for him. That name perfectly describes me. In the late spring of my fourteenth year, I found out that I had a mother. I ran for miles with a pounding heart, but I returned chilled. I expected to be greeted by the warm love of a mother, but heard these words from Ilyeop, the monk:

Do not call me "Mother."

A mother should be a spiritual refuge from the isolation and trouble of the world. My loneliness and disappointment, my pleasure and hope—all were embodied in my mother. Because of her, I felt both thirst and fulfillment. But her words pushed me away as I tried to cling to her skirts.

"Mother!"

Because of that one word, my yearning snowballed, and became one immense and gushing tear. My longing for her put my life in shadow, but also gave me my power to live. Though I realized now that my mother was not going to be close to me, I still struggled with my love and my hate for her.

At one time I cared about what people said regarding my mother and me, but after twenty years as a Buddhist disciple myself, I came to realize that all this was in vain. But, still, in my heart is a mother's place, no longer a arid field, but a fertile meadow gleaming in morning dew.

In the past, I struggled with the longing that distorted my life, but now my heart is bigger, and I can embrace our story, and tell it. Now, the icy cold memory of Mother, yearning, thirst, love and hate melt alike into a murmuring springtime stream. That is what Buddhist teaching has brought to me.

July, 2002
Iltang, Kim Tae-Shin, in prayer.

3) Letter to My Mother by author

Mother, it has been a long time since I called you "Mother." When I was young, you scolded me for calling you that. You are always fully in my mind, but it requires courage for me to show you to the world in my book. I worried about whether I would disgrace your name, but please look upon this work kindly, as a song of Iltang.

You and I were mother and son, but it was always a special kind of relationship. I always ached with longing because I could not call you Mother, and I always had to look at you from a distance. Your son sent his longing to you over the mountains and the ocean, but you only folded it in your hands, and sat quietly regarding the Buddha. You were cold, but I knew that the love in your heart was deepest of all. I knew that I was like Buddha's son, Rahula, to you, hampering your search for truth. Now I realize that, because of our relationship, one of the issues of your enlightenment became clarified, and you gained energy to approach your devotions.

Mother, the mountain in my paintings is no ordinary mountain. Mother is always there in that mountain, and our teacher, Buddha, is there as well. There is also a temple, and the temple bell. Despite that, my mountain omitted everything else, and was only a mountain.

Mother, my father, Oda Seizo, died in the same year as you did yourself, while serving as a special envoy in Germany. All his life he missed you, and died a lonely man. I worry that his solitary spirit is wandering around in Hades. Please call that spirit up from the nether regions into Heaven.

It has been thirty years since your passing; I have become a Buddhist monk, following in your path. As a disciple of Buddha, and also of yours, until I see you in paradise, I will do my best, without shame, to emerge from being your Rahula. You are already gone, but you will always be my precious mother, and the model Seu-nim for many people. Today, I am thankful for that. Please watch over me as a mother and as a teacher until I finish my life. Blessings on you.

July, 2002
Iltang, Kim Taesin

4) Letter to translator from Choi Yongjin, Senior Director, The Korea Society in New York

For twenty years I have worked to add Korean Studies to the curriculum in American public schools. My aim is that American textbooks offer accurate information about Korea, and I have been meeting with editors, authors, teachers and those who make educational policy. I have trained them, taken them on trips to Korea, etc., in order to develop new approaches to teaching about Korea.

For the past twenty years, educators have been given only two recommended texts for the teaching of Korea-related issues. One is *Lost Names: Scenes from a Korean Boyhood,* by Richard Kim, published in 1998, and *Years of Impossible Goodbyes,* by Choi Sukyeol, published in 1991.

In America, for educational purposes, the story of personal lives is preferred over the usual history textbook. That is the reason I recommended this book [*The Lost Mother*] to textbook selection committees.

This book tells of the youth and development of Iltang (Kim Tae Sin), whose mother was Kim Ilyeop and whose father was Oda Seizo, who grew up to be a famous artist of both Korea and Japan. It shows the process of becoming a painter in Korea and in Japan, the effects of the Second World War, the partition of Korea, the Korean war, and outlines his efforts to reconcile his two nations. It is an autobiographical novel which clearly portrays a specific historical period.

This book could be used in the following curriculum areas:

1. The book introduces the poetry of Kim Ilyeop, which deals with the Women's Movement of the 1930s, a setting which can be studied through the lives of Kim Ilyeop, and her friend, Na Hyeseok.

2. There is a special love story between the Korean Kim Ilyeop and the Japanese, Oda Seizo, which transcended the era in which they lived, showing the historical background of the doomed relationship. The concepts of dating and marriage depicted would be useful in the study of world history and culture.

3. There is the story of the growing-up of Kim Tae Shin, who is looking for his parents, and meets many Buddhist masters during his search, learning about them and their spiritual identities. This story would be of use in classes of world history, religion and culture.

4. Iltang develops his artistic abilities by training in both Korea and Japan. He recognizes that the lessons of his masters come both from their artis-

tic and their spiritual beings. This concept would be of interest in social studies classes.

5. Iltang remained loyal to and concerned about the foster parents in his early life, Song Gisu and Kim Bongyul, to whom he felt a special obligation. This, too, is of interest in a social studies perspective.

6. Also in the realm of history and social studies is the view of the Korean independence movement, in which Iltang participated as a young boy, helping to smuggle money to the activists.

7. During the Japanese occupation, there was an attempt to destroy the culture of Korea, for example by the oppression of Korean Buddhism. There was also the effort to destroy the Korean language, as illustrated in Richard Kim's *Lost Names.*

8. Also of historical interest is the episode in Iltang's life when he, a Korean drafted into the Japanese army, at the end of the war led two hundred Korean prisoners of war from Japan back to Korea.

9. After WWII, Korea was partitioned, and Iltang was imprisoned by the North Koreans when he went there attempting to find his bourgeois foster family to move them to the South. He pictures his life in prison and his escape back to the South, illustrating the realities of the cold war between North and South Korea.

10. Iltang struggled with his divided identity, living back and forth between Korea and Japan, and eventually arriving at a level of comfort with his own identity. This process may be of help to Korean children living in America, who find adjustment to adoptive or foster parents difficult due to language and assimilation problems, in finding their own personal selves.

In summary, this book is not simply a coming-of-age story, but is a depiction of huge historical events and their effect on one man's life. The meeting of his mother, a feminist pioneer in Korea, and his father, a Japanese aristocrat, resulted in his birth and abandonment; in his search for his mother he meets many people, including great masters, whose lives, like his, represent the tragic history of Korea and its scarred relationship with its Japanese neighbor. It is a contribution to world literature in its portrayal of the life and philosophy of one elderly monk.

I sincerely hope that this book may be offered as reading material for American middle and high school students.

5) Letter to translator from Hyangsoon Yi, Ph.D., Associate Professor of Comparative Literature at the University of Georgia:

He was a child left behind in the world by the woman who took the path of enlightenment, aspiring to be like the Bodhisattva of Mercy. Out of that harsh life of contradiction did the boy ironically opt to follow in the footsteps of his birth mother by renouncing the life of an artist and joining a Buddhist monastic community. I encountered *The Lost Mother* while collecting research material on Iryop who is a prominent Zen nun in modern Korea. Better known by her pen-name Iryop, the New Woman Kim Wonju spawned sensational stories about her "radical" lifestyle in the early days of Korea's modern era. Memoirs about her often fail to disentangle fact from fiction. On the contrary, personal recollections tend to confound them further. It is thus out of curiosity and of due suspicion that I picked up *The Lost Mother*, the autobiography of the monk who claimed for long that he was Iryop's biological son. The first few pages of Iltang's book, however, were sufficient enough; to my surprise, I was absorbed into the extraordinary narrative of the boy who had been cast into the vortex of life due to the secrecy surrounding his birth.
Iltang's memoir is full of dramatic events and untold anecdotes about well known figures who lived through Korea's tumultuous transition to the modern period. High hopes and deep despair that coexisted in the rapidly changing society are compressed into the private history of the person who refused to yield to life's insurmountable challenges, struggling to uphold his passion for art. Painstakingly recorded, Iltang's life story thus offers a new point of view on Korea's modernity and its multi-faceted meanings. What makes this autobiography especially moving is the author's ability to reflect on his identity with unstinting candor and thoroughness. The root of his contemplative power, of course, goes back to his eternal longing for his lost mother. Such longing, however, can be understood broadly as our fundamental existential question on our origins. Here lies the universal truth of Iltang's journey in life.

The Lost Mother can be approached from diverse angles. First and foremost, this book traces the tortuous life of one who was born in the tragic circumstances. As a personal memoir, it presents a human side of the highly regarded Buddhist monks and nuns of our time, including Master Mangong and his disciples as well as Iryop. Their portraits as "blood-and-flesh" enable readers to get a rare glimpse into the Buddhist community of the mid-twentieth century. It is a unique picture caught in the eyes of the precocious boy who crisscrossed the two worlds: the secular and sacred. Iltang's book contains valuable information on Korean society at large. His life story, personal as it is, cannot be adequately understood without paying attention to its historical, social, and political backgrounds. Of particular importance are the conflict-ridden relation between Japan and Korea as the colonizer and colonized and the tragic confrontation between South and North Korea as capitalist and communist states. The intellectuals and artists who appear in Iltang's book, including the author himself, provide readers with great opportunities to probe a complex relationship between the individual and nation in East Asia at the time of the disintegration of its traditional social order. Written in a simple style, Iltang's *The Lost Mother* is accessible to a wide range of readers from various walks of life. It will appeal to them on many different levels by providing them with an unusual cross-cultural experience.

978-0-595-44194-5
0-595-44194-7

Printed in the United States
110422LV00005B/13-18/P